BAR EXAM

MPT

PREPARATION

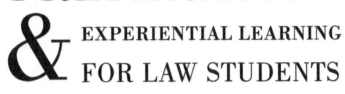

& EXPERIENTIAL LEARNING

FOR LAW STUDENTS

PROFESSOR SARA J. BERMAN, ESQ.

BAR EXAM

MPT

PREPARATION

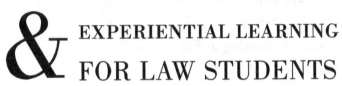

& EXPERIENTIAL LEARNING FOR LAW STUDENTS

Interactive Performance Test Training

PROFESSOR SARA J. BERMAN, ESQ.

Printed in the United States of America.

21 20 19   5 4 3 2

ISBN: 978-1-63425-845-6
e-ISBN: 978-1-63425-846-3

Library of Congress Cataloging-in-Publication Data

Names: Berman, Sara J., author.
Title: Bar exam MPT preparation and experiential learning for law students : interactive performance test training / Sara J. Berman.
Description: Chicago, Ill. : American Bar Association, 2017. | Includes bibliographical references and index.
Identifiers: LCCN 2017008507 (print) | LCCN 2017012080 (ebook) | ISBN 9781634258463 (ebook) | ISBN 9781634258456 (soft cover : alk. paper)
Subjects: LCSH: Bar examinations—United States—Study guides. | LCGFT: Study guides.
Classification: LCC KF303 (ebook) | LCC KF303 .B448 2017 (print) | DDC 340.076—dc23
LC record available at https://lccn.loc.gov/2017008507

Discounts are available for books ordered in bulk. Special consideration is given to state bars, CLE programs, and other bar-related organizations. Inquire at Book Publishing, ABA Publishing, American Bar Association, 321 N. Clark Street, Chicago, Illinois 60654-7598.

www.ShopABA.org

DEDICATION

To UCLA Law Professor Emeritus Paul Bergman—the greatest teacher, co-author, friend, and role model ever—and the funniest too!

CONTENTS

ACKNOWLEDGMENTS

I begin with deep gratitude on behalf of myself and the ABA to the National Conference of Bar Examiners and to the California Committee of Bar Examiners for permission to use past exams as part of this book. It is my hope that these brilliant examples of meaningful testing will help legal educators nationwide to train law students to become practice-ready ethical professionals.

I would never have written about performance tests in the first place had it not been for my extraordinary UCLA Law School professors, particularly Paul Bergman, David Binder, and Carrie Menkel-Meadow. My love of PTs started at UCLA Law School and flourished when in 1991 Professor Paul Bergman not only did not laugh, but encouraged and fully supported my creation of the first performance test preparation course, the *Performance Test Review*.

I could never have completed this book without the help of many people: first and foremost my editors and the entire staff of ABA Publishing, including but not limited to Bryan Kay, Jon Malysiak, John Palmer, and my first ABA editor Erin Nevius. For their invaluable assistance critiquing chapters of this book, my profound thanks to Miriam Billington, Esq.; Christine Francis, Esq.; The Honorable Judge Mark Juhas, Esq.; Professor Michele Tobenkin, Esq.; David Cook, Esq.; and Jacqueline Neumann, Esq.

There are also many people whose work has helped shape my ideas about bar exam success generally and whom I credit accordingly: first and foremost, my students. It really is all about you. Second, my professors, some of whom I have already mentioned, but all of whom I will thank until I take my last breath. Next, my passlaw.com partners and dearest friends Steve Bracci Esq., Craig Gold Esq., and Bruce Landau Esq. You have each taught me so much about the bar exam and legal education, and Craig, about technology as well. Anyone who has not heard a Professor Bracci bar review lecture is missing out! Thanks also to my Concord and Kaplan colleagues for the opportunity to teach thousands of students to pass bar exams nationwide. I hesitate to name anyone for fear of leaving too many out, but I must at the very least note with great appreciation some of many attorneys who opened invaluable teaching doors, including Barry Currier, Dean Emeritus and currently Managing Director of Accreditation and Legal Education for the American Bar Association Section of Legal Education and Admissions to the Bar, Dean Emeritus Gregory Brandes, Donna Skibbe, Bob Hull, Steve Marietti, Tammi Rice, Michael Power, Chris Fromm, Chris DeSantis, Amit Schlesinger, Nicole Lefton, and Micol Small. Thanks too to Concord Law School Dean Martin H. Pritikin for his support and for his work in experiential learning, embracing technology, and flipped classrooms. Thanks to Whittier Associate Dean Andrea Funk for shining a bright light on the importance of assessment and for her review of the Professor's Guide to this book. And, thanks to Dean Emeritus Penelope Bryan for her unwavering support of my teaching and writing, and for her friendship.

My heartfelt thanks to all of my NSU Shepard Broad College of Law colleagues, most especially Dean Jon M. Garon, for welcoming me with open arms and allowing me the opportunity to use my creative energy to help even more students pass the bar exam and become thriving members of the legal community.

A very special thank-you to my dear friend Arthur R. Miller. Longtime Harvard Law School Professor and now University Professor at NYU, one of the nation's most distinguished legal scholars, notably in the area of civil procedure. Arthur Miller, with his casebooks, hornbooks, treatises, lectures, and Emmy Award–winning legal television, has directly or indirectly influenced nearly every lawyer and judge in this country. Professor Miller also remains the clearest voice ever in preparing students for success on bar exams nationwide. Arthur, you inspire me. Your work, from the highest levels of scholarship to television and everywhere in between, reminds us that legal education is a vehicle for positive change that extends well beyond the four corners of law school buildings.

Last but not least, I thank my family, particularly my children, Daniel and Julia, for making me want to get up every day to write, teach, and share ideas, in the hopes of in some small way making the world a better place. With you both here, I know the world is filled with goodness.

1

HOW TO GET THE MOST OUT OF THIS BOOK

This book is for law students—especially if after you graduate, your bar exam will include an MPT (multistate performance test) or a state-specific performance test. (Most bar exams include a performance test or "PT" and many of the jurisdictions that do not yet include a PT are thinking about eventually moving in that direction.) Reading the book during law school,

- You will gain critical exposure to practical lawyering skills that will help you to pass the bar and transition effectively to law practice.
- You will begin to see yourself not just as a student but as a practicing attorney. In the role-play simulations in this book, you will "represent" almost a dozen clients. As examples:
  - You will help a teenage boy who was injured from wires that fell on him while he was swimming in a local river. (Was he swimming when he should have been in school? You may need to find out!)
  - You will represent a local school board trying desperately to keep its high school free of profanity, plays with sexualized content, and scandalous news reporting in the school paper. (Whatever your own free-speech views are, this exam will test your ability to think in terms of what your client wants and needs.)
  - You will act as a prosecutor in two cases, one involving a possible criminal trespass and the other a murder case in which the defendant seeks to suppress evidence alleging that the police violated his *Miranda* rights.
  - You will counsel a local politician who has gotten into hot water from a string of potential ethical violations.
- You will gain practical writing experience by drafting a host of documents (some of which you might be able to adapt and use as writing samples for job interviews), including:
  - Legal memos
  - Briefs to the court

- Discovery and fact-gathering plans
- A cross-examination plan to question (and discredit!) a key witness at trial
- You will give yourself a down payment for success on the bar exam
- You will find that law school comes alive, especially if you have thus far seen it as "just" reading and briefing cases

Taking performance tests (abbreviated as PTs) during law school brings the law to life. In my many doctrinal courses where I taught using a typical casebook, I liked to think the classes were as engaged as possible. When I began introducing PTs into the curriculum to complement the case readings, though, students suddenly showed a profoundly different level of engagement. They were excited to see how theories and rules we had discussed in the abstract applied to "their clients." And they had fun. (Fun? In law school? Yes!)

Once you are comfortable with PTs, you too may find this part of the bar exam—dare I say—enjoyable! Please understand that I am not knocking the case method; I am a big fan. I loved law school and learning via the Socratic method. Cases are as real as it gets; this stuff actually happened to people! Cases are "reality reading." Still, PTs are interactive and a bit like theater: you not only read, but you also role-play, acting the part of a real lawyer.

Who else is this book for?

Attorneys, law professors, college students, and future law students will also benefit from this book:

- Attorneys: You may use some of the exams in this book as part of an interview process to select competent new associates. Reading how the applicants respond to PTs under timed conditions may well give you a sense of how they would perform in practice.
- Law professors: You may want to introduce PTs into your skills or doctrinal courses.
- College students in mock trial or other prelaw programs: You will find the book helpful to train your analytical, persuasive, and writing skills.
- Readers thinking about applying to law school: You will find valuable information and help in deciding whether law is the path for you.
- Anyone interested in law generally will enjoy this book and the online practice tests.

THIS BOOK'S APPROACH

Readers, I am writing directly to you just as I would speak with you if you visited me during office hours. I am intentionally setting aside formalities with the hope that I can motivate you to really get *into* these exams and enjoy them.

If you have read my book *Pass the Bar Exam,*[1] you know that my philosophy is one of empowerment. Unlike many who describe the bar exam as "torture," I believe that studying for the bar exam can be one of the most positive and empowering experiences imaginable, if you approach it that way.

Doing the work that is necessary to become test-ready (poised to pass your bar exam just as an Olympic high diver stands ready to plunge gracefully into the pool below), involves a mental strength-training process that will leave you feeling like you can conquer anything. Take a moment and close your eyes. Picture yourself as that diver, on the high board, your confidence stemming from years of training and a fundamental belief in yourself. By the time you take your bar exam, you too will have had years of training.

Notice that nowhere do I say that confidence will come to you "just because." I do not say, "Hope for the best and you will automatically do well." Not at all! I am all about the work, the training, and the practice tests. When you pass, though, all that effort pays off with a lifelong positive ripple effect. You will embody your own "can-do" potential. You will know that you can do virtually anything you set your mind and efforts to.

So, throughout this book, as we drill down into the performance test portion of the bar exam, just as in *Pass the Bar Exam*, we will focus on the positives. We will acknowledge what is tough about this exam, and help you do the "heavy lifting" necessary to become test-ready—but we will do all that with a sense of humor. I will encourage you every step of the way. You can think of me as your "trainer," using the metaphor of practice tests as workouts at the legal gym.

Please read on, and get ready to master the performance test portion of your bar exam!

START STUDYING FOR THE BAR EXAM DURING LAW SCHOOL

Law students often assume that the bar exam is something far off in the future, a test to be studied for after law school. In years past, many successful law students did not think about the bar exam until after graduation; at that time, they hibernated and did nothing but study for two months, then took and passed the exam. Those days are history! It is different for you. Today's law students have more pressure, more riding on outcomes, and much more student loan debt than prior generations. Today's law students must start early, during law school, and do everything to ensure success. You cannot risk having to retake the exam.

---

[1] Sara J. Berman, *Pass the Bar Exam: A Practical Guide to Achieving Academic & Professional Goals* (American Bar Association, 2014).

On a personal note, I was lucky enough to have law professors, experts in clinical legal education, who had the foresight to incorporate performance tests in our 1L Legal Writing and Contracts classes. To this day, I am certain that my early exposure to the PT was instrumental in my success on the bar exam. I watched colleagues from other law schools in bar review who were terror-struck when they saw their first PTs in late June. PTs are not hard when you train and are prepared for them, as I was beginning in 1L. Trust me, you do not want to see your first PT in bar review just before your exam.

DO EVERYTHING YOU CAN TO AVOID FAILING THE BAR EXAM

The bar exam is not "just another test." Yes, many very successful people have had to repeat the bar exam, but failing the exam now, especially with the cost of legal education and student loans coming due shortly after graduation, can have long-lasting financial and psychological repercussions.[2] This is entirely unnecessary when there are so many proactive steps you can take during law school to prepare to pass the bar exam first time around. Why not commit to success?! If you sit for the exam having done everything possible to prepare and still do not pass, it is easier to accept those results, refocus, and pass the next time. If you "wing it" on the bar exam, not only will you likely fail, but that failure may also be much harder to accept and recover from.

So, how do you get that head start? What can you do during school? A lot! The most critical step is to get into the habit of effectively completing practice tests. That is what this book is all about: slow and steady practice training so that you "win the race." (The bar exam is in some ways very similar to a marathon race.) The bar exam is too comprehensive an exam to leave anything to the last minute. Starting early is a must.

Certain parts of bar exams are closed book; they depend on your having learned and memorized relevant rules of law. In contrast, the performance test, the part of the bar exam this book focuses on, is open book. By the end of your first year, you should be able to understand and complete these PT exams. Your finished product may not yet be passing quality, but maintain a practice schedule all through law school, taking even

---

[2] *See* Jane Yakowitz, *Marooned: An Empirical Investigation of Law School Graduates Who Failed the Bar Exam*, 60 J. LEGAL EDUC. 1 (August 2010).

just a couple of practice PTs each semester, and you will "build the muscle" you need for success on the actual exam. Gaining exposure to and practicing PTs during law school can also free up extra time that you will need in the months just prior to the exam to review all the legal rules you know and learn whatever you have not yet learned.

Why do I keep stressing the need to "free up" time during the two months prior to the bar exam? Because as much as you may think you are busy now, during bar review you will likely feel far more time-crunched than ever before—and PT practice takes time. You will have to work to carve out that time now, but you should be able to find it. During bar review, you will look at the 90-minute block you need to complete just one PT (and the additional time to review and study the sample answer), and think, "I could take 50 practice Multistate Bar Examinations (MBEs) during this same time! How can I spend it on one PT?" (With 100 MBE questions in 3 hours, you have an average of 1.8 minutes per question.) Beware: Neglecting the PT can come at a hefty price.

WHAT ELSE TO DO AS EARLY PREPARATION TO PASS THE BAR EXAM?

In addition to working through the practice tests for this book in the Online Question and Answer Bank at **http://ambar.org/barexamprep**:

- Familiarize yourself with all the subjects tested on your bar exam. Fill in any knowledge gaps. If there are bar-tested courses you did not take or understand during law school, study them on your own at least briefly before you graduate.
- Make sure that "bar review" is really a *review* and not *bar learning*. It can cause tremendous (wholly avoidable) anxiety to see subjects for the first time in bar review, especially heavily tested subjects, that you either did not take or did not understand well during law school.
- Complete whatever moral character requirements there are in your jurisdiction, including taking and passing the Multistate Professional Responsibility Examination (MPRE). When you get the news that you passed the bar exam, you want to be sworn in without delay.
- Take the necessary steps to clear your calendar, prepare your friends and family, and give yourself the tools you will need for success.
- Read *Pass the Bar Exam: A Practical Guide to Achieving Academic & Professional Goals*,[3] which details bar exam success strategies and

---

[3] *See supra* note 1.

confidence building. If you do not believe that you can pass the bar exam, *Pass the Bar Exam* will help you work through doubts and approach the exam from a position of strength.

Taking practice tests is a bit like going to the gym, for a legal workout. Once you have committed to passing the bar exam, and once you believe beyond a reasonable doubt that you will pass, the most important step is to train by regularly completing the types of questions that will be on your bar exam: multiple-choice questions, essay exams, and performance tests. Go to www.ncbex.org for information on preparing for the Multistate Bar Examination (MBE), the Multistate Essay Examination (MEE), the Multistate Performance Test (MPT), and/or the Multistate Professional Responsibility Examination (MPRE). Your bar exam may also include state-specific questions; if so, practice those regularly as well. You can find information on how to prepare for state-specific portions of your bar exam on your state bar's website and by talking with your academic support faculty.

All the practice performance tests you need to complete the work in this book can be found in the Online Question and Answer Bank at **http://ambar.org/barexamprep**. In Chapter 2, you will learn what PTs are and how to complete them most effectively. Subsequent chapters will guide you through actual practice PTs. In each chapter, I will tell you which practice PT to download from the Online Question and Answer Bank at **http://ambar.org/barexamprep**. After completing the assigned practice exam, return to the chapter with a copy of the question and your answer to review my step-by-step, detailed but easy-to-understand debriefing of that exam.

Again, you will find both the PT question and sample answers for each chapter online at **http://ambar.org/barexamprep**. You will use my debrief to assess your understanding of the question and you will use the answers to self-assess your own answer. Note that the answers in the Online Question and Answer Bank are sample answers but not "model" answers, meaning they are passing quality but not perfect answers. Compare and contrast these sample answers to your own to determine whether your answer was well-organized, thorough, and, most important, whether your answer was responsive to the instructions. In other words, did you produce the task(s) requested? Be sure to complete the question on your own before reading answers.

You must complete many practice MBEs and essays, and study quality answers to these questions in order to self-assess your work and learn to improve. Taking all types of bar exam practice questions and studying sample answers helps you develop critical reading, factual and legal analysis, time management, and other lawyering skills. Unlike PTs, which are open book, MBEs and essays are closed-book exams.

Passing MBEs and essays necessarily depends on both skill *and* memory. Because there is only so much information your memory can store, and you will have quick recall of applicable rules for only so long, you must to some extent "cram" in the months before your bar.

Caveat on cramming: "Cramming" for two months is very different from cramming the night before an exam. It should be called "sustained intensive learning." Do not think that you can give bar study only a couple of weeks and still pass. Most people who pass study for 8 weeks or more, 10 to 12 hours a day, for 6 to 7 days per week. Living and breathing the bar exam for two full months, you learn, review, and memorize rules from dozens of subjects and train by applying those rules with thousands of practice questions. Nothing about the bar exam should be last minute. Because the PT is an open-book test, you can master the PT portion of the bar exam much earlier on, in law school, so that during intensive bar preparation you can focus more fully on those portions of the exam that require memory: essays and multiple-choice questions.

There's no way around it; memory fades. Even if you had every rule memorized by the March prior to the July bar exam, you would likely forget certain rules by the actual exam time. Make no mistake: To effectively *memorize* the rules for instant recall on your bar exam, you must have already *learned* the concepts and be fluent with all the main rules and principles. This learning you can and must do during the years and months prior to intensive bar review. So, do not interpret what I am saying here about early PT work as a suggestion to leave essay and multiple-choice work until the end. Not at all. Just know that you will continue to do *some* memorization even at the end. (I call memorization "frosting the cake." Learning is like going to the store, buying all the ingredients, and baking the cake itself. You bake the cake all through law school; you frost it in those last months before the bar exam.)

TIMING OF BAR EXAMS

Most law students graduate in May and take the July bar exam. The bar exam is offered twice annually, in July and in February. The MBE, or Multistate Bar Examination, is administered the last Wednesday in July and the last Wednesday in February, respectively. For graduates taking the February bar exam, as you read this book, substitute references to "July" with "February." Advice for the months preceding the July bar will be largely the same as for the February bar.

In addition to learning the substantive law during law school, you can also train MBE and essay *skills* (reading, analysis, and writing) well ahead of the final stretch. Even when you feel you have not yet learned and memorized enough to take practice essays, you can still write them as practice, open book. You can also get used to the phrasing and style of MBEs by reading and answering a few questions each day (and studying explanatory answers). This helps you see how tricky they are. I often advise my students to begin, many months before the bar exam, by completing 5 MBEs each day with their morning coffee or tea. On the bar exam, you must complete 5 MBEs in approximately 9 minutes. If you carve out just 15 to 20 minutes a day, you will have enough time to complete a set of 5 questions and review the answers. Painless. Easy. You can afford 15 minutes each day, right?

PTs differ from essays and MBEs. PTs are open book and closed universe (meaning you do not need to reference authorities outside of what the examiners provide in the exam materials). Thus, PTs are truly skills-based exams. Success on the PT does not require any last-minute training. Mastering PT skills is like learning to ride a bicycle: You do not forget how to do it. Therefore, you *can*, very effectively, train your PT skills while in law school—and you should. Again, the earlier you master the PT, the more time you free up during the months prior to the bar exam when memorization for essays and MBE training demands the majority of your time and energy.

For all these reasons, I hope you will use this book throughout law school, to practice PTs and get a real head start on the bar exam. In doing so, you will build a rich down payment for future success, both on the bar exam and in law practice.

PERFORMANCE TESTS: THE BEST PART
OF YOUR BAR EXAM

Many bar exams include a performance test component. At the time this book was written, more than 45 jurisdictions (including U.S. states and territories) have bar exams that include a PT component. If you are lucky enough to be taking the bar exam in a jurisdiction where you must complete one or more performance tests, you will find this book particularly helpful.

> **Note:** I am *not* being sarcastic when I say "lucky." I truly believe that PTs are a gift: both because they are more "fair" in the sense that they do not depend on memory, and because they are realistic and help prepare you for actual legal work *while* studying for the bar exam.

> In some ways, PTs are like puzzles. I predict that by the end of this book, especially if you complete the online practice tests, review the debriefings, and study the online sample answers, you will find PTs "fun." (I cannot begin to tell you how much I smile when, each July, students email me saying, "You will never believe this, but I am actually enjoying these PTs. Finally!" And I get many of these emails.)

Even if your bar exam does not include a PT, this book is still important. Training with practice PTs helps bolster your analytical and writing skills generally, which in turn helps you to succeed on bar exam essay questions and in law practice. Also, bar exam essays in some jurisdictions include PT-like aspects. For example, at the time of this writing, some jurisdictions such as Florida do not include actual PTs on their bar exams, but certain Florida bar essays include role-play components, requiring a similar sort of PT mindset.

Additionally, the work in each chapter of this book will help sharpen your writing, and your analytical, time-management, and problem-solving skills, many of which are directly transferable to essay and multiple-choice testing, as well as to law practice. Completing the work in this book may also help prepare you for your first law jobs, be they internships during school or new attorney work after graduation. You may be able to use the work you complete in one or more of the chapters in this book as a writing sample for a job interview.

Again, why do I say PTs are the best parts of bar exams?

- Because they are open book, they do not put crazy pressure on your memory.
- They are realistic.
- They mirror the type of work you do as a beginning lawyer.
- They allow you to think and write creatively.

Some readers may not welcome this last point. (You know who you are, MBE fans!) You don't want options or "creativity" on exams. You want bright lines, blackletter law. Rest assured, once you understand what the bar examiners are up to, you will quickly see that many performance tests, at their core, require a type of logical writing style similar to that used for bar essays. Even on PTs, often you will write using some form of IRAC: Issue, Rule, Analysis/Argument/Application, Conclusion. You will likely find that you can produce passing PT answers without having to think too far outside the box. But, for those of you who happily receive the news about being *allowed* to think and write creatively (and often being rewarded handsomely for doing so), trust me when I say that you will particularly like the PT portion of the bar exam.

If you yearn to see yourself dealing with real people who have real problems, considering all of the wants and needs of your clients, you will like PTs. If you are eager to investigate and develop potentially useful facts and not simply analyze whether "frozen" fact patterns include evidence of each element of memorized rules and theories, you may love the PT.

One of my mentors, Louis M. Brown, Esq., used to describe facts before or during trial as "hot facts," suggesting that they were still malleable, but said facts became "frozen" by the time of appeal. Similarly, on bar essays and MBEs, facts are frozen. You cannot question them or ignore them, and nearly all of them are relevant. In contrast, on PTs, there may be both cold and hot facts. Also, as you will soon learn, PTs typically include many irrelevant facts that you must learn to sift through and separate out.

PTs may end up being your favorite part of the bar exam, or you may remain an MBE fan. Nevertheless, every reader, whether you see yourself more as a "left brainer" or a "right brainer," can grow to appreciate the PT form of testing, if you:

1. Train the underlying skills required to effectively complete PTs
2. Complete many practice PTs under timed conditions
3. Study quality sample answers, working steadily to improve your efficiency and work product

Notice I say that you can "grow to" appreciate PTs. Why? They are open book, but they are not easy! PTs require you to sort through a large amount of material; to absorb, understand, and organize facts and law; and to package your thinking into a well-written, logical, and thoughtful answer in a relatively short amount of time.

Completing PTs within the time limits feels like running a race. Expect your first performance tests to be overwhelming. Some of my best students have literally cried the first time they tackled a PT. By exam time, however, most of my students come to welcome this piece of their bar exam with open arms. One former student referred to the PT with the memorable phrase, a "points volcano," because of the potential grading cushion this open-book exam provides, especially given the possibility of that unpredictable moment on an essay or MBE when you know but forget a rule.[4]

Know, too, that although the first PTs you complete will seem tough, they get easier with practice—much easier. If you complete all the PTs that are part of this book, you will gain confidence in your fundamental lawyering skills. With continued training, you will get to a place where you can handle and produce a passing answer to any PT thrown at you on your bar exam.

STRATEGIC TRAINING OVER TIME IS THE KEY TO SUCCESS ON PTs

As noted earlier, I believe in success, but I am also all about hard work. I want you to win, and I want to help you get there. I have designed this book precisely with that goal in mind, and with the soundest strategy possible to help you achieve your goal. The strategy is based on stamina building.

The first part of this stamina training is to start early, as already discussed, while you are in law school, and not wait until bar review to begin PT training. The second part is to practice with longer and more difficult exams than you will have to complete on your bar exam. Think of it this way: If you want to easily and effortlessly run five laps around the track, start with one lap, build to two, and eventually practice on a regular basis running ten laps each day. If you are used to running ten laps, five will

---

[4] Credit here to Miriam Billington, Esq.

seem easy. My nephew ran track for years. When his varsity team competed in 3-mile events, his coach made them regularly train with 10- to 15-mile practice runs, and sometimes at high altitudes, to make the practice even more difficult than the main event. That is the type of success training I want for you![5]

If your bar exam includes a PT component, it will consist of one or two 90-minute PT exams. In this book, you will train with both 90-minute PTs and 3-hour PTs. Both involve the same skills and the same approach, but training for 90-minute exams with some 3-hour exams will build your stamina and focus. The longer exams include more law and facts to read, sort through, analyze, organize, and write about. After even some initial training with longer exams, your 90-minute PT exam will seem fairly easy by comparison. (As noted in this book's acknowledgments, we owe a huge debt of gratitude to the National Conference of Bar Examiners and the California Committee of Bar Examiners for their permission to use these exams.)

TIME CRUNCH SHORTCUTS: A LITTLE PRACTICE IS MUCH BETTER THAN NONE AT ALL!

Full-out stamina training is, no doubt, a great way to succeed. But I also know and respect that you are all busy. Therefore, in each chapter I have included "Time Crunch Shortcuts." These describe how to do productive work on that chapter's practice exam, even if you do not have time to complete the entire practice test. Again, let's consider a fitness metaphor. If you are looking to get fit, it may well be ideal to commit serious blocks of time each day to working out. Still, even a 10-minute jog around the block, on a day when you don't have time for more, is much better than nothing at all. For that reason, I will give details of these time-saving tips so that you can make sure you have time to gain exposure to PTs during law school, no matter how busy you are. You can also mix and match your practice sessions. For some chapters you can do a "full workout" and complete the entire exam; for others, you can take the shortcut, and come back to that PT when you have more time.

A last word, for now, on stamina training: Whatever you are working on, be it reading cases to prepare for class, getting a head start for bar success, writing a paper

---

[5]Thanks to Roger Berman for recounting his stamina training strategies.

for a seminar, or clerking at a law firm, practice concentrating for three-hour stretches of time, without breaks. We live in a fast-paced, multitasking society. Most of us stop every few minutes to check our phones, send messages, watch videos, eat or drink, or engage in any number of other distractions. But bar exams include several-hour testing sessions, in both the mornings and afternoons. (Even if your bar includes only one 90-minute PT, you will have other test questions to complete in each session.) Many jurisdictions present three hours of essay testing; in that time, some include three 1-hour essays, others have six 30-minute essays, still others have a greater number of short essays. Furthermore, the MBE consists of three hours in the morning and three hours in the afternoon, each block testing you on 100 questions. This requires enormous concentration and endurance.

There's no way around it: to succeed on the bar exam, you will have to sit and focus for several-hour blocks of time, with no breaks. Start training early, and train to win. Even in social settings, practice stopping yourself from checking your phone every few minutes (especially during your 3L year as you get close to the bar exam). If you think I am urging you to study in a way I would not do myself, think again: I forced myself, for all of June and July before my exam, to sit and focus for *four-hour* blocks of time, without breaks. My reasoning was that if I got used to concentrating for four-hour stretches, three hours of doing so in bar sessions would be easier. Now, that may seem hard-core, but all I know is that this system of early training worked well for me, and it has worked well for the thousands of students whom I have helped pass bar exams nationwide.

WHAT IS IN THE REST OF THIS BOOK, AND HOW TO USE THE MATERIAL DURING LAW SCHOOL

Chapter 2 of this book serves as a primer on how to take performance tests. I describe the skills that PTs test, and I walk you step-by-step through a logical approach to successfully tackling any performance test question you might encounter.

The rest of this book is divided into chapters that correspond to law school courses. I have chosen subjects that are heavily tested on bar exams: criminal law, criminal procedure, torts, contracts, civil procedure, evidence, constitutional law, professional responsibility, real property, and family law. In each of those chapters you will find a quick overview of the subject and a debriefing of a practice PT from that area of law. All practice questions and sample answers to those questions are in the Online Question and Answer Bank, which you can access at **http://ambar.org/barexamprep**. Do not review the answers until after you have completed the practice tests!

In each chapter, you will also find "spin-off" exercises, which are suggestions for additional assignments to complete based on that chapter's practice PT to provide more exposure to potential testable tasks. Each chapter ends with "key takeaway" points, to reinforce and cement your learning.

Do not study PTs to help you master specific rules of law. Reviewing rules in PT Libraries may help bolster your general knowledge of a subject and sharpen your legal analysis skills within the context of that doctrinal area. However, you must *not* expect to use practice PTs to learn particular rules for your bar exam. Why? First, bar examiners may use fictitious law for PT exam purposes. (The examiners explicitly warn that they may change case holdings.) Second, the PT rules may come from a different jurisdiction and thus not be applicable on your bar exam essays. Third, the law in a PT may be outdated. So remember, practice PTs provide excellent *skills training* within the context of subjects you need to learn, and they help you gain general fluency in areas of law that will in turn help when you master the rules tested in your jurisdiction—but do not rely on the accuracy of the law in PT Libraries.

Ideally, readers will use this book throughout law school. You may also want to refer back to the book during bar review. You can complete the exams in any order you like. You can:

- Work through the chapters in chronological order
- Read each chapter while you are taking the corresponding course in law school (e.g., complete the torts PT while you are studying torts)
- Complete the chapters corresponding to all your 1L courses just after you complete your first year, while you are still very familiar with them
- Work through the entire book during your last year of law school, and re-read it in bar review to refresh your recollection. (Well, I guess that would be in the evidence chapter! Pun intended.)

If you work through this book in chapter order from beginning to end:

- You will first take four 3-hour PTs in criminal law, criminal procedure, torts, and contracts. You will access all of the PT practice questions for this book in the Online Question and Answer Bank at **http://ambar.org/barexamprep**.
- Then, you will take your first 90-minute PT (in civil procedure); trust me, you will notice and appreciate how much shorter it is! You will see how well prepared you are *because* you trained more intensively to begin with.
- The next chapter (evidence) includes a 3-hour PT that breaks evenly into two 90-minute PTs. You can go to the Online Question and Answer Bank and take the evidence PT exam in one 3-hour sitting for endurance and stamina training, or take it as two separate 90-minute PTs to simulate your actual exam timing.
- Next, you will go to the Online Question and Answer Bank to take another 90-minute PT on constitutional law.
- The last three PTs, for the professional responsibility (PR), real property, and family law chapters, are also 3-hour PTs, providing still more of the stamina and endurance training that is so essential for bar passage.

- Professional responsibility (PR) is also tested in many ways on most bar exams, so it can only help to give yourself an additional three hours of exposure to PR, and the practice exam for PR in that chapter is a great one.
- I chose the practice PT for the real property chapter as the ultimate empowerment tool. Along the same lines as running 10 laps to get ready to easily run 5 laps, it is an excellent strategy to at least see the worst-case scenario and know that you will be OK. In real property, for many students the worst case would be an exam on the rule against perpetuities, a most dreaded rule. So what did I choose for you? Of course! A PT that allows you to face the rule against perpetuities for three hours. Tackle this PT, and you will know you can handle anything the examiners throw at you.
- The last chapter, on family law, includes a final 3-hour PT, but this is one that you can easily shave off time with if you cannot afford to dedicate the full three hours. The family law PT is a creative and interesting exam that demands thinking outside the box, and also provides excellent reinforcement of element-based analysis skills. The task in this family law PT is an investigation/discovery plan and thus provides exposure to both family law and civil procedure.

Note again that each chapter provides time-saving tips on how to complete a variation on the practice test if you cannot find time to complete the entire exam. Remember, though, after graduation and during bar review, you will train exclusively with 90-minute PT exams. Thus, during law school is the time to use three-hour PTs to build muscle and stamina and prepare to easily pass this portion of your bar exam. So, although I provide time-crunch tips, please do try to complete as many of the full three-hour PTs in the Online Question and Answer Bank as possible.

You might also find it interesting to work through each chapter as you are taking the corresponding class in school. You may have further insights into the client's situation, and you may enjoy seeing cases in that area "come to life." Nevertheless, because each PT has a closed-universe Library, you do not have to have studied a subject to do well on a PT that is set in any particular area of doctrinal law. Because the examiners provide the necessary legal rules, any subject is fair game on the PT. Your bar exam may include a PT set in a tax law context, for example, or one that deals with sports law, environmental law, or bankruptcy—subjects that are typically electives and not required courses in law school.

General legal reasoning and basic concepts you learn in law school will help tremendously on the PT, but avoid referencing outside law, even if you are aware of additional relevant authorities. As you will learn in Chapter 2, the only rules beyond the official Library to which you may need to refer are rules of professional responsibility. That is true in part because you are expected to come to PT role-plays as a competent lawyer (albeit usually a new or beginning lawyer), one who knows his or her ethical obligations.

CAVEAT

This book is not designed as any sort of substantive law outline, and, as noted earlier, you are not to rely on PT Libraries to master law or rules tested on your bar exam. You may use this book in individual chapter units, completing PTs in certain areas as you study those subjects, beginning in 1L. You may wait and complete all the PTs in this book in your final year of law school to get a head start on bar review. You may also use or review this book as a supplement to your bar review course. Here, though, is the big caveat: However you use the book, and whenever you take the practice PTs, **use them for skills-based learning and *not* to learn the law**. A PT Library may contain real cases or statutes, or authorities that are "made up" for that exam. The examiners may provide rules that are outdated or not applicable in your jurisdiction. They may even change the holding of a well-known case. Therefore, do not rely on PTs to master legal rules. Rather, use PT Files and Libraries as a platform to train your legal and factual analysis skills, and to gain a comfort level with drafting legal documents such as legal memoranda, briefs, opening statements and closing arguments, discovery plans, letters to clients, and more.

KEY TAKEAWAYS

- Practice PTs during law school are one of the best investments of time and energy you can make to set you up for success in bar review, help you pass the bar exam, and thrive in law practice.
- PTs are hard but fair. They are open-book exams, testing skills but not memory.
- Stamina training should be your key success strategy. Work harder than you will need to in practice test sessions so that you are ready for the bar exam "marathon" when the actual time comes.

PTs can be fun. They provide realistic lawyering scenarios where you jump into role-plays and have the chance to show the grader not only that you know how to read cases, but also that you know how to help clients. If you do not yet believe you are ready for that, read on! You will be soon.

2

WHAT PERFORMANCE TESTS ARE AND HOW TO PASS THEM

This chapter explains what a performance test (PT) is and how to successfully complete this type of exam. If you are already familiar with PTs, this chapter may provide new ways of thinking about your approach to tackling any given PT. If you have never worked on a PT, this chapter will provide the foundation you will need before testing yourself with the practice exam work in the remaining chapters.

Whether initially familiar with the PT or not, you may find it helpful to return to this chapter as you complete your practice tests. Why? With each re-read, you will gain new strategic insights and confirm your mastery of those skills required to produce passing answers to any new exam you encounter.

OVERVIEW OF PERFORMANCE TESTS

Performance tests are examinations based on simulated case files. Unlike real-world lawyering, where you must often complete extensive legal research, PTs come in neat packages with (almost) all the facts and law you need to draft the required tasks. (I say "almost" because some PTs involve discovery or fact-gathering tasks, as will be discussed later in this chapter.)

Performance tests provide:

1. **Instructions:** Detailed directions on how to complete your assignment. Typical assignments include memoranda of law, briefs to the court in support of or opposing motions, declarations, statements of facts, closing arguments, opinion letters, letters to clients, discovery plans, and settlement offers.

Note: PT tasks are judged by the examiners to be work that a beginning lawyer could perform. Do not be concerned if you are not yet familiar with all of these documents, just read on.[1]

2. **Facts:** Usually in the form of original source documents such as transcripts of interviews, police reports, letters, and contract excerpts, rather than the preset hypothetical fact patterns that are typical of law school and bar exam essays.
3. **Law:** Most often in a "Library" that includes cases and statutes. You will read, brief, and analyze these legal authorities, and use them to draft your assigned task(s). The PT is thus an open-book test; virtually all the law you need to know is in your PT Library. (More on PT Libraries follows.) Compare this PT approach with essay and multiple-choice testing where you must find the relevant rules in your own memory.

Your first and most important job in successfully completing a PT is to pull together these instructions, facts, and law, as if they were puzzle pieces; organize them logically; and then use them to produce whatever document(s) you are directed to write.

SUCCESS TIP

Most PTs include only these components: Instructions, File, and Library. Rarely, a PT might include an additional set of materials, such as an exhibit or jury instructions. (One PT included jury instructions instead of a Library.) If your PT includes other materials, the Instructions will so specify and/or they will be listed in the Table of Contents. Start by carefully reading all Instructions and find out what your "universe" consists of. Students are sometimes taught to skip the Instructions and jump right into the File and Library. This is bad advice. The short amount of time necessary to read Instructions is worth the investment.

At first, PTs seem like a lengthy mish-mash of unrelated pages. The more PTs you practice taking, the more you will come to trust that all the materials "fit" together, somewhat like a puzzle. There is a framework, and at least one logical organizational structure.

---

[1]An easy way to get a crash-course overview of civil litigation and the criminal justice systems is by reading two books I co-authored with my law professor Paul Bergman: *Represent Yourself in Court: How to Prepare and Try a Winning Case*, and *The Criminal Law Handbook: Know Your Rights, Survive the System*. These two books, published by Nolo.com and written for laypeople, are light reads for law students but tremendously helpful in getting a clear picture of the system, from pretrial discovery to appeal on the civil side and arrest to appeal on the criminal side. Many of my former students have found these two books invaluable in helping them prepare for performance tests.

You typically find an organizing structure in either the Instructions or the Library, or a combination of both. This makes sense. Facts are not relevant in a vacuum; rather, facts are relevant as they prove or disprove elements of rules of law. To help visualize the organization of a typical PT, think of the underlying client matter in a PT as a "tree." The "trunk" is a legal theory, cause of action, or crime. The "branches" are elements or factors. The "leaves" on each branch are facts relevant to proving that particular element or factor. A PT answer may have one or several legal "trees" or organizing principles. (More on organization follows later in this chapter, as does information regarding variations on organization for PTs set in transactional rather than litigation contexts.)

YOUR ROLE AS LAWYER: PRACTICAL ASPECTS OF PERFORMANCE TESTS

In a typical PT, you find yourself acting as a junior associate in a private law firm. Some PTs set you in a government law office as a prosecutor or public defender. You may also role-play as counsel for a nonprofit organization, as a mediator, or as a clerk to a judge or legislator. (Think quickly: How might your tone and ethical obligations differ when assuming these different roles?)

As counsel, you have clients. Your client may be one or more individuals, a business, or another entity. You learn whom you represent in the Instructions. Just as in practice, you will be expected to be attentive to your client's wants and needs. In a PT, that means taking note every time a File document mentions your client's objectives and concerns. You must be aware of, and sometimes predict, obstacles that may hinder your client's ability to achieve desired outcomes.

PT Instructions will direct you to perform tasks such as analyzing issues, advising and counseling clients or colleagues, or persuading a judge or jurors to decide a matter in your client's favor. You may be called upon to investigate facts or negotiate with opposing counsel. You may have to draft or edit documents.

I often think that if bar examiners had limitless funding, they would call applicants in to appear in person and observe them actually interviewing people posing as clients, reporting to actors posing as colleagues, or arguing in a mock court setting. Instead, they use the performance test as a "paper interview." The examiners determine how you handle yourself as a lawyer by reading the documents you draft.

You must be aware at all times of your own professional responsibilities. PTs were designed in part as a vehicle to test ethical rules. In many of the exams, ethical issues arise—and where they do, bar graders will be looking at your PT responses to assess whether you are ready to be responsible for real clients.

> **Note:** Professional responsibility, or PR, is the only aspect of PTs that is not necessarily open book. You will not be expected to cite statutes by number, but you will be expected to know basics about your professional responsibilities. More on this later.

A DETAILED LOOK AT THE PERFORMANCE TEST

Bar exams typically include essays, multiple-choice questions, and/or performance tests. Essay exams and multiple-choice testing are familiar formats, but you may just be learning what a performance test is. If so, you are in good company. Performance tests are fairly new to bar testing and still not a routine part of the curriculum in most law schools.

PT HISTORY

The first PTs were launched experimentally in 1980 and became a standard part of the California Bar Exam in July 1983. Until 2017, the California Bar Exam included two 3-hour PTs; the California Bar now includes one 90-minute exam. (You can find information about the California Bar Exam at http://admissions. calbar.ca.gov/.) Some years after California launched its PT, the National Conference of Bar Examiners created the Multistate Performance Test (MPT), modeled after California's PT but half the length. MPTs have similar though slightly different Instructions, File, and Library components. (More on the MPT at http://www. ncbex.org/exams/mpt.) Pennsylvania also created its own 90-minute PT that is much like the MPT (see http://www.pabarexam.org/bar_exam_information/ testsubjects.htm).

Performance tests require examinees to be proficient in a number of lawyering skills. Principal among these are (you will find a descriptive list of MPT-specific skills at http://www.ncbex.org/exams/mpt/preparing):

- Legal analysis and reasoning
- Factual analysis
- Awareness of professional responsibility: recognizing and resolving ethical dilemmas
- Problem solving
- Communication, including critical reading and effective writing
- Organization and management of a legal task, including time management

We will discuss, and you will train in, each of these skills as you work through the book and the practice exams in the Online Question and Answer Bank.

PT APPROACH: HOW TO FINISH A PT IN 90 MINUTES

The following presents an efficient and effective approach to the materials in a PT. Note that because each person thinks differently, and each performance test is unique, all times are approximate. The examiners recommend that you spend 45 minutes on reading and outlining, leaving 45 minutes to produce your answer. Some people are slower readers and need more time to fully understand the File and Library before they are able to write a passing answer. Others are slower typists; they read quickly but take more time to set out a legible and well-organized answer. True story: one former student who was following the recommended timing and was also failing all her practice tests, tried increasing the time she spent reading, thinking, and outlining to nearly 60 minutes. She was a fast enough typist that she was not only able to complete the exams in the remaining 30 minutes but produced much better quality answers. Most people do well with the recommended 45/45 split, but, bottom line: these times are guidelines; experiment with timing as you practice and adjust the suggested times based on your own strengths and weaknesses.

1. **S**tudy any General Instructions, study the Task Memo, and review any Format pages. (3-5 min.)

General Instructions provide broad guidelines for taking the exam; the Task Memo describes your client's situation, tells you who you are in the exam role-play, and tells you which document(s) you must draft in your answer. The Task Memo is the most important document in the PT. (Some analogize it to "the call of the question" in a law essay.) You may find information in the Task Memo or separate formatting information that tells you how to set up your answer. If there is nothing specific on format, just choose a logical organization. (Much more on how to organize commonly tested tasks appears later in this chapter.)

2. **S**kim the File, to get a sense of your client's situation. Then re-read the Task Memo to focus your Library reading on what is critical to your task(s). (8-10 min.)
3. **B**rief the Library authorities—typically cases and statutes, but sometimes PT Libraries include other authorities. (10-15 min.)
4. **R**e-read the Task Memo to remind yourself of exactly what you are to draft. Re-read the File; it should be much easier to spot relevant facts now that you know the law. Think about how the Instructions, Library, and File logically fit together. Re-read the File, Library, and Task Memo again, as necessary. (10-15 min.)
5. **O**utline your task(s). (5 min.)
6. **W**rite your answer (45 min.). Re-read the Task Memo any time you pause in your writing to make sure you are following directions and answering the question(s) asked. Be sure to proofread your answer using any time remaining.

If this seems like too many steps, you can remember them with the acronym SS-BROW: Study, Skim, Brief, Re-Read, Outline, and Write. Easy!

- **S**tudy the Instructions
- **S**kim the File
- **B**rief the Library Authorities

- **Re**-Read Instructions, File, and Library as needed
- **O**utline
- **W**rite

You've got this! SS-BROW. Simple.

Remember, time flies when you are writing PTs. There is a lot of material to sort through, synthesize, and write about intelligently. So, it is critical to master an efficient approach to the material and to complete many practice tests under timed conditions. Note that for the 3-hour practice PTs in this book, you will employ the same SS-BROW approach but *double the time* for each step. In those exams, it is recommended that you spend approximately 90 minutes to read and outline, leaving 90 minutes to produce your answer.

PERFORMANCE TESTS AS TRAINING FOR THE TIME PRESSURES OF LAW PRACTICE

Some critics believe that the artificial time constraints of PTs make them unfair and unrealistic. They contend that there is too much emphasis on finishing within the allotted time, rather than on producing quality work product. It is true that law practice may not obligate attorneys to achieve the rapid turnaround of work product that is required for the PT. However, it is also true that as an attorney in today's fast-paced society, you will likely have to act and react very quickly on many occasions. Clients frequently want instantaneous answers to legal questions. Email and even texting have become a routine part of law practice. Gone are the days when lawyers could leisurely ponder questions before giving advice. That is why, despite them seeming like a lot of material to process in a relatively short amount of time, PTs are realistic exams and tremendously useful learning tools.

THE PT APPROACH IN DETAIL

Now let's take a closer look at the steps for mastering a PT, starting with the Instructions.

Note: You will see samples of all of these PT components in practice exams when you complete the work in later chapters. For now, just think about what each part is and how it will help you answer the question.

You must complete a very specific task(s) in a very limited amount of time, so it is critical to have a precise picture of what the examiners want before you start writing. Additionally, the examiners expect you to deliver a concise, responsive, well-written, and well-organized answer. For these reasons, the most important parts of every performance test are the Instructions.

Instructions

Performance test instructions take the following forms: General Instructions, a Task Memo, and sometimes one or more format pages.

General Instructions

General Instructions are largely boilerplate, meaning the same or similar in every exam. They describe the performance test, tell you how long you have to complete the exam, note what jurisdiction you are in, and provide a few other important details. The trend, especially with the MPT, has been to keep these Instructions entirely boilerplate. See a copy of the MPT Instructions at http://www.ncbex.org/exams/mpt/preparing.[2]

Despite this trend, I would still advise at least quickly skimming the General Instructions because some critical information could be located only in the General Instructions.

---

[2]The Instructions read:

MULTISTATE PERFORMANCE TEST DIRECTIONS

You will be instructed when to begin and when to stop this test. Do not break the seal on this booklet until you are told to begin. This test is designed to evaluate your ability to handle a select number of legal authorities in the context of a factual problem involving a client.

The problem is set in the fictitious state of Franklin, in the fictitious Fifteenth Circuit of the United States. Columbia and Olympia are also fictitious states in the Fifteenth Circuit. In Franklin, the trial court of general jurisdiction is the District Court, the intermediate appellate court is the Court of Appeal, and the highest court is the Supreme Court.

You will have two kinds of materials with which to work: a File and a Library. The first document in the File is a memorandum containing the instructions for the task you are to complete. The other documents in the File contain factual information about your case and may include some facts that are not relevant.

The Library contains the legal authorities needed to complete the task and may also include some authorities that are not relevant. Any cases may be real, modified, or written solely for the purpose of this examination. If the cases appear familiar to you, do not assume that they are precisely the same as you have read before. Read them thoroughly, as if they all were new to you. You should assume that the cases were decided in the jurisdictions and on the dates shown. In citing cases from the Library, you may use abbreviations and omit page references.

Your response must be written in the answer book provided. If you are using a laptop computer to answer the questions, your jurisdiction will provide you with specific instructions. In answering this performance test, you should concentrate on the materials in the File and Library. What you have learned in law school and elsewhere provides the general background for analyzing the problem; the File and Library provide the specific materials with which you must work.

Although there are no restrictions on how you apportion your time, you should allocate approximately half your time to reading and digesting the materials and to organizing your answer before you begin writing it. You may make notes anywhere in the test materials; blank pages are provided at the end of the booklet. You may not tear pages from the question booklet.

Do not include your actual name anywhere in the work product required by the task memorandum.

This performance test will be graded on your responsiveness to the instructions regarding the task you are to complete, which are given to you in the first memorandum in the File, and on the content, thoroughness, and organization of your response.

First, the General Instructions tell you what jurisdiction the problem is set in; this is essential to knowing which Library authorities will be binding. Second, General Instructions tell you how many sets of materials you have to work with. Almost always, that is a File and Library. But it is worth confirming that your closed universe consists only of a File and Library because on rare past occasions applicants were given a third set of materials (such as, in one past PT, a set of draft trusts) which some Applicants who had not read the Instructions mistook for scratch paper. Also in at a couple of past PTs, there was no Library; the law was provided in something other than a Library, such as in jury instructions located in the File. Third, on many PTs, you only draft one document in your answer. But, if you are assigned multiple tasks, how much each task is worth will likely be indicated in either the General Instructions or the Task Memo. This information is critical to how you apportion your writing time. So, again, just give any General Instructions a cursory review before moving on to the Task Memo.

Task Memo

The Task Memo is the most important part of the Instructions, and arguably the most important part of the entire PT. The Task Memo is to the PT what the "interrogatories" (or "calls of the question") are to an essay exam.

The Task Memo is written to you ("Bar Applicant") from the person giving the assignment. Often, that is a senior partner in the fictitious law firm where you work in this PT role-play. For that reason, many people call the Task Memo the "Senior Partner Memo." I refer to it more neutrally as the "Task Memo" because your assignment may come from someone other than a senior partner. You may not even work in a private firm. You may work in a government office or a nonprofit organization, or you may clerk for a judge. So, in addition to telling you what your assignment is, the Task Memo also tells you who you are. Knowing your role can be critical to drafting an appropriately worded and complete answer.

In a rare past PT, bar applicants were to play the role of a more experienced lawyer writing to a beginning lawyer. The appropriate tone on that PT was heavily influenced by the fact that applicants were supposed to have had more experience than the person to whom they were writing.

Bottom line: The Task Memo is your key to success on the performance test! It must be your bible, your guide, and your constant companion. Refer back to the Task Memo frequently. Glance back at it after you read the File, after you study the

Library, and again periodically as you organize and draft your answers. The further you get into a PT, the more helpful hints you will notice in the Task Memo.

MARKING THE TASK MEMO PAGE

You may *not* bring sticky notes, paper, or anything you could write on into bar exams. **MPT instructions specifically forbid ripping or tearing any pages.** You may fold the corner of the Task Memo page (without tearing it) or clip it with a paper clip if you are allowed to bring in paper clips, in order to easily flip back to the Task Memo. But, remember, it is usually one of the first pages, so easy to find. **Be sure to verify your state's rules about what you may and may not bring into the exam, and be certain you know all other testing rules for your bar exam.**

Format Pages

Some performance tests include an additional instructional page, one that provides a "format" and sometimes a sample of how to structure the document you are to draft. A format page may follow the Task Memo, or formatting instructions may be a part of the Task Memo itself. (If they give you any specific formatting instructions, be happy! That is a gift. If they don't, worry not: just read on. Every PT has some logical organizing principle.) Formats may be drafted as internal office memoranda that start with language such as, "Our firm follows the practice of drafting [the particular document type] as follows...." You will see sample format pages in some of the practice tests in the Online Question and Answer Bank.

If a PT exam provides guidance on how to set up your answer, follow that guidance. **Do not disregard instructions and format the document your own way.** Among other key parts of what bar exams test is your ability to follow directions. People frequently fail PTs because they fail to do as instructed. I have counseled many attorneys who were licensed in one jurisdiction, took the bar in another, and failed because they formatted PT documents as they had in practice and not as directed on the exam.

LAW PRACTICE NOTE

Formats, including form books and documents drafted by other lawyers in your law firm, can also be invaluable in law practice. As a practicing lawyer, you often do not need to start from scratch when drafting a motion or other document.

Also, in many law firms it is common practice for new lawyers to ask more senior lawyers for similar documents from previous cases to use as samples for guidance when beginning new projects.

What if a PT does not provide a specific format? When there is no suggested or required format, the key is to know what you are writing, for whom, and why, and then simply to choose a *logical and responsive way* to organize and present the information requested. If there is no distinct format guide, there will most likely be organizational clues in either the Instructions or the Library. (More on this later.)

File

Next, after carefully reviewing all instructional documents, skim the rest of the documents in the File.

> **Note:** You will re-read the File later, but the first pass through should be a quick read or skim.

Why such a quick read or skim? Because reading every word of each File document now, before you have read the Library, wastes time.

Let me explain why it makes so much sense to skim, rather than read the File carefully, on your first pass through the File. The File will include a great deal of information that you will not need to draft your answer. One major skill tested by a PT is your ability to sort relevant from irrelevant facts. If you read the File carefully, without having any context for the facts, you will likely get mired in irrelevant detours. Only *after* you have studied the Library, and are familiar with governing law, will you readily see what is and what is not relevant in the File. Once you know the law, you will be able to identify important facts much more quickly.

You may be asking yourself, "Then why not read the Library first?" Great question! The answer is a bit complicated but the bottom line is, again, that you will also waste precious time wandering in the Library if you do not first have at least a sense of your client's situation before reading cases and statutes. You see, which to read first, File or Library, poses a "chicken and egg" challenge: You really cannot sort relevant from irrelevant information in the File until you know the law; but you also cannot effectively determine how the legal authorities apply to your client until you know at least a little about your client's case. For these reasons, the best method is to *skim* the File to get a sense of your client's factual circumstances, then study the Library to see which law applies, then go back and re-read the File. During that re-read, you will readily (and much more quickly) be able to identify relevant facts, and start plugging those facts into the legal framework (your outline).

Think of it this way: PTs require you to be on a precision mission rather than a fishing expedition. What does that mean? When you read and brief cases in law school, you are reading every word of each case with an eye toward anticipating any possible question the professor might ask, about any part of the court's decision. If you proceed straight to the Library in a PT without knowing your client's circumstances, you head off on a similar sort of "fishing expedition," finding the cases interesting perhaps, but not knowing what you are looking for in them or how they relate to your case or task. Instead, you want to read PT Libraries like a lawyer, not a law student. Go into the Library not on the student's fishing expedition, but rather on a lawyer's precision mission. Reading the Library while armed with a sense of what has happened to your client and what your client wants, you will be able to immediately assess whether case law favors your client or not. You will be able to see where a case is factually analogous to or distinguishable from your client's case. Perhaps most importantly, you will understand how to use the authorities in your PT answer.

Skimming the File first may also provide hints about how much time to spend on each Library case. Why? If the law supports your client's position, you may be able to quickly get in and out with a holding to cite in your answer. However, if the court has ruled in a manner that would hurt your client, you will likely need to read more closely to see if you can factually distinguish the case from your client's situation.

I hope that you are starting to see now why the read/skim method makes sense. It will come together as you complete practice tests. In the meantime, you may still be wondering how thorough your initial "skim" should be. How much should someone know after studying the Instructions and skimming the File? This varies from exam to exam, but typically after first skimming the File, you will have a sense of the following:

- Who you work for (private law firm, government, or other entity)
- Who you represent, and some of the basic facts about your client's current situation and problem (What are your client's goals, and what or who is preventing your client from getting what he/she/it wants?)
- What the basic dispute is, if this is a litigation-based problem; or what document is to be drafted or edited to achieve which goals, if a transactional problem
- Where you are located (what fictional state and, if applicable, what fictional federal circuit)
- How many documents the File contains and what sort of information is in the File (e.g., hearing transcript, report, interview or deposition of a witness or party, a map, a photo, a contract, a newspaper article, etc.)
- What type of document(s) you are to draft; if more than one, how much each is worth; and some basic information on format for each task you are to complete

From your skim, you may have learned more than the preceding points suggest, but as you begin reading the Library, you should at least have a basic sense of your client's situation and your assigned task(s).

In the Library, note what types of authorities have been provided: cases, statutes, jury instructions, excerpts from a treatise, or some other source of law. As you study the Library, extract the relevant rules and principles from those authorities (paying attention to the precedential weight of those authorities). Notice how surgical that sounds: "extract relevant rules." Very different from leisurely reading where you might peruse every fascinating aspect of a case!

Now, once you know what basic rules of law govern your case, you will go back to the File and see how the PT puzzle pieces fit together. After re-reading the File, you can begin your outline and soon start drafting your answer.

Be patient. You may need to re-read parts of the Library and File several times, and re-read the Task Memo, in order to effectively create a working outline. Keep reading, keep reasoning, and trust that the examiners have crafted a doable exam. Believe that it is a puzzle that fits together, and just keep looking to see how it does.

PT PARTICIPANTS AS CAST OF CHARACTERS IN PLAY

As part of your initial skim, start a "cast of characters" list on your scratch paper or in the table of contents. Sketch the players in the PT as one would the actors in a program for a play, so you have a quick reference guide if you forget someone's role. For example:

Carl Corporate: my client, the defendant in present action

Ms. Bigg: senior partner I work for

Mr. Big-Headed: opposing counsel who represents the plaintiff

Wendy Whistleblower: the plaintiff, fired from her job at my client's company

Library

After skimming the File, check back in quickly with the Task Memo to focus your thinking on your precise mission before you head in to the Library to read the legal authorities. The PT is an open-book test. Unlike in the movie *Mission Impossible*, where the directions self-destruct, your Task Memo is always available. Bar examiners consistently state that one of the most common reasons people fail the PT is not following directions. So, keep that Task Memo handy as you read and write. Consult it frequently.

Library Table of Contents

Once inside your PT Library, start with a quick review of the table of contents to see what sorts of authorities the Library includes.

> **Note:** Note that MPTs usually include one table of contents page for both the File and Library, unlike California PTs which include a separate table of contents for the File and Library. You will see these in the practice tests in the Online Question and Answer Bank.

I suggest taking notes about each case directly on the table of contents page. If your handwritten notes are hard to read, it can be particularly helpful to use the table of contents, or to type your notes right into your first draft of your answer. (If you do the latter, be sure on your bar exam to delete anything that is not part of your final answer before uploading the file.)

Using the table of contents for note taking is advantageous because all the main case names are printed neatly and all your thoughts about the law are then in one place. (As discussed earlier, assuming that you are permitted to bring them into the exam, you can paper-clip the table of contents page to easily locate it while you are working.)

You can either rewrite the case holdings in your own words on that table of contents page, or jot down the page numbers corresponding to where you "book-briefed" in the Library authorities. For example, you can underline or star the holding of a case on the page where it appears and then make a notation such as "H @ p.3" on the contents page next to the case name.

Briefing the Library Authorities

If your Library includes cases, determine before you read them whether they are binding or persuasive. Then, begin reading each case, paying attention to the dates each case was decided. Summarize each case using the "surgical briefing" system discussed later in this section to get into and out of each with just the information you need to use on your exam. You can always go back and re-read cases if you need more detail, but you do not want to waste time with too slow a Library read; that is time you cannot get back.

I always read the PT Library cases in the order they appear, but some people find it helpful to read them in reverse-chronological order from most recent to oldest. Sometimes a later case will refer to an earlier case, and some PTs include cases that have been overruled by later cases. In one instance, a theory stated in an earlier case had not yet been adopted in the jurisdiction, but was embraced by a later case in the same jurisdiction.

In your answer, you will want to cite all the main cases—meaning those listed in the table of contents. You may, but do not have to, cite cases within cases. Recognize that when cases cite other cases, the cited cases may be helpful. If so, reference them in your answer as follows: "*Jones* as cited in *Cray*." (*Cray* was the main case, and *Jones* was a case cited in *Cray*.) Again, you should strive at a minimum to use all the main Library cases. As you read each case, look for key facts, law, and reasoning, and incorporate them into your answer along with rules and, where appropriate, policy considerations and/or the court's rationale.

As you read each main case, determine three Ws: **Who, What,** and **Where:**[3]

- **Who** is suing whom, and which party is in the position analogous to your client? (You must know which party in a case is in a similar position to your client to determine if the court's ruling helps or hurts your client. If the case hurts your client, look further into the facts to try to distinguish the case from your client's situation.)
- **What** did the court rule, and why did it so rule? (To help you keep your case briefing short and surgical, you can combine the holding and rationale.)
- **Where** does the rule from this case fit in your answer? As soon as you know how the rule applies to your client's situation, you can put a reference to the case in your outline. (You may have to come back to this question of where to mention the case after you have read all the law, re-read the facts, and are putting together your final outline.)

Pay attention to the relative weights of the authorities. If a case that is unfavorable for your client is merely persuasive, it is easy to note in your answer that the decision need not be followed. Do not expect that, though. Usually bar examiners make things more difficult for you. The best authority for your client may be merely persuasive and those authorities that tend to lean against your client's position may be binding. When you are faced with a binding decision that is bad for your client, you must usually distinguish the facts of that case from the facts of your client's case. The graders want to see that you can do this! (In rare instances, you may have a good faith argument that the law is outdated and should be overturned, despite its being binding.)

---

[3] I gratefully credit Professor Steve Bracci for this case-briefing method.

Be sure to read every PT Library case as if it were new to you. Even if a case seems familiar, read it carefully. Do not assume that you know its key facts or holding. The examiners explicitly state that they may change or edit cases for exam purposes.

If the Library provides selected statutes and/or statutes from a subject not on your bar exam, read those too as if they were new to you. Read carefully. Pull the rules out of the statutes; they will likely be key building blocks in your answer. Just as you brief cases and extract the holdings, underline the elements of such statutes and make sure you understand what they require or prohibit. Circle all the "and" and "or" words so you know whether components of each statute are conjunctive or disjunctive.

If, however, instead of selected statutes, a PT Library provides a block of rules or a series of statutes from a code that you are already charged with knowing for the bar exam, such as the Federal Rules of Civil Procedure, you may want to skim rather than read each statute. Look at the provision headings, and know that the precise rules are there for your reference if you need them. Some people call this sort of Library a "reference Library." The statutes are there to consult whenever you need to look up the details of a particular section, just as you would search online or in a code book in practice.

Remember that cases never form a "reference" Library. In other words, you should always read Library cases as if they were new, even if they seem familiar, because the examiners may edit them for the exam, changing facts and/or the holding. (PT Instructions state this clearly.)

Re-read, Think, and Outline

After reading the Library and extracting rules from cases and/or statutes, consult the Task Memo again. Ask yourself: (1) What document(s) must I draft? and (2) How does the law in the Library fit together?

Look for an organizing principle. There must be a logical organization. There may be more than one, but there is at least one sensible structure in every PT. The examiners create PTs as solvable puzzles.

The Library may contain three to five different theories to support a single cause of action or defense theory. It may include different elements of a single claim, or several possible legal claims. The authorities may include one main rule and exceptions to that rule. There may be a guiding theory or principle with multiple factors or a multipart test.

Whatever the Library includes, the disparate threads of law will fall into an order; you just have to find it. So, after you have looked through all the authorities, stop and take a moment to think about how the cases, statutes, and/or other Library rules fit together. I tell my students at this point to, figuratively, "Put your feet up on the desk, *pretend* that you have all the time in the world, and just think—read and think, really hard."

Re-read the Task Memo. Think back to what you are being asked to draft and determine how the authorities help you draft it. If you are drafting a discovery plan, for example, does the Library include statutes about different discovery devices? If you are drafting a memo, does the Library include cases that all relate to one cause of action, but perhaps address several different elements? Try to see how the authorities can help you form a legal structure into which you will weave the facts when you ultimately write your answer.

If, after thinking for a few minutes, you do not see a pattern or structure emerging, keep moving forward with the process described in the following sections of this chapter and trust that an organization will come into focus. If you see only a partial pattern—for example, you see how some but not all the cases fit together—start your outline using the pieces you have, and build on them as you proceed.

For your outline, your goal is not to craft a very detailed outline but rather a basic roadmap, preferably including points that you will use as headings and subheadings in your main answers. (The grader will only review your final answer, not your scratch paper.) You will see sample outlines in later chapters.

TREES AND HIGHWAYS: METAPHORS FOR OUTLINING PTs

You can think of your outline as one or more trees with particular branches. The tree trunk(s) are causes of action or defense claims; the elements or factors of those theories are branches. (A torts tree might have a trunk called "negligence" with four branches: duty, breach, causation, and damages. The "causation" branch might itself have two limbs: actual cause and proximate cause.) The "leaves" that cover those branches will be facts from the File. (The kinds of "leaves" that might appear on a "damages" branch could include hospital bills or photos of your client's injuries following an accident.) Your Library may include one tree with a bunch of branches, or several trees.

If you prefer a more urban metaphor, think of your headings and outline as a highway map. There are typically between one and five main legal "highways" in a PT Library. (To finish in the allotted time, and write in an organized way, you need to find them so that you don't get lost on the "side streets.") The main highways will form the main headings or major components of your outline. Each highway may have main roads or side streets that branch out from that highway. The "cars" that drive on those highways are File facts.

After you practice with all the PTs in this book, you will get comfortable with finding the "trees" or "highways"—that is, with identifying the organizing principles in each PT.

Review the File

Now, go back and re-read the File. You will be surprised at how relevant facts just pop out at you. Before reading the Library, the File seemed filled with random details. Now, as one of my former students put it, your search through the File feels like an Easter egg hunt: you are just pulling out pieces of chocolate![4]

Put It All Together

Re-read the Task and Format Memos. Make certain you understand the exact document or documents you are to produce, for whom you are writing, and why.

What is your goal, who is your immediate audience, and who is your ultimate audience? For example, you might have to draft a brief in support of a motion along with several declarations for your senior partner to file with the court. (The senior partner is your immediate audience; your ultimate audience is the court.) Or, you might have to draft a letter for your boss to send to your client. (Your boss is the immediate audience; the ultimate audience is your client.) Always remember that the truly ultimate audience is your bar grader. The burden is on you to produce a well-organized, responsive answer. Make it easy on that grader to want to pass you. Do not give the grader reasons to want to fail you, such as not following directions or writing in a disorganized manner.

Think first, and then think some more. Think hard. Then, outline your answer before you start writing. Your outline need not be detailed, but it should include all your main headings. It should also note where the main cases and/or other legal rules fit in.

Get organized before you write. (This is especially true of those who hand write on the bar exam.) The clearer you are about what you are to produce, the clearer your answer will be. Organized, thoughtful writing is what creates passing PT answers.

As you think and outline, refer back to the File, the Library, and any notes you have taken in the margins and/or on scratch paper. Remember that your grader will not consider your notes. You only get credit for your final answers that appear in your final submission, either in an uploaded file or a handwritten bluebook. So, take selective notes, and organize them in a way that you will be able to read and use quickly and easily.

This takes a lot of practice. It is easy to take too many notes. Always remember, though: The PT is an open-book test, so you can go back into any document in the File or Library to pick up details or specific language.

Your Answer

Beware! Graders generally spend very little time grading answers, so write just what the instructions direct and in the order requested. As you write, refer back to the Task Memo and any format guidance to make sure your answer is complete and responsive.

---

[4] Credit to Ross Mitchell, Esq.

WHAT IF I DON'T KNOW WHETHER TO INCLUDE A POINT OR NOT?

My general rule is that so long as you finish, it is better to err on the side of including something that may not be relevant than to miss something that is relevant and critical. So, if you think of a point that you are not certain should be included and can quickly write it, go ahead, as long as you have a logical tie-in to your answer. If it is a longer point, note it on your scratch paper and decide whether or not to include it after you have written everything you know is critical.

Given that graders are pressed for time, make it easy for them to see your points. Write short sentences and use frequent paragraph breaks. Make your organization explicit, with clearly marked headings and subheadings to indicate main topics and subtopics within a document. (You do not have to do this with a fancy numbering system. You can use any logical system that visually sets out your organization. For example, some students left-align all main headings, indent all subheadings once, and indent all sub-subheadings twice.)

Type clearly. Try your best to spell key legal terms and names of the parties in your PT correctly. Graders understand and will forgive some typos, but because lawyers are detail oriented, you want to try to keep your presentation as neat as possible. Remember my earlier analogy of the PT to a paper interview: just as you would wear a clean suit to meet with your prospective employer, so too must you present well-organized, neatly drafted documents on your PT.

Those who are writing by hand *must* write legibly. If the graders cannot easily read your answers, they likely will not try too hard to decipher what you have written. Handwriters mostly feel disadvantaged because they cannot "cut and paste." If you are handwriting and think of something that relates back to a section of your answer that you have completed, go back and simply insert a number and write the new thought as a corresponding footnote if you left room at the bottom of the page, or as an endnote if you only have room at the end of the document. That way you can get full credit for "afterthoughts" by indicating the logical place where they belong.

Your Tone

Whatever your role, part of the test is to see that you approach the task from the perspective of a professional dealing with your client, not as a law student. In other words, when writing a letter to a lay client, you will be judged on your ability to use plain English and define all legal jargon. When preparing a document for court submission, you will be expected to adopt a more formal tone, and use language and legal authorities in a lawyer-like manner.

You will typically adopt a more neutral, balanced, and analytical approach when writing in-house documents (those where you are writing to someone in your own law office or perhaps an investigator or other professional your firm hired). You will employ a more persuasive tone when you are writing to the court, opposing counsel, or someone who is not "on your side."

A general rule is to avoid slang and to spell out abbreviations the first time you use them. You may use lists in certain documents, such as in-house fact-gathering assignments, but on most PTs you will want to write in complete sentences and complete paragraphs. You will learn much more about appropriate style by completing all the practice exams in this book.

> Do not write your name or other self-identifying information in your answer. Grading is anonymous and you will be identified only by the number you are given. Further, avoid humor and politics; the bar grader may not share your views and may take offense to something you write.

HOW TO COMPLETE PERFORMANCE TESTS UNDER TIMED CONDITIONS

Now that we have a basic approach, let's look at what is perhaps the most challenging aspect of the PT: how to finish within the time constraints.

After your first practice PT, you may find yourself saying, "I could do this if I had a full day! No problem." Do not be discouraged if you exceed the time limit on your first few PTs. You may have had several weeks to complete a similar type of assignment in a first-year "Legal Research and Writing" course. You must train to complete PTs in a timely fashion. It is not easy!

There are two ways to master PT timing. One, always attempt to complete all practice tests under simulated test conditions. Your first practice PT will likely not be passing quality, but you will improve the quality of your answers with each practice exam. With this strategy, you force yourself to produce better and better quality, within a consistent time frame. Two, complete your first practice PT taking as much time as you need to produce a passing quality answer. Then, with each subsequent practice test, shave off time. It may take four hours to complete your first PT, the next one you might finish in two hours, and so on. After several practice exams, you will get your timing under control.

If you opt for the second strategy, keep close tabs on how far over the time limit you went with each practice exam. If, after completing a half dozen, you exceed the limit by just a few minutes, keep practicing and do not worry. You will have what I call the "adrenaline advantage" on the actual exam. However, if you are consistently taking well more than the allotted time:

1. Keep working to improve your efficiency.
2. Pay attention to time-saving tips and strategies throughout this book.
3. Use the red-pen approach.

The red-pen approach works like this: Write until the time limit is reached, then note where you are, then finish. After printing your answer, or on your paper if you are handwriting, draw a big thick red line where you hit the time limit. See how many paragraphs or pages fall below the red line. With each subsequent practice test, try to move that red line closer to the end of your answer. Visualizing how much over time you are often helps you internalize how much faster you must work to complete the exam in time.

Another great thing to do to speed up your timing is to study or even re-type sample answers. Often you will see that something you spent a long time writing was stated much more succinctly—yet still effectively—in a sample answer. Comparing your own work to passing answers will help you see how to improve both your timing and your content.

CHOPPED!

I liken the PT to the TV cooking show *Chopped*, where chefs compete to pre-pare a three-course meal with each dish featuring all the foods in a particular basket of ingredients. The time limits are strictly enforced. On the TV show when the time limit has passed to prepare a particular dish the host says, "Stop cooking. Put your knives down. Step away from your dishes," just as bar exam proctors will call out, "Time" and say, "Stop typing." On the PT, your "basket of ingredients" includes the Instructions, File, and Library. Just as the *Chopped* judges expect contestants to produce a tasty, well-prepared, and beautifully presented meal in a very short amount of time, bar graders expect test-takers to craft well-reasoned, carefully drafted documents that are responsive to the instructions. Chef contestants sweat to finish; so, too, do bar applicants race against the clock. But, just as nearly all the contestants on TV complete each course using all the required ingredients, so too will you. With enough practice, you will become not only proficient but also comfortable completing these PT tasks within the required time frames. *Caveat:* On the very odd chance you run out of time on the actual bar exam, *never* indicate in your answer that you ran out of time. When you see that you have only a few moments to finish, conclude the paragraph you are writing. Skip a line, write the heading, "Conclusion," and finish off as best you can.

Selected Time-Saving Tips

First, figure out where in the process you get delayed: reading, outlining, or writing?

If you are reading too slowly:

- Resist the temptation to force yourself to "just read faster." It is counterintuitive, but sometimes taking more time to read will actually help you answer faster because you understand more clearly what you intend to write about when you put fingers to keyboard. Consider giving yourself more than the suggested reading time, if you can still manage to complete your writing in less than the suggested time. To put this in numbers, it is typically recommended that applicants spend half the exam reading and outlining and half writing. Some people just do not have a thorough enough handle on the problem halfway in, but, by taking an extra 5 or even 10 minutes to read and think, they are better positioned to knock out a good answer in the remaining time. This strategy may work well if you are a slow reader and a fast typist.
- Read more generally, in and out of law school. The more you read, the faster you will become at reading. Read a news website or blog every day. Try to summarize in a single sentence the main thesis of at least one article or posting each day. (This is yet another reason to start bar preparation while in law school rather than waiting until intensive bar review.)

If note-taking and outlining bog you down:

- Use skeletal outlines. Your outline should read like a summary of contents rather than a full table of contents; include just headings and subheadings, not every detail.
- Your grader will only read your answer; your outline and notes go in the trash. So, practice writing bare "roadmap" style notes and outlines. What you want in your outline are the main points that will become the headings and subheadings in your answer. Only write a more detailed outline if you are typing and your outline effectively becomes the first draft of your answer.

- Take notes on scratch paper sparingly. The grader will not see your scratch paper, so you will not get credit for even the most brilliant thoughts unless they are transferred to your official exam answer. Try underlining or starring key points you want to quote in the actual File or Library document, and just note on your scratch paper the page number where you have marked those points. (Remember that, generally, bar graders do not want to see long passages quoted from the File or Library. Short quotes are fine, but for longer points, it is better to summarize facts or law in your own words.)
- If you plan to type your answer, use your outline as the first draft or template of your answer; type key points or quotes directly under the relevant headings in your draft answer, rather than typing once in an outline and again in your final answer.

If writing itself takes too much time:

- Follow directions. If they tell you not to draft a Statement of Facts, do not include one. Give the examiners what they want, and only what they want. Bar examiners design these problems to make them writable within the given time frame; if you do "extra" work, you will likely not finish. (Also, such extra work will not impress the graders. Instead, you will look like someone who does not follow directions.)
- Use short cites. They tell you that you may do this. You will not appear more knowledgeable by taking extra time to include formal citations.
- Finish, and then go back and polish any rough sections. Do not try to write perfectly. To complete the exam in time, you may have to submit what you view as a draft rather than a finished product. That may be fine. Remember, bar exams are pass-fail tests. While in law school you worked continuously to get "A"s; here you are striving to do your best, but with an ultimate goal of simply passing—and remember, your quality will improve with continued practice.

Time-saving tips are great … in theory. I recognize, though, that sharing these suggestions is a bit like telling you how to run faster in a race. I can explain the theory forever: The real trick is to train. The more "fit" you are, the faster you will run. So, let's get running! Next we will look at the fundamental skills you need to pass the PT, and then you will go on to subsequent chapters to practice with actual exams. I am confident that once you see what the examiners really want, you will be reassured that these really are all skills you have learned in law school (and in life!).

FUNDAMENTAL LAWYERING SKILLS TESTED ON PTs

The four core competencies or skills tested on the PT are factual analysis, legal analysis, awareness of professional responsibility, and problem solving. (See www.ncbex. org/exams/mpt/preparing.)

Factual Analysis

You can think of PT factual analysis as a two-part process:

1. Separating relevant from irrelevant facts
2. Tying relevant facts to applicable rules of law

Compare this for a moment to bar exam essays. Because most facts on bar exam essay questions are relevant, the first part of the process (separating relevant from irrelevant facts) is not heavily tested on essays. The second part, however, should sound familiar; it mirrors the "A" ("Analysis," or some say "Application") in the logical writing system abbreviated as IRAC which stands for Issue, Rule, Analysis or Application, Conclusion. The factual analysis competency, in the words of bar examiners, is: "Given knowledge of legal rules and preliminary identification of legal issues, the ability to identify areas of factual inquiry, assess facts and marshal facts in support of legal arguments."[5]

In plain English, your tasks in performing factual or fact analysis are to consider, given the legal rules: (1) What facts do you have, and are those facts credible? (2) What further facts do you need? (3) How do these facts relate to and prove or disprove each element of each cause of action, or each factor or element of each legal theory?

Factual analysis in PTs fundamentally differs from work with facts on law essays or multistate bar exam (MBE) questions. On PTs, relevant facts generally come from (and may be buried in between irrelevant facts in) original source documents. You will hunt for relevant facts within File documents such as letters, depositions or court transcripts, interview excerpts, articles, medical reports, photos, arrest records, notes, minutes, or statements.

Contrast that with essays and MBEs, where facts come from artificially constructed hypothetical fact patterns that you must take as true. Professors sometimes say, "Do not fight the facts." Whoever drafted the exam put each fact in the fact pattern for a reason. Though some law school exams include "red herrings" (or distracter facts) on essays, on bar essays, and MBEs, you are generally not being asked to cull out irrelevant facts or assess the credibility of facts. Still, those are critical components of the factual analysis skill tested by the PT.

PTs also contain much more information than you will actually need to complete your assigned task(s). Many facts are duplicative or irrelevant to your task. This makes

---

[5] Quoted from Section II.B. of a pamphlet published by the State Bar of California called *Information Regarding Performance Tests*. This pamphlet notes that: "The description of competencies is based in large part on the work of H. Russel Cort and Jack L. Sammons, described in "The Search for 'Good Lawyering': A Concept and Model of Lawyering Competencies," 29 CLEVELAND STATE LAW REVIEW 397."

perfect sense. A bar exam essay question is often one-half to one full page in length. A PT File alone may include about six to eight pages of factual information; that is about six to ten times the amount of material in three times the amount of time. (Multistate Essay Exam [MEE] essays are 30 minutes and the MPT is 90 minutes.) What can we deduce from this? Many facts *must* be either duplicative or irrelevant.

PT Facts versus Essay Facts

Again, some law professors love "red herrings," or facts meant to distract you, but bar exam essays typically contain few irrelevant facts. In contrast, one of the key PT skills is your ability to sort relevant from irrelevant facts. Expect to have to weed out a great deal of information in the File in order to finish in time. Knowing how facts are used in different forms of testing helps you develop appropriate test-taking strategies. On essay questions, read the fact pattern and ask yourself why each fact was included and what rule it triggers. (On essays, you have no "Library." The rules must be memorized.) For example, in a criminal law essay, seeing facts such as a "broken" window or "dim lighting" might trigger you to ask yourself if burglary is a discussable issue. *Burglary* at common law was the breaking and entering of the dwelling house of another in the nighttime with intent to commit a felony therein. You would then compare the facts to each element of that rule and analyze whether there is sufficient proof of each element to conclude that the crime has been committed.

It is likely that some elements will be clear and others ambiguous. For instance, the facts may clearly state that the defendant broke and entered the requisite structure at the requisite time, but it may be unclear what her intent was upon entry. There may be facts from which an inference of felonious intent could be drawn, and other facts that refute that inference. In that instance, you may have to analyze the issues from both sides and conclude by showing why the facts logically point toward one or the other party prevailing.

> **Note:** On many states' bar exam essays, it will be fine to conclude that one or the other party will "likely" prevail (so long as that conclusion logically flows from your thorough and complete analysis). In other states, the examiners expect a definitive conclusion. Read the call of the question very carefully to get insight into what is expected on a particular question, and study as many released passing bar exam essay answers from your jurisdiction as possible to determine the expectations of your bar examiners. Also, heed the advice of your academic support and bar support faculty.

Notice, even where facts "cut both ways" on an essay question, you do not question the reliability of those facts. Back to the preceding burglary example: You would never ask, "Well, what if the window wasn't really broken?" You would not fight the facts and say, "I bet the lighting wasn't really all that dim." No! If essay facts tell you the lighting was dim or the window was broken, those are the facts you must use. Period. The facts on essays, as in appellate course cases, are frozen. The grader wants to see how you analyze the particular facts given.

In PTs, we know that all the facts will *not* be relevant to our task. (The examiners tell us this!) Hence, there is no way you want to waste time combing through all the facts to see which legal issues the facts trigger, as you would when approaching an essay question. Reverse the thinking process on PTs: Learn the law to see which facts are relevant. Study the Library to determine which legal rules you are working with. Then sift through the facts to pick up the "wheat" (facts that are relevant to elements of those Library rules), and leave aside the "chaff" (irrelevant facts).

File documents in PTs may also include contradictory facts or unreliable facts, leading you to question their credibility. (For example, in a statutory rape–related PT where the age of the victim is critical, you might not take the victim's word about how old she was but suggest your law firm obtain her birth certificate to prove her age.) Keep in mind as you read PTs whether any biases or holes make facts unreliable. As noted earlier, this is the exact opposite of the wholesale acceptance of the fact pattern "as is" that you must do on bar essays.

Also, on some PTs, you may need to think "outside the (factual) box." In other words, part of your PT task may be to discuss what additional pieces of evidence are needed and how they might be gathered, such as in a discovery-related assignment. Again, this is a very different way of thinking about facts than what you do on bar essays—but this sort of factual investigation and analysis are precisely what many lawyers do.

Legal Analysis

Legal analysis skills on performance tests include "[t]he ability to analyze and evaluate legal authority, identify legal issues, and generate, assess, and justify the relative merits of alternate or competing legal positions."[6] This skill requires that you read and extract rules from cases and statutes, sift holdings from dicta, and determine the precedential weight of various authorities. You then apply these rules to the factual context in which the client is situated.

Some authorities (sources of law) are binding or mandatory; a court *must* follow them. Others are permissive; if a court finds them persuasive, it *may*, but does not have to, follow them. In order to anticipate how a court will rule or argue how it should rule in your client's matter, you must know these distinctions.

---

[6] State Bar of California, *Information Regarding Performance Tests*. See descriptive list of MPT-specific Legal Analysis Skills at http://www.ncbex.org/exams/mpt/preparing.

LEGAL AUTHORITIES

Primary authorities (which may be either persuasive or mandatory) that you may see in your PT Library include:

- Legislative authorities, such as constitutions, statutes, court rules, charters, or ordinances
- Judicial authorities, including cases and some court rules
- Administrative authorities, including decisions and regulations

Performance tests are typically set in a fictional state sometimes called Franklin, Columbia, or Olympia, or in a fictional federal circuit often at the district court or trial court level. The Instructions provide the name of the fictional state or fictional federal circuit so you can determine which authorities are binding in that jurisdiction. In general, primary legislative authorities are mandatory if enacted by the legislature in the jurisdiction. Primary judicial authorities in state courts are generally mandatory if they are decided by the court itself or a higher court in the same jurisdiction (or the Supreme Court if a federal issue) and are still good law, meaning the law has not been overruled. In federal courts, primary judicial authorities are binding if decided by the same court, the relevant federal circuit court, or the Supreme Court, and are still good law.)

As distinguished from primary authorities, secondary authorities are never mandatory; however, they can often be quite persuasive. Secondary authorities you might see in a PT Library include dictionaries, treatises, encyclopedias, legal periodicals, *A.L.R.* annotations, law review articles, restatements, and legislative history.

Cases

Cases are enforceable decisions made by judges that explain, based on a particular set of facts, what result or outcome applies to the litigating parties and why. *Case holdings* are rulings the court makes that are necessary to the decision's outcome. There may be other legal rules stated in court decisions that are parenthetical and not essential to the particular outcome at hand; these are called *dicta*. (One of my favorite professors in law school, my Nolo.com co-author Paul Bergman, refers to dicta as "Oh, by the way, comments.") You can reference rules from dicta if they are helpful in your PT answer, but do not cite them as holdings.

Using legal precedent involves referring to past cases to see if a court has already decided the same or an analogous issue to predict how a court would rule in the given new situation. In our judicial system, the core premise is that like situations should be treated alike. As an advocate and as a bar applicant on the PT, you will often be trying to show either that the facts are alike enough for the previous rule to apply, or that they are different enough that a different rule should apply.

In the real world you have many cases to consider, especially because new decisions are handed down regularly. Lawyers must conduct extensive searches to be sure that they have looked into every relevant case. However, PT Libraries typically only include a few cases, making it easy to compare and contrast the facts of the Library cases to your client's situation.

Do not be surprised if the bar examiners give you binding authority (controlling decisions that must be followed) that is bad for or unfavorable to your client, and persuasive nonbinding authority that is good for your client. If you are writing to a court, your job will then be to distinguish the cases and show why they are so factually different that the court you are addressing should not follow this binding rule.

However, remember that on a PT you are not always writing to a court. Often you will be writing a memo or other internal document to someone on your side (your senior partner, your investigator, or your client). Therefore, you may be tasked with exposing the weaknesses as well as the strengths of your client's case, perhaps counseling your client to settle rather than litigate given the facts and unfavorable law.

However you handle bad law, on the bar exam and in practice, *do so ethically*. Do not lie, and do not misrepresent what a case (or a statute) says. If binding law does not favor your client's position, deal with that as a zealous, responsible, honest advocate would: argue why it should not apply in this circumstance, make a good faith argument that the law should be overruled or changed if applicable, or (as noted earlier), counsel the client against taking a particular position. Bar graders do, should, and will continue to fail applicants who advocate unethical positions on bar exam answers.

Statutes

Statutes, like cases, are primary authority; statutes are created by legislatures, whereas cases are decisions written by judges. Generally, statutes provide rules to govern future matters, and are meant to apply to a category of persons (or entities), whereas cases resolve past disputes between specific parties.

As discussed earlier, statutes may be included in PT Libraries in blocks of code sections that you are familiar with, for your reference. For example, there may be a number of sections excerpted from the Federal Rules of Civil Procedure or the Federal Rules of Evidence. Or, a Library may include one or more selected statutes, such as a section of an environmental regulation, from an area you are not charged with knowing for another part of your bar exam. When given blocks of statutes you know, they are in the Library for your reference. You may skim them and then re-read whichever passages you need to consult. However, when given selected statutes, read every word of each law and assume that it is purposeful. There is no dicta in statutes.

You must read statutory language carefully, section by section, in order. The first sections often define terms used in the body of the law. As you read statutory language, circle every "and" and "or" to know whether provisions are conjunctive or disjunctive.

Also consider legislative intent and public policy, if relevant. Who did the legislature want the statute to affect, and why? Do these rules apply to your client? Would application of the rule to your client have the effect the legislature intended? Would such application be fair and logical?

Concluding our walk through PT Libraries, remember that on performance tests, you will *use* cases and statutes differently from the way in which you used them in most law school classes. You will read and analyze cases and/or statutes from the Library, not with the general purpose of avoiding embarrassment should the professor call on you, but with the explicit purpose of learning how the law has treated people whose problems were similar to those of your client, and predicting how a court (or opposing counsel for settlement purposes) will likely treat your client's matter.

Get into the Library, pull out rules from the authorities, and you will start seeing how the facts plug into (and prove or disprove) the relevant rules of law. Do not feel that you must master the Library authorities on your first read. This is an open-book test. You can go back to the Library any time you want and as many times as you need.

Marshalling or Organizing Facts into Legal Structures

We looked at factual analysis and we looked at legal analysis. How do these two skills fit together? On PTs, typically they mesh when you "marshal" or organize facts into legal structures. *Legal structures* include legal theories, causes of action, defenses, and other ways of organizing facts into legally significant frameworks. To *marshal evidence* means to group facts or evidence together so as to help prove or disprove a particular legal element, factual proposition, or factor.

VISUALIZING A LEGAL STRUCTURE

Tree trunk = cause of action, crime, defense, or other legal liability theory

Branches = elements or factors

Leaves = facts

One of the most important skills you are demonstrating on a PT is your ability to show how facts relate to each component of the applicable law. Let's illustrate with a simple contract case. A new client tells you he agreed to loan his business partner $50,000 but the partner never repaid him. The client wants your advice. Even without looking at a Library, you know that for your client to bring a lawsuit to recover the money, you must establish that there was a valid contract that was performed and breached.

You are a lawyer (well, almost!), so you naturally think "formation, performance, breach, and damages." But what *facts* would a jury of lay people have to find in order for those legal elements to be proven?

1. To prove *formation*, jurors would have to find that Client agreed to lend Partner money, and that Partner agreed to pay Client back. (In other words, jurors as factfinders do not "find formation." Rather, they find that certain facts have been established which counsel will argue prove that a valid contract was formed.)
2. To prove *performance*, jurors would have to be satisfied that the evidence shows Client actually lent the money in question.
3. To prove *breach*, jurors must find that Partner failed to repay Client.
4. To prove *damages*, the jury would have to determine that Client is out of pocket $50,000 (perhaps plus interest).

How does this example relate to PTs? Typically, on PTs, you extract applicable rules from the Library authorities and break them down into component or element parts. Then, you search the File to find particular facts in your client's situation that "match up" to (prove or disprove) each part of each rule. Often, to prove to a bar grader that you have a command of the case, your analysis or argument, just like the preceding contracts example, must be simple and straightforward enough that a juror or client could follow your reasoning.

You may also be asked on a PT to gather additional facts. If so, you will want to show how that new potential evidence relates to the elements of the applicable rule(s). For example, earlier we said that "formation" would be established by showing that your client agreed to lend his partner money and the partner agreed to pay your client back.

What evidence would prove this? (1) Testimony that a witness saw or heard the deal being made; (2) Client's or Partner's calendar noting the date an agreement was made; or (3) a written contract, agreement, or IOU that documents the loan in writing.

What evidence might you look for to prove that your client actually lent the money? (1) A withdrawal in Client's bank account at the time of the loan; (2) a deposit in Partner's account at the time of the loan; and/or (3) evidence that Partner needed the money at the time of the loan.

You might go through the same sort of reasoning to decide what evidence you would use to prove the remaining elements of the cause of action and to anticipate potential defenses. For example, anticipating that Partner might allege that the contract offer was invalid and thus the contract was never validly formed, you might determine if both parties were sober when the deal was allegedly made. You might find out where they were when the deal was struck (a bar, an office?). What other evidence can you think of that might help, or hurt, your client's case?

We take the time here to make our reasoning explicit because in PT fact-gathering documents, you may be asked to state the evidence you intend to discover, the element it helps prove, and why. You may also be asked to engage in this sort of marshalling of evidence to assess potential facts you want to develop and/or determine the relevance of facts you already have in the File. You will see examples of fact-gathering and marshalling assignments in Chapter 3 (criminal law), Chapter 5 (torts), and Chapter 12 (family law) of this book.

Awareness of Professional Responsibility

In the context of performance testing, professional responsibility (PR) awareness is described as "[t]he ability to recognize ethical considerations in a factual situation, analyze and evaluate their implications for present and future actions, and behave in a manner facilitates the timely assertion of the client's rights."[7]

All PTs involve legal analysis and factual analysis. Not all PTs have ethics or PR issues, but PTs may be used to examine your knowledge of ethical rules as well as your sensitivity to general client concerns and your sense of good lawyering practices. In other words, you should note and comment appropriately if you see any ethical rule violations in a PT File. Also, you should be aware of, and urge where appropriate, clear and timely communication with clients and other best practices.

I have repeatedly said throughout this book that PTs are open-book tests, meaning that all the law you need is in the Library. Here's where I have to backtrack: *Nearly* all the law you need is in the Library. You are expected to come to the PT as an ethical lawyer who is already aware of his or her professional responsibilities. So, keep your PR antennae up. If, as you read the File, you notice that someone (perhaps even someone in your own office) has committed an ethical violation:

1. Identify the concern; that is, describe the problem and whom it affects.
2. State the rules. (You need not reference a code section number or case name unless those rules are in the Library, but simply state that ethics rules bar the behavior, and/or professional responsibilities require certain action.)
3. Suggest ways you and/or your firm might resolve the issues.

---

[7] State Bar of California, *Information Regarding Performance Tests*. Note that another version of the same pamphlet modified the last part, adding "and behave in a manner that is consistent with law and ethics while facilitating the timely assertion of the client's rights."

Sometimes the entire PT is about an ethics matter, and the Library will contain PR authorities. Other times, an unethical or unprofessional action will be suggested somewhere in the File and you will have to call someone or some action out and propose ways to correct the problem.

Ethical issues in PTs may include: (1) a client pursuing an unlawful or unethical objective, such as defrauding a creditor, and trying to get an attorney to go along with this; (2) an attorney breaching client confidentiality; (3) attorneys who are in actual or potential conflicts of interest in representing clients; (4) problems with attorney fees, such as the client's fees being paid by a third party (testing your knowledge of your duties to your client); and (5) obligations of candor and duties to reveal certain information. (Chapter 10 in this book, on professional responsibility, includes an excellent practice PT that poses a myriad of ethical issues.)

In PTs, ethical concerns can often be resolved by obtaining client consent. You can show the grader that you understand there is a problem, and recommend a cure, yet continue to finish the assigned tasks. Even if in real life you might consider withdrawing from a case, do not do that on the bar exam and "write yourself out of the question." Bring the problem to the attention of the person for whom you are writing your assignment (usually a senior partner or head lawyer in your office), and then move on.

If your ultimate audience is the court or opposing counsel, and you have spotted an ethical issue that you want to flag for your boss only, before the document is filed or sent out, write your concern in a short introductory paragraph. Put your note in brackets, addressed only to your senior partner, before writing the rest of your assigned task.

EXERCISE

In the following spaces, list at least five things a lawyer may generally not do, and then think of five more actions specifically prohibited during trial. This exercise will help sharpen your PR antennae and spot ethical issues that arise on PTs.

Questions

1. Generally, a lawyer may not:

_____

_____

_____

_____

_____

2. Specifically during trial, a lawyer may not:

_____

_____

_____

_____

_____

Answers

These answers are drawn from PR issues that have arisen in past PTs.

1. Generally, a lawyer:

   - May not counsel or assist in fraudulent or criminal conduct

   - May not use false evidence

   - May not reveal client confidences

   - May not assist a client in committing perjury

   - May not force a client to make decisions regarding defenses, settlements, or pleas

   - May not litigate in bad faith

   - May not talk directly to the represented opposing party

2. Specifically during trial, a lawyer:

   - May not assert personal knowledge of contested facts

   - May not assert personal opinions regarding credibility of witnesses, justness of a cause, guilt or innocence of an accused

   - May not abuse the court process

   - May not violate court orders

   - May not secure the absence or noncooperation of a witness

   - May not pay a witness (except for travel, meals, lodging, loss of time, or expert fees)

   - May not suppress or tamper with evidence

   - May not falsify evidence or assist in perjury

If you spotted at least five for each of these, great! You are likely to see these if they arise on a PT. If not, review these examples and be aware of the types of ethical issues that may be "planted" in a PT on your bar exam.

In addition to concerns that are clear violations of ethical rules, someone in a PT File may suggest actions that are just not good practice, such as deliberately stalling in returning someone's call or replying to an email. Call such actions out the same way you would a PR rule violation. Explain why the behavior is not professional and suggest the best way to proceed. Again, you can sometimes write such a comment in brackets in a note to the person to whom your PT assignment is addressed, either at the beginning or the end of your task.

Problem Solving

All PTs require competency in the legal analysis and factual analysis skills described earlier. Not all PTs involve PR, as just discussed, or the problem-solving skill discussed here. Nevertheless, perhaps because many complaints are lodged against the practicing bar due to failure to adequately listen to (and hear) client concerns, or perhaps because it is just good practice, listening to clients and helping them accomplish their objectives are themes that have been stressed on some past performance tests. Problem solving on PTs involves "[t]he ability to identify and diagnose problems in terms of client objectives and to suggest measures to achieve those client objectives."[8]

On past exams, problem-solving skills have been tested in many different tasks, including in-house memoranda, client letters, and memos to investigators. Applicants have had to identify client concerns and think about ways to meet client objectives in various contexts, such as client counseling and interviewing, negotiation, settlement, mediation and other ADR, as well as in drafting or revising contracts and estate planning documents such as wills and trust instruments.

It may be helpful to think about problem-solving tasks by breaking the definition into two parts:

1. Figure out what the client's problem is (*identify and diagnose problems in terms of client objectives*), and
2. Solve the problem (*suggest measures to achieve those client objectives*).

---

[8] *See* State Bar of California, *Information Regarding Performance Tests.* Another version of the same pamphlet identified the skill as "[t]he ability to identify and diagnose issues in terms of client goals and to develop lawful suggestions for how best to achieve the client's objectives" (State Bar of California, *Information Regarding Performance Tests.*) See descriptive list of MPT-specific Problem Solving Skills at http://www.ncbex.org/exams/mpt/preparing.

To competently perform the first part of problem-solving tasks (the identification and diagnosis of problems), you must find those facts from the File that tell you what your client needs and wants. You may see details about the client's concerns, values, and/or priorities in the Task Memo, in letters to or from the client, in transcripts of interviews with the client, or in other client-related documents. Pay attention to these details. At the same time, as you read the Task Memo and File, keep the following big-picture questions in mind:

1. Who is my client?
2. Who is suing or plans to sue whom over what, if the problem involves litigation? With whom is my client dealing, and about what specific concerns, if the PT involves a transactional matter?
3. What can I suggest to help my client achieve his/her/its objectives?

Note: It will ultimately be up to the client to decide what choices to make, so better PT answers often include *more than one way* for the client to achieve his/her/its objectives and discuss the pros and cons of each alternative. You may also be called upon to suggest which action is preferable and why.

In some performance tests, the types of solutions will be fairly generic. For example, you might suggest that the client settle, sue, or mediate. In other performance tests, the solutions are more case-specific. For instance, the client may not be able to have certain goods shipped and delivered on time, so may negotiate a reduced future shipment price to compensate for losses due to delays.

PROBLEM SOLVING

Recall our earlier hypothetical about a client who lent money to his business partner and wants it back. How might that client accomplish his goal? Of course, he could bring a lawsuit alleging breach of contract. But he could also ask for the money back, if he has not yet done so. He could write a formal letter of demand (copying you as his lawyer on the letter), or have you write a demand letter. He could propose a payment plan or settle for a smaller sum in cash. Think of and write in the following spaces just a few pros and cons of each of these solutions:

Lawsuit Pros:

Lawsuit Cons:

_____

_____

Mediation Pros:

_____

_____

Mediation Cons:

_____

_____

Arbitration Pros:

_____

_____

Arbitration Cons:

_____

_____

After trying to think of pros and cons on your own, read these suggestions.

Lawsuit Pros:
- If the case is strong, your client may win and be paid back in full.
- It is possible that just filing a complaint will show that your client means business and encourage the business partner to pay up.
- Your client may also feel a sense that justice has been served by bringing the matter to court.

Lawsuit Cons:
- Costs. Attorney fees and costs could easily eat up much of the $50,000 even if the client wins.
- The possibility of losing. No case is a "slam dunk."
- Time. Win or lose, litigation takes a long time.
- Last but not least, being in an adversarial situation with a business partner will likely destroy the relationship.

Mediation: Your client and his business partner could go together to a neutral third party to resolve their dispute.

Mediation Pros:
- May result in an amicable solution that will help if the two want to remain business partners.
- May be quicker and less costly than litigation.

Mediation Cons:
- May require both sides compromising, with no clear "winner" or "loser."

Arbitration: Your client and his partner could select someone to arbitrate their dispute (similar to litigation but less formal).

Arbitration Pros:
- May be quicker, less formal, and less costly than litigation.

Arbitration Cons:
- May still not be easy for parties to work together after going through this adversarial process.

In writing the pros and cons of those dispute resolution scenarios, did any other solutions come to mind? How about:
- *Using a guarantor or providing security:* Perhaps your client's partner could find someone else to guarantee the obligation. Or, maybe the partner could provide your client with some collateral or security for the $50,000.
- *Performing services in lieu of payment:* Maybe the partner could do something for your client in exchange for the money.
- *Force or fear:* Your client could send a thug to rough up his friend and coerce the money out of him. **No way!** I just wrote this to see if you were still awake and reading carefully. No matter what you see on the latest TV law dramas, *do not suggest anything unethical or illegal.* If you do, you may well fail. Likewise, *do not even joke about anything unethical or illegal;* bar graders may not share your sense of humor or realize that you were joking.

You can see that even in a very simple breach-of-contract scenario there may be many solutions. On performance tests, because time is so severely limited, usually thinking of even two alternatives to help the client achieve the client's objectives is enough to answer the question adequately.

Problem solving, though not tested on every PT, is one of the most creative and fun skills tested on these exams. The more you practice, the easier it will become.

TYPICAL PT TASKS

Now that you have a sense of the basic skills in which you must demonstrate competency for PT success, let's look at frequently tested tasks. On your PT, you will be asked to complete one or more documents that a beginning lawyer might draft in practice. You will likely have specific instructions and may even have a "Format" Memo to guide you. Nonetheless, the more familiar you are with frequently tested tasks, the more prepared and confident you will be.

Here, we look briefly at some of the tasks tested on past PTs. You may want to skip this part of the chapter now and come back to it after having completed a few practice performance tests, or you may read it now and then again after you complete some exams.

For those who have taken trial advocacy or other clinical classes, some of this information will be familiar. If you have not taken such courses and/or want additional background in litigation-related documents, the following may be helpful resources: *Represent Yourself in Court: How to Prepare & Try a Winning Case* (Bergman and Berman, Nolo.com, 9th ed., 2016) and *The Criminal Law Handbook: Know Your Rights, Survive the System* (Bergman and Berman, Nolo.com, 15th ed., 2017).

TEST YOUR KNOWLEDGE OF COMMON PT TASKS

In the following spaces, without looking anything up, write what you know about each document type: its purpose, rules limiting its usage, its typical content or format, and the context in which such a task would be drafted.

NEGOTIATION LETTER:

_____

_____

_____

MEMORANDUM OF POINTS AND AUTHORITIES:

_____

_____

_____

POSITION PAPER:

_____

_____

_____

APPELLATE BRIEF:

_____

_____

_____

DEMAND LETTER:

_____

_____

_____

MEMORANDUM OF LAW:

_____

_____

_____

DISCOVERY PLAN:

_____

_____

_____

CLOSING ARGUMENT:

_____

_____

_____

TRIAL BRIEF:

_____

_____

_____

INTERROGATORIES:

_____

_____

_____

DECLARATION:

_____

_____

_____

AFFIDAVIT:

_____

_____

_____

CONTRACT:

_____

_____

_____

WILL:

_____

_____

_____

TRUST:

_____

_____

_____

STATUTE:

_____

_____

_____

The next subsections contain brief descriptions of selected documents you may be asked to draft, and some strategies for effectively completing these tasks on PTs. On most PTs, you are asked to draft one or two documents.

Legal Memo

This may be called a memorandum of law, memo or memorandum, or analytical memorandum. Memos frequently appear as tasks on PTs. Most students have drafted legal memos in law school legal research courses, so you may have a reasonable comfort level with this task. Nonetheless, be sure to study the PT instructions carefully. A PT memo may require fewer formalities than your legal writing professor required and you would waste time providing anything that was not requested.

You may be asked to draft only a memo, or a memo along with another task or tasks. Depending on the law in the Library, your memo may center on exploring how solid a case your client will have asserting a particular cause of action, legal theory, or potential defense. You may be asked to explore a conflict of laws. You may assess whether and under what theories certain evidence may be admitted. There are infinite legal issues that could form the basis of this type of assignment, but they will all have their foundation in the Library. Study the Task Memo and the Library to determine exactly what the issues are and how to outline your assignment.

A typical legal memo on a PT is written to someone in your office, usually the senior partner or another colleague. You will adopt a balanced tone, explaining the law and, if appropriate and relevant to the task, the strengths and weaknesses of your client's position.

Caveat: Just because a task is called a "memorandum" may not mean it is the classic legal memo you are familiar with. Be certain to ascertain for whom and for what purpose this piece of writing is intended. If it is not an in-house strategizing document, but rather a document you are to file with the court, then it is likely to be a persuasive presentation in disguise. For example, in certain jurisdictions, a persuasive "brief" is called a "memorandum of points and authorities."

You may also be asked specifically to evaluate the likely success of a particular course of action and/or propose alternative solutions for handling your client's problems. *Read the directions carefully.* If you are asked to analyze and then make a recommendation, but all you provide is a neutral discussion, no matter how thorough that discussion/analysis is, you will likely not do well because you failed to follow directions.

Format

If the examiners give you a specific format, *follow it*. If they do not provide a format, include an introduction with a simple header as outlined in this subsection, a body that provides an analysis of issues (separated into sections, by issue, if you are addressing more than one question), and a conclusion (short, no more than one paragraph).

Start your memo as indicated in the following, then move into the body of your analysis:

To:

From: [your name on the bar exam is "Bar Applicant" or "Applicant"]

Re:

Date:

Please find the memo you requested regarding [state the general issue, for example, admissibility of evidence] below. If after reviewing it you have additional questions, please let me know and I will be happy to research those.

Unless the instructions tell you otherwise, you need not spend time on "questions presented," "short answers," or other formal parts of a memo that you may have been taught to draft in legal writing courses. In fact, many passing answers on PT memos omit the statement of facts altogether unless it is specifically requested.

If you are asked to write a statement of facts, select only those facts that are relevant to the issues you will analyze. You may want to write the body of your analysis first and then quickly draft the statement of facts, because by that time you will know exactly which facts you used. (If you are typing, it is easy to place the statement of facts above the analysis. If you are writing by hand, you can leave space to insert the statement of facts.)

Be alert for directions that instruct you to omit a statement of facts and proceed directly to your analysis. Follow those directions. You will not "wow" the grader with a superb statement of facts if the directions told you not to include one; in fact, the opposite is likely.

If the directions are silent as to format, and you are not specifically asked to draft a statement of facts, you may typically omit that section and jump straight into the body of the memo (your analysis). But, when you are not told to omit a statement of facts, drafting a short factual summary may help if you are not ready to begin drafting the body of your analysis; starting with a brief statement of facts may unblock your writing and get your creative juices flowing. Again, though, if not specifically requested, do not spend any length of time on this section of the memo; get immediately to what is directly instructed. And, if directed to omit this, leave it out.

Because a legal memo is typically an in-house document, you will want to expose facts that support your client's positions as well as facts that do not. This is very different from the "Statement of Facts" portion of a persuasive brief where your goal is to select those facts that, though stated accurately, paint a picture that helps persuade the reader of the strength of your client's position.

In an in-house legal memo on a PT, you may well end up concluding that your client's position is not supportable, that you do not expect to win on a particular argument, and that therefore you recommend settling or even withdrawing a complaint if necessary.

> **Note:** As always, abide by applicable rules of professional responsibility and ethics. In other words, on PTs (and in law practice), *do not* counsel or suggest pursuing a claim that is not well grounded in law and fact.

Following the header and the statement of facts (if requested), organize your analysis around each main legal theory, or each element of each cause of action or defense. To make it easy for your grader to see your main points, give each subsection an appropriate heading.

Headings in legal memos can typically be short, descriptive phrases, similar to headings in typical law essay exams. Their purpose is not to summarize your analysis but to provide a roadmap to the organization of your memo.

Be sure to conclude, briefly, to show the grader that you completed your task.

Persuasive Brief

In this type of task, you are typically writing a legal argument to a judge in order to persuade that judge to make a particular decision or ruling. Related tasks may be a brief in support of a motion, a memorandum of points and authorities, a trial brief, and/or appellate brief.

The PT may be set in state or federal court, or some other quasi-judicial body such as an administrative agency. You may be asked to draft a brief covering any area of substantive or procedural law.

You want to use respectful, formal language when addressing a court, just as one would in practice. For example, write out terms in full that you might abbreviate in an informal, in-house memorandum. You may use bullet points where appropriate; for example, in listing reasons for supporting a position that you intend to develop in a later part of your brief. However, do not write in outline style. Rather, write in basic prose, with complete sentences and paragraphs. (By contrast, using more of an outline style might be the perfect format for an in-house investigation or discovery plan task.)

You will not be expected to prepare tables or indices. However, you may be asked to start with a statement of jurisdictional basis. (Unless you are specifically asked to draft this section, leave it out.) If you are asked to draft this section and, for example, your case is set in federal court, you will need to briefly state how your client has satisfied the jurisdictional requirements of either diversity or subject matter jurisdiction. (You would know these basic rules about jurisdiction by the time you get to the bar exam, and the facts would tell you enough about your case to know whether the parties are diverse or suing about a federal question.)

The next part of a persuasive brief-type task is typically a statement of facts. As noted earlier with respect to legal memos, if instructed to omit this section, leave it out. (You will take precious time away from your argument and be graded against others who followed the directions and jumped right into their argument.)

If instructed to draft a statement of facts as part of a persuasive assignment, draft this by summarizing any facts that are relevant to and support your client's legal arguments. Do not distort or fabricate facts. Do be selective, in both the facts you choose and the order in which you present them, to maximize the persuasiveness for your client's position. Look for either explicit directions or descriptive clues about the appropriate length of the statement of facts. Usually it will be relatively short compared to the argument portion of a brief, but it could be a featured part of the PT assignment. As noted earlier with respect to fact statements in legal memos, it can be helpful in persuasive briefs as well to come back and draft the fact statement last, after completing the body of your assignment.

Next in a brief or persuasive memo is the body of your argument. The most important part of this section on a PT is often your persuasive headings.

Past PT instructions have described headings in persuasive briefs as "carefully crafted subject headings that illustrate the arguments they cover. The argument heading should succinctly summarize the reasons the tribunal should take the position you are advocating. A heading should be a specific application of a rule of law to the facts of the case and not a bare legal or factual conclusion or a statement of an abstract principle."[9]

---

[9]This guideline and the following examples, taken directly from past California PTs, are extremely useful to see what is expected on this sort of assignment.

EXAMPLES FROM PAST PTs OF PROPER AND IMPROPER PERSUASIVE HEADINGS

Improper: Defendant had sufficient minimum contacts to establish personal jurisdiction.

Proper: A radio station located in the State of Franklin that broadcasts into the State of Columbia, receives revenue from advertisers located in the State of Columbia, and holds its annual meeting in the State of Columbia, has sufficient minimum contacts to allow Columbia courts to assert personal jurisdiction.

Improper: The evidence is sufficient to convict the defendant.

Proper: Evidence of entry through an open window is sufficient to satisfy the "breaking" element of burglary.

Improper: The plaintiff is not entitled to back pay.

Proper: Because Plaintiff refused to accept Defendant's offer to place her on administrative leave, she is not entitled to back pay.

Improper: The prisoner's rights were violated.

Proper: Requiring the petitioner to take psychotropic medication in the absence of a hearing establishing violent behavior constitutes cruel and unusual punishment under the Eighth Amendment.

Improper: The underlying facts establish Plaintiff's claim of right.

Proper: By placing a chain across the driveway, by refusing access to others, and by posting a "No Trespassing" sign, Plaintiff has established a claim of right.

Under each heading, write the rest of your argument, interweaving facts and law. **Do not list and summarize cases!** Argue why the law and facts together prove that your client should prevail on each particular issue in question.

At the end of your argument section, be sure to include a short conclusion so that the court is reminded of the relief you are seeking and to show the grader that you finished the assignment.

Declaration/Affidavit

In a declaration (also called an *affidavit*), you are presenting facts in the name of a witness (called the declarant or affiant, respectively), facts which that person could testify to if he or she were called to the witness stand in court. In other words, you are writing facts that are personally known to the witness and are truthful and relevant. Declarations often provide the supporting documentation that go along with persuasive briefs. Though they are recitations of facts, they are persuasive in nature in that you are selecting those facts that are necessary to and helpful to support your client's legal position.

Format

You will typically be given a format to use, but for PT purposes, a declaration may be presented quite simply, as the following examples indicate.

I, [insert name of Declarant], declare as follows:

1.

2.

3.

Signed,

Declarant

I, Sara Berman, declare as follows:

1. I have taught as a law professor for more than 20 years.

2. I currently serve as the director of the academic success program at Nova Southeastern's Shepard Broad College of Law.

3. I attended the UCLA School of Law where I studied with professors, experts in clinical legal education, who helped in the creation of the first performance tests.

4. Since law school, I have been interested in and passionate about performance tests.

5. I wrote this book to help law students learn from performance tests and do well on that portion of the bar exam.

I declare that the information above is true and correct to the best of my knowledge,

Sara Berman

Note that the first numbered paragraph often contains background information on the declarant and may include the person's connection to the case (for example, whether that person is a party or a witness). The remaining numbered paragraphs each recite important facts that are relevant, truthful, and within the declarant's personal knowledge. (Think: what did the declarant personally observe by sight, hearing, smell, or touch and how are those points helpful to proving something relevant to the case?)

Look for examples within the File itself. On a practice PT that I recently administered to my students, they had to draft declarations for the plaintiff and several witnesses. Some students panicked because they had never drafted a declaration. Others remained calm; they noticed that the File included the defendant's declaration, so they studied that declaration as a sample, and used it along with the formatting instructions to get a handle on how to draft the assigned documents.

Closing Argument

This type of assignment is usually a closing argument in court to a jury or judge, but you might be asked to draft a concluding statement in an administrative or other sort of hearing.

For this task, you are expected to write out what you would say at the close of a trial to convince the trier of fact (typically the judge or jurors) to decide in your client's favor, given the evidence presented and the relevant legal rules. You use helpful evidence supporting your client and refute harmful evidence presented by your adversary. You may reference the credibility (or lack thereof) of particular witnesses. And, you attempt to convince the judge or jurors that your client has met its burden of proof and/or that the opposing side has failed to meet its burden of proof.

If you are to write a closing argument to a jury, remember that your audience is composed of lay people. Avoid jargon and define any legal terms you use. For example, when discussing the burden of proof, explain carefully terms such as "preponderance of the evidence" or "beyond a reasonable doubt." Use examples. Refer to the ultimate facts that must be proven, perhaps quoting briefly from the jury instructions that the jurors will themselves have to follow, rather than citing cases or statutes.

When drafting a closing argument to the court in a "bench trial" (or trial without a jury) you may (possibly extensively) cite cases and/or statutes in addition to proving how the facts satisfy the elements of those applicable legal rules. When writing to the court, feel free to use legal terms.

You can be less formal when writing to jurors than when you address a judge. However, in a closing argument to a judge or jury, be sure to write in as organized as possible a fashion so that the factfinder (and the bar grader!) can easily follow your points. Even though in a real-life oral argument you would be talking, and one does not generally speak aloud with headings, you still want headings, perhaps in brackets, for the grader to identify your main points.

Your organization will almost always be an element-by-element approach under each respective crime, cause of action, and/or defense theory. If the PT Library or File (as part of the trial transcript) includes jury instructions, let these be your guide as to which legal elements must be proven. If not, find the elements that must be proven from other Library authorities. Then, using facts that were established as evidence in trial, lay out explicitly for the jurors those inferences you want them to draw from the evidence.

Be sure to anticipate and rebut arguments the other side would make. Even if in the real world you may have a chance to speak again (what is known as "rebuttal"), you will likely only be drafting one document on the PT.

WHAT ARE ULTIMATE FACTS?

In the instructions, you may be prompted to marshal or organize the evidence around what may be referred to as the "ultimate facts." These are plain factual statements of each legal element. For example, in a negligence action where the elements are duty, breach, causation, and damages, "the fact that the plaintiff suffered medical injuries for which she had to pay doctors $100,000" is an ultimate fact; it is the factual restating of the legal element of "damages."

Opening Statement

An opening statement is a sort of roadmap or preview that you are giving to jurors at the beginning of a trial to let them know what evidence you intend to present. You can only discuss evidence that you believe, in good faith, will be presented at trial. In other words, you may not discuss evidence that you believe will be found inadmissible.

Format: The Task Memo and/or Format Memos will likely give you a sense of how you are to set up the opening statement, but often you will begin by introducing yourself, and then proceed, witness by witness, to discuss the evidence. An example of the type of language that may be used follows:

> *Ladies and Gentlemen, my name is Applicant. I represent _____, the plaintiff in this case, and will be talking to you today about some of the evidence you are going to hear in the coming days. First, you will hear from Mr. _____. Mr. _____ will testify about _____. Next, you will hear from Ms. _____, who will tell you*

about _____. *Last, you will see documentation of* _____ [and you may discuss any exhibits or documentary evidence that will be presented at trial].

In a closing argument you may ask jurors to draw inferences from facts; in an opening statement you may not. You therefore have much more of an opportunity to show your ability to reason in a closing argument assignment. Closing arguments have been tested regularly on past PTs. You may not see an opening statement task on a PT, but if you do, you now know the basics of what it is.[10]

Jury Instructions

It is unlikely, but possible, that you could be asked to draft jury instructions. You could also be given proposed jury instructions and asked to edit them to ensure that they comply with relevant, binding case law.

In such a document, you are to present the law or ultimate facts that jurors must find in order to decide the case. Often these instructions are presented in paragraphs or bulleted lists, each paragraph or bullet point discussing one legal element or ultimate fact.

According to the Format Memo in one PT that asked applicants to draft jury instructions: *The objective [of jury instructions] is to fairly state the law while emphasizing factors that support a favorable result for our client.*[11] That same PT gave examples of jury instructions for cases in tort involving issues of negligent infliction of emotional distress, two of which were as follows:

> *If you find that Harry Jones, as an adjacent landowner to the Chesterfield airport, suffered emotional distress as a result of the noise from aircraft landing, taking off and in-flight, you may award damages to the plaintiff.*

> *If you find that the employee of the defendant, Speedy Process Service, made an invalid service of the writ on Mary Williams and thereafter knowingly filed a false affidavit of valid service, you may award damages to the plaintiff for negligent infliction of emotional distress.*

Witness Cross- or Direct Examination

Direct examination is the process in which counsel elicits (in question-and-answer form) relevant admissible evidence from counsel's own witnesses. Usually this helps establish facts that support one's case. In *cross-examination*, counsel questions the

---

[10] If you seek more detailed explanations of how to draft closing arguments, opening statements, and other litigation-related items, see Sara J. Berman & Paul Bergman, *Represent Yourself in Court: How to Prepare & Try a Winning Case* (9th ed., Nolo Press, 2016).

[11] California Performance Test, February 1996.

opposing party's witnesses, with the goal of getting those witnesses to make statements about or admit to facts that support the other side's version of events, or in order to cast doubt on someone's credibility (often the credibility of the witness testifying).

Similar to closing argument, in this sort of task you draft your written answer exactly as the words will be spoken in court. Again, though, do include headings and subheadings to provide a roadmap for graders, even if you would not say aloud in court what is in the headings.

You may be asked to draft an examination (cross or direct) that you or another lawyer in your law firm would conduct. Alternatively, you could be asked to draft questions you think opposing counsel is likely to ask your witnesses and plan for how to respond. In either case, the Instructions will typically give you a precise format to use, one that helps you lay out both the questions and the anticipated responses.

For each witness, you may be asked to list the subject that the questions address, and then write out the questions and anticipated answers in full. After that, you may be asked to note any evidentiary objections that you or opposing counsel might make, give responses to those objections, and finish with the judge's likely ruling as to whether each objection will be sustained or overruled and accordingly whether or not the witness will have to answer each question.

As you can see, the examiners' asking you to draft a cross-examination or direct examination is a backdoor way of also testing you on evidence. Because relevance is one of the most fundamental concepts in evidence, it may be helpful to keep in mind (and, where appropriate, to write out explicitly) why a question is relevant. For instance, assume that you are counsel for the plaintiff in a personal injury action based on alleged domestic violence. You are questioning the witness, a police officer, whose version of events contradicts that of your client. If, in questioning the officer, you were to elicit the fact that the officer was once employed as a personal security guard for the defendant, this would be highly relevant in impeaching the witness's credibility.

I always think students are going to be put off by the rigidity of cross-examination tasks, but inevitably students enjoy drafting them. Chapter 8 of this book, on evidence, includes a PT in which one of the tasks is to draft a cross-examination plan. Practice with that assignment and get comfortable in case this type of task appears on your bar exam.

Discovery/Investigation Plan

Applicants have been tested on both informal fact investigation and "discovery" or formal fact-gathering. In either context, first set out each of the elements to be proven. Then, under each element, list the evidence you wish to locate and why. (State succinctly why the evidence is relevant or what it would help to establish.)

Next, list the possible sources you would look to, or tools you might use, to obtain each particular item of evidence. Note that the instructions may ask you to point out any evidentiary concerns with regard to getting a statement or physical evidence admitted into evidence. For instance, you may get credit for noting, in conjunction with the listing of a certain letter that you wish to obtain, that the letter must be authenticated before it will be received into evidence by the court.

For formal discovery, recall that:

- You may depose parties and/or nonparty witnesses. Depositions involve questioning, under oath, with a court reporter making a transcript. You are typically seeking information from the deponent that is within the deponent's personal knowledge about what happened, when, why, and how. You may also ask the deponent about documentary or physical evidence.
- You may only send *interrogatories* to parties. These are written questions asking about facts within the party's knowledge (what happened, when, why, and how), and/or about documentary or physical evidence to which the party may have access. Note that it is generally much less expensive to send interrogatories than to take depositions, because you do not need to hire a court reporter.
- You might send *requests for admission*. These are written questions that ask a party to admit or deny certain facts.
- You might send written requests for a party to *produce documents*. Remember, this discovery tool can only be used for parties, but you can subpoena documents you want from nonparties.

As for informal fact-gathering on PTs, consider everything from talking to anyone who may have relevant information to reviewing public records, social media, or documents obtained via the Freedom of Information Act. However, *do not* suggest talking directly with someone who is represented by counsel; this violates ethical rules. You may suggest examining scientific data (with or without the assistance of an expert), taking pictures or measurements, or doing other sorts of physical testing.

Caveat: Only suggest lawful and ethical ways of obtaining evidence. Do not look to the law students in the television show *How to Get Away with Murder* for ideas on how to gather evidence.

Letter to Client

In order to write an effective client letter for a PT, determine before you begin the exact purpose of the letter. Know why whoever is assigning this task wants you to write to the client.

It may be that your goal is to render some legal opinion to the client. For example, you might need to tell the client how likely the client is to succeed with a particular course of action. If so, you might organize the letter by possible courses of action and then discuss the pros and cons of each. To do this, you must be keenly aware of your client's needs and desires. If you think of different ways to help the client achieve his or her goals, explain the benefits and risks of any proposed course of action in simple, plain English. Take into account the psychological and financial implications, in addition to the legal aspects, of anything you propose. (Review the problem-solving skills discussed earlier; be alert to any language in the File about what the client wants or needs.) If your client expressly or impliedly suggested some course of action that is illegal or unethical, you must counsel the client as to why that action may not be pursued.

You may be writing to update your client on what has happened in his or her case. If so, you might summarize events to date chronologically, or from most important to least important.

You may be helping to prepare the client for an upcoming court hearing, deposition, or interview. If this is your assignment, you should describe the purpose of the proceeding and tell your client what he or she must do to get ready. Your client will almost always be a nonlawyer or lay person, so this task typically tests your ability to use simple language. Remember to define all legal jargon/terms in plain English.

Client or Witness Interview

You may be asked to write out a plan for interviewing your own client or another person who was involved in, observed, or knew about your client and/or the client's story. (On one past performance test, applicants were asked to critique an interview plan that a more junior member of their law firm had drafted.)

If you are asked to write or critique an interview plan, you will likely be given a format or guidelines to follow. If you are not given more specific guidance, consider the goals of an interview and set up your answer in a way that logically meets those goals.

Generally, in the first part of an interview plan, you want to include language that puts the client or witness at ease as much as possible. For example, tell the person how long the meeting is likely to be and the topics you expect to cover.

If you are meeting for the first time with your own client, this initial interview should also include discussions of fee arrangements. Tell the client how much and on what basis (hourly, contingency, or other) your firm charges.

Next, it may be helpful to try to establish a chronology of events: what happened, what was observed, and when. After that, you may probe one or more areas of questioning further to develop a particular legal or factual theory that is helpful to your client and/or to find out more about something that may be potentially damaging to your client.

Lastly, before the client or witness leaves, it may be important to conclude by confirming any particularly important information that came out during the interview and to thank the person. You may also need to have the person sign something or take documents to review, sign, and return later. You may want to conclude by arranging to meet again and/or to have the person follow-up by sending you physical or documentary evidence that the person has in his or her possession.

Client Counseling

Lawyers counsel clients in both litigation and nonlitigation contexts. In each, the lawyer tries to help the client make an informed decision about a particular problem, issue, choice, or path. In a performance test, you could be asked to counsel your client by writing a letter to the client, writing an internal memo about counseling the client, or in the context of writing some plan for meeting with the client. Follow whatever specific format or guidelines you are given about how to set up the document. If you are not provided a detailed format, write in an organized, logical manner, keeping in mind the following basics for client counseling.

Start by identifying the client's problems and clarifying the client's goals. (You may do this with the client, or by reading information from the File, such as the transcript of a previous interview with the client or a letter from the client.)

Next, in light of the client's goals, articulate alternative courses of action or competing solutions to the client's problems. Identify the legal consequences of each of these alternatives. You will also want to consider, and likely write about, any important nonlegal consequences to the client, such as the possible effects of these alternatives on the client's business and social life.

Last, you will want to give the client any guidance you can to help the client choose among the various solutions, making certain that you abide by relevant rules of professional responsibility, and, if necessary, request relevant additional information from the client.

Negotiation or Settlement

A negotiation or settlement task usually asks you to develop a compromise or settlement offer that helps resolve a number of different areas of conflict that exist between your client and an adversary.

If a format is provided, follow it. If a format is not given, remember that the basics of this type of task involve setting out the factual context for the settlement, what both parties agree to, and what the parties disagree about. Follow that with a specific proposal. Your tone will differ radically depending on whether you are writing an internal (in-house) memo about what to possibly propose by way of settlement or whether you are writing a letter to opposing counsel urging the opposing party to agree to your proposal.

Keep in mind some generally positive aspects to settling a case:

- Cost savings (as compared with litigation)
- Increased privacy (court documents are public records, unless sealed, but you may agree to keep settlement-related documents private)
- Speed (a settlement can resolve matters quickly; litigation is typically a very lengthy process)

Before you can negotiate a successful deal, you must first learn your client's goals and needs. This involves the same first steps as counseling. Then, you will move on and try to persuade the other side either to accept your client's terms or to come to some agreement that is acceptable to all parties.

In practice, you often learn about clients by talking with them. Your client is your first and most helpful source of information. You may also need to talk with others and/or review documents. PT Files may contain notes from meetings with your client, documents the client produced, or notes the client wrote. Often, you will need more information than what is given in the File. If that is so, you may be asked to detail such potential additional evidence or information in a memo to the senior partner or an investigator your firm has hired, or in a letter to your client.

Generally, when you negotiate on behalf of a client, your primary job as counsel is to present the client's claims, concerns, and proposals to the other side, and try to get the other side to accept your client's terms. Remember, your client must consent to any final agreement or bargain reached in the negotiation process.

As with interviewing and counseling, lawyers negotiate for their clients in both litigation and nonlitigation contexts. When a dispute is resolved in the litigation context, the standard legal remedies for a prevailing party come in the form of money damages. In negotiating solutions to clients' problems (both in litigation settlements and in alternate forms of dispute resolution), you may be able to fashion agreements that involve nonmonetary terms or deals, either in addition to or instead of money damages. Often such terms will suit your client's needs better than money damages.

A classic litigation example, using a defamation lawsuit, is where the client really wants an apology more than money. Imagine a situation in which your wealthy client was slandered in some tabloid press. (If you are thinking that, technically, this is libel because it is in writing, I am proud of you!) Given your client's finances, negotiating with the newspaper's counsel for a public apology and retraction of its statements, perhaps in a full-page *New York Times* advertisement, might be a perfectly acceptable solution to both parties. Your client's reputation could be restored, at least in the eyes of those who read the *New York Times;* the tabloid, although it may have paid a lot for the ad, probably paid less than it would have paid in legal fees and costs (and possibly a hefty judgment) had the case gone to trial.

In a sales context, suppose that your client is involved in a contract dispute with a regular supplier about the purchase of certain goods. As part of negotiating about damages for goods already shipped, consider shaping an agreement by bargaining about other terms in future deals, such as delivery time, place, or quantity; timing of payment; exchange for related products or services; or anything else your client might want.

Bottom line: Think creatively to find mutually agreeable solutions that meet the financial as well as the legal and psychological needs of all the parties.

In addition to knowing what *your* client wants, you should know how a court would likely decide the dispute; that is, what are the legal rights and remedies of each party. Even if you fashion a creative agreement, such as those described earlier, knowing the law is vital. It may give you leverage in the negotiation process. If your research shows that your client is not entitled to any legal relief, make sure that you do not file a complaint; if one has already been filed, make sure you withdraw it, because filing a frivolous lawsuit is sanctionable conduct.

You should also consider the amount of time and money it will take for the dispute to be resolved, and how important time, money, and other considerations are to the respective parties. Try to learn as much as you can about the opposing party's wants and needs; this will help you know what to press for and what to concede.

As to tactics and strategies, when you finally sit down to negotiate with the other side after counseling your own client and conducting any necessary legal research (on your PT, that means after reading and analyzing the File, Library, and any other documents), you can take several approaches. One is to start with an assertive, but realistic, position and make only a few concessions. When you concede on a small point, you may lose little and in turn get the other side to give in on some terms that really matter to your client. Another strategy is to start with an aggressive stance, expecting to give in on many terms. A third strategy is to ask for something reasonable that you know the other side will accept, then forcefully state that yours is a "take it or leave it" offer from the outset and you will not bend. Further, show the opposition why the offer is reasonable and why they should accept it as is.

What is essential on this type of a performance test task is not to adopt one or another strategy, but to make explicit the reasoning for whatever strategy you choose. (The bar graders want to see that you can think like a lawyer, not necessarily that you have "the right answer," especially in negotiation situations where there often is no one right answer.)

As you read documents in your PT File, note the terms and conditions that your client seems adamant about and those about which your client seems open to compromise. Show the grader how your thoughts, critiques, and proposals attempt to meet and fulfill your client's needs and goals. It is vital to demonstrate to the bar grader your ability to act in a *zealous yet ethical manner* on behalf of your clients.

Other Transactional Tasks

Although the litigation context is a more common setting for performance tests, there have been tests involving or set in other areas. Also, given ongoing trends away from costly, time-consuming litigation and toward both alternative methods of dispute resolution and preventive law (education and planning to stop legal problems from ever arising in the first place), it is quite likely that performance tests of the future will be set more frequently in these areas and contexts.

You may be asked to draft documents that cover a broad range of planning, counseling, or deal making, in either a business or a personal context. Business clients may seek advice concerning proposed agreements with other persons or entities, compliance with government regulations, or applications to various government agencies and offices for licenses. Individuals may come to you or your firm regarding the purchase and sale of property, premarital agreements, or estate planning.

On past performance tests, applicants have been asked to draft estate plans, evaluate business-related proposals, write marital settlement agreements, and more. For many such assignments, you will be given specific instructions in the Task Memo guiding you on how to format your answer. If not, in order to begin such a task, you would use the same sorts of logical reasoning approaches discussed earlier with respect to counseling, interviewing, and negotiation.

In particular, you would start by developing a clear understanding of your client's objectives and concerns. You begin this process by gathering information from the File. Locate any documents from the client or about the client's situation from other sources (interview transcripts, letters, contracts, property descriptions, and photographs).

Then, identify the legal and nonlegal issues that are actually and/or potentially raised by the proposed transaction(s). Look at the Task Memo, and study the Library for clues as to the main legal problems or issues you are expected to discuss. Information from the File about the client's goals and desires will help steer you toward the nonlegal problems.

The next part of an analysis of a typical transactional performance test will likely involve drafting or editing some proposed agreement or statement of your client's position. You may have to present this to other parties (for example, in negotiating with them), or you may be asked simply to counsel your own client about his, her, or its options. Typically such documents are organized paragraph by paragraph. The practice test in the constitutional law chapter of this book (Chapter 9) will help you with this sort of a task.

Analysis/Editing of a Contract, Will, Trust, or Statute

Applicants asked to handle tasks relating to contracts, wills, trusts, or statutes have typically been asked to review a document that someone else drafted, looking provision by provision to determine whether the agreement is valid, enforceable, and most advantageously worded for your client. From the File, you can determine your client's specific goals, what terms are essential to your client and what terms your client is willing to yield on, and the strength of your client's bargaining power. The practice test in Chapter 6 of this book, on contracts, will help you with this sort of a task.

As always, if the examiners give you a format, follow it. If not, you should proceed through the document, paragraph by paragraph, and suggest what language should be deleted, added, and modified; in each instance, say why. You may also edit the document for ambiguities and ensure that it fits the law provided by legal authorities from the Library. (An example I often give students about editing for ambiguity is when a PT asks you to draft or edit a will and your client wants to disinherit his two children, Sam and Dave, and give his entire estate to charity. Let's say the operative provision says, "I leave nothing to my children." What is wrong with that? It is not against the law or incorrect per se. However, it is vague. Your client may some day have a third child whom he adores. For this reason, the provision should be edited to specify the names and identities of the children he wants to disinherit. "I leave nothing to my twin sons born in 1993, Sam and Dave.")

Alternative Dispute Resolution (ADR)

In a performance test, if you were asked to prepare a client for a mediation and/or arbitration, would you be comfortable doing so? What are arbitration and mediation?

Although in practice there are great differences between these two, for purposes of preparing and completing performance tests set in this context, you may generally think about preparing for mediation as you would for a settlement conference, and for arbitration as you would for trial. Knowing at least a bit about ADR and understanding some of the practical differences between litigation and alternatives, however, may broaden your base of problem-solving skills and help you with a PT task that involves ADR or settlement.

In *arbitration*, the parties agree to let a neutral third party (often someone knowledgeable about the subject matter of the dispute) make a final and binding decision. Arbitration resembles courtroom litigation but is less formal; for example, rules of evidence may not be adhered to as strictly as in a court proceeding.

In *mediation*, parties also go voluntarily before a neutral third party, the mediator. Unlike arbitrators or judges, however, mediators do not impose a binding decision on the parties. Rather, mediators try to facilitate dialogue between the disputing participants and allow them to come to their own mutually agreeable solution, instead of rendering a judgment for one party. A mediator may also help the parties draft a written memorandum of the agreement reached, which usually takes the form of a binding contract. If you are unfamiliar with mediation, see the sidebar on "The Mediation Process."

Mediation resembles negotiation; however, rather than simply pushing one or another party to make concessions in order to arrive at an agreement, the goal is to discover the underlying needs of each side and attempt to find a mutually satisfying resolution. The classic mediation example is two people fighting over one orange. Both want the fruit. In litigation, one would prevail and win the entire orange. In a settlement, the orange might be cut in half. But, if a mediation were to reveal that one party wanted the orange for its juice and the other for its zest, then both might be completely satisfied by splitting the fruit such that the juice is squeezed for one and the entire peel goes to the other. On a PT, you will seek to understand what each party wants and/or needs by carefully reading the File documents and zeroing in on any information about both parties.

If your client is open to contemplating ADR, some of the reasons to consider mediation include:

- Less cost to the client.
- Informality: parties are not bound by evidence rules.
- More control: the parties themselves, not a judge, make the ultimate decisions. Thus, there is truly the potential to get to the parties' underlying needs, as discussed in the preceding example concerning the orange.
- Convenience: parties also may be able to schedule ADR sessions at times that are more convenient to them, rather than simply when the court clerk places the matter on the judge's calendar.
- Privacy: There is greater privacy in mediation, as there are no court-filed documents that become public record.

THE MEDIATION PROCESS

This information is slightly adapted from U.S. Department of Health and Human Services, Departmental Appeals Board (DAB), October 2, 2016, available at http://www.hhs.gov/dab/divisions/adr/mediation/process.html.

Conceptually, mediation includes three general phases:

Introductory: During this part of the process, the mediator helps the parties create a safe environment in which to discuss difficult topics. Depending on the parties' experience with mediation, the mediator may provide a process overview: the role of the mediator, what will happen in the various mediation sessions, and confidentiality. During this phase, the parties may agree to ground rules for the conduct of the mediation (e.g., ensuring that only one person speaks at a time) and a general timetable for the process. This phase includes a joint session among the parties, during which opposing sides have an opportunity to state their views and desired outcomes.

Problem-Solving Stage: During this stage, the mediator helps the parties together to focus on issues, interests, options for resolution, and criteria for evaluating those options. The parties may also meet separately with the mediator to share confidences and fully consider options in private.

Closure: During this phase, the parties decide whether and on what terms to resolve the dispute. The mediator may help them draft a document that reflects any commitments they wish to make. As needed, the agreement then may be passed to others for approval. If the parties do not reach agreement, the mediator makes sure they understand why and what next steps are available to them.

Legislation

Because lawyers also act as legislators, some past performance test tasks have included redrafting statutes and advocating amendments to legislation. As with lawyering tasks, if you are asked to draft or revise/edit legislation on a performance test, focus on content and follow any form or format-related instructions that are provided.

Your tone should be formal, similar to how you would write to a court. If you are instructed to advocate the endorsement or passage of certain legislation, your tone should be partisan and persuasive. However, if you are instructed to evaluate the pros and cons of certain legislation, adopt an objective, neutral tone. If you are to edit or draft legislation, consider the suggestions made in the preceding sections on transactional matters and document analysis. Often, the best way to approach this type of assignment is to proceed paragraph by paragraph.

Unusual or Unfamiliar Tasks

The material in this chapter will help you familiarize yourself with commonly tested documents. Occasionally, though, bar examiners task you with drafting a document that you have never heard of. If this happens on your exam, stay calm, read the instructions carefully, and follow them as closely as possible. It may well be that once you get into the exam, the instructions and assignment will start resembling a task you have seen before, perhaps just called by an unfamiliar name. For example, in California, briefs in support of motions are typically called "Memoranda of Points and Authorities." If you had never heard the term "Points and Authorities," you could nonetheless clearly see from reading the instructions and putting the task in context that really the examiners are just asking you to draft a "brief."

DRAFTING A TASK YOU HAVE NEVER SEEN BEFORE

When faced with an unfamiliar task, stay calm and think logically. Begin by studying the instructions. Even before you learn the facts from the File and the law from the Library, you can likely get a pretty good idea of what you need to write by simply thinking things through. Whether your task is determining *how* to draft some document, or strategizing about *when* to do or perform various acts, think and reason through the issues, and you will likely see a way to formulate a responsive answer. For example, let's say you are asked to draft a discovery plan—and that is something you have never done. You don't know what it should look like. How should you proceed? Whatever you do, do not worry. Just stay calm and think. Ask yourself: "What am I being asked to write and why?" Your thinking might proceed as follows:

> *I am being asked to draft a discovery plan. I am supposed to be an associate in a law firm. The senior partner said the client is contemplating filing a lawsuit after suffering severe physical injury while trespassing on the defendant's property. I know that discovery is the formal process that allows our client, as a party to a lawsuit, to obtain information, documents, or things that are now in the other side's possession, and which will help us understand the strengths and weaknesses of their case, our case, or both. The partner wants me to plan or strategize about how we are going to get that information—that is, which tools of discovery we will use (depositions, interrogatories, requests for admission, etc.), when we will use them, and why, and what information we are looking for.*

Already, you can begin to see that in asking you to draft a discovery plan, what the examiners are really testing is your ability to analyze the strengths and weaknesses of your client's and the opposing party's cases, and find out more information about them. You can handle that! You can figure out a logical organization if they do not provide a format.

Let's take the example one step further. In considering *when* to use which discovery tools, context and logic will help your analysis. Your internal thought process might continue as follows:

> *If we send interrogatories <u>first</u>, we will learn how to proceed with the rest of our discovery; we might find out who has further information and thus learn who to depose and where potential deponents are located. We might learn about documents we will want to review, and more. In addition, interrogatories will be much less expensive than depositions (as they do not involve court reporters and all that attorney time for preparing and for sitting through the sessions). We should start with less expensive discovery tools and proceed to more costly ones if we need them. We should consult our client before spending more money than we need to.*

You would continue talking yourself through the problem, returning frequently to the instructions, and produce something thoughtful, well-organized, and responsive—exactly what you need to do to pass.

No matter how many times you read the Instructions and Task Memo, a new document may be unfamiliar. If so, don't panic. The key to success on the PT is and will always be in reading and carefully following whatever instructions they give you. Look for any clues they do give you about what you are writing, to whom, and why, and pick any logical organization for your responsive writing. Fall back on your general approach, organizing facts around legal principles. Look to the Library for structure and think:

- Tree trunk = cause of action, crime, defense, or other legal liability theory
- Branches = elements or factors
- Leaves = facts

Remember, if the task is unfamiliar to you, it is likely unfamiliar to everyone else around you. Remember too that after completing all ten practice exams in the Online Question and Answer Bank, you will have been exposed to many of the types of tasks that might appear on your bar exam.

By now, we hope you know a bit about what a performance test is and how to complete one, at least in theory. Let's move now from theory to practice. Read on with me. Start working through the exams in each of the subsequent chapters to develop your practical knowledge and hone your PT skills. By the time you reach the end of the book, I am confident you will agree that the performance test is not only wholly doable but it is the best part of the bar exam.

KEY TAKEAWAYS

- PTs would be much easier were it not for the time constraints of the exam. Do not get discouraged if you are not completing practice tests in the allotted time; keep up the practice and follow the many time-saving tips detailed in this chapter.
- Master the steps in SS-BROW, a logical approach to handling any PT. (SS-Brow stands for: **S**tudy the Instructions; **S**kim the File; **B**rief the Library Authorities; **R**e-read the Instructions, File, and Library; **O**utline; and **W**rite the tasks as directed.)
- Familiarize yourself with commonly tested tasks such as briefs, memos, letters, fact investigation plans, arguments to the judge or jury, and the other documents discussed in this chapter. Have a strategy for drafting unfamiliar tasks. Bottom line: Be prepared to write any sort of task that might appear on your bar

exam. (In the concluding chapter of this book, after completing all the practice test chapters, we will sum up and I will show you the one-page "strategy sheet" that I developed to prepare for bar exam PTs.)

- PTs test several basic lawyering skills: legal analysis, factual analysis, awareness of professional responsibility, and problem solving. Along with these, PTs test practical skills such as reading comprehension, time management, and clear and effective writing.[12]

---

[12]The PT skills that are tested are listed at www.ncbex.org/exams/mpt/preparing.

3

CRIMINAL LAW

OVERVIEW OF CRIMINAL LAW

In law school, criminal law and criminal procedure are very different courses. For that reason, you will find separate chapters for each in this book. On bar exams, however, they are often considered one subject, as they are on the Multistate Bar Examination (MBE) portion of the exam.

Criminal procedure courses in law school typically focus on studying the Fourth, Fifth, and Sixth Amendments to the Constitution, looking at defendants' rights in cases of arrest and search and seizure of evidence, and considering constitutional rights with respect to defendants' statements. You learn about the history and evolution of the rights, how they have been guaranteed, when and where exceptions have been carved out, and more. You study mostly Supreme Court cases in law school criminal procedure courses.

In typical criminal law courses, you study the elements of crimes, including:

- Homicidal offenses such as murder and manslaughter
- Structure crimes such as burglary and arson
- Theft crimes such as larceny and embezzlement
- Preliminary (or inchoate) crimes such as solicitation, attempt, and conspiracy
- Defense theories, such as self-defense and insanity

For a more comprehensive list of the topics covered on the MBE in criminal law and procedure, consult the most recent MBE Subject Matter Outlines published by the National Conference of Bar Examiners on their website at ncbex.org/exams/mbe/preparing/. In criminal law courses, you most often read appellate cases that focus on what is required for proof of certain elements of certain crimes. For teaching purposes, those cases are heavily edited to drill down into particular aspects of each concept. You may read cases illustrating different tests that have been adopted in different jurisdictions to establish certain legal theories. For instance, you will likely read about a number of tests for the insanity defense. You may also study the differing approaches various jurisdictions have taken to establish that a defendant has engaged in sufficient action (when coupled with the requisite intent) to support a conviction for attempt crimes. Casebooks often include historical perspectives, so you can see how the law has evolved over time in certain areas. You may study decisions that illustrate how courts may create exceptions to rules to mitigate the harshness of certain results, such as restricting criminal liability under the felony murder rule.

In bar exam criminal law essay questions, you are typically given a set of facts from which you have to determine the defendant's guilt with regard to one or more offenses. The interrogatory or query at the end of the fact pattern may ask if a defendant is guilty of particular crimes, or, simply, whether or not any crimes have been committed. To determine this, you will consider both the elements of relevant crimes themselves and relevant defenses. In criminal procedure essays, you are often considering whether the defendant's arrest, statements, or evidence seized from the defendant (or others) may be used against the defendant at trial, or whether such evidence will be suppressed.

The following are some of the many possible scenarios that could be tested on criminal law and procedure PTs:

- You may be asked to role-play as either a government attorney (a prosecutor) or a defense lawyer. As a prosecutor, you may have to determine whether the law and evidence support charging the defendant and/or convicting the defendant of particular crimes. As a defense attorney, you may be asked to prepare the defense case or prepare to plea bargain.
- You may be given statutory law and/or cases that specify what must be proven beyond a reasonable doubt, and you may have to study testimony or documentary evidence to determine the likelihood of conviction.
- You may have to write an investigation plan to determine how evidence may be obtained to prosecute or defend against a conviction.
- You may be asked to draft an argument to a judge to suppress evidence before a trial, or to draft a closing argument to a judge or jury to urge a conviction or argue that the prosecution has not met its burden of proof at the close of a criminal trial.
- You may be asked to draft an appellate brief arguing that a conviction at the trial level should be overturned, or, if you represent the government, that the conviction should be upheld.

SIMULATED CRIMINAL LAW–BASED PERFORMANCE TEST

Take three hours and complete the exam called *State v. Burke* in the Online Question and Answer Bank at **http://ambar.org/barexamprep**. I strongly recommend that you complete this exam in full under timed conditions. If you do not have time, however, and prefer to take this exam in shorter sittings, read the following Time-Crunch Tips.

Note that the debriefing in the rest of this chapter assumes that you have taken the entire practice test.

TIME-CRUNCH TIPS

You will see that *State v. Burke* involves two drafting tasks, both of which relate to several crimes the defendant may be charged with. To divide the exam into two practice tests, in your first sitting complete the part of Task A that relates to the possible violations of Columbia Criminal Code §§ 18-602(D) and 18-602(F), and also complete the part of Task B that relates to those same charges. In your second sitting, complete the part of Task A that relates to the possible violation of Columbia Criminal Code § 18-745 and the part of Task B that relates to that same charge. The Library divides neatly: the *Wallace* and *Zerbe* cases relate to the § 18-602 charges and the *Polin* and *Lathus* cases relate to the § 18-745 charge. You will need to read the entire File to write about all three charges, but because it will be familiar when you go to complete your second "practice test," you may need to spend about 100 minutes on §§ 18-602(D) and 18-602(F), and only 80 minutes on § 18-745. If you have even less time, just complete the document requested in Task A for the crimes in Columbia Criminal Code §§ 18-602(D) and 18-602(F), referring only to *Wallace* and *Zerbe* (about 60 minutes total), and then complete only Task A for the crime in Columbia Criminal Code § 18-745, referring only to *Polin* and *Lathus* (about 30 minutes).

INSIDE THIS TEST: DEBRIEFING, TIPS, AND STRATEGIES

Note: Read this section only after completing the *State v. Burke* assignments.

Why *State v. Burke* as a practice criminal law exam? I chose *State v. Burke* for a few reasons. The first is that this test provides a superb review of one of the most fundamental underpinnings of criminal law: the requirement of proof beyond a reasonable doubt. Next, the highly structured tasks in *Burke* also remind us that crimes (like torts and many other areas of law) are element based. Typically, each element of each cause of action in a civil case must be proven by a preponderance of the evidence; each element of each crime must be proven beyond a reasonable doubt. Third, the *Burke* exam provides exposure to some crimes that one may not study in criminal law classes: criminal trespass and assault with a deadly weapon. Finally, the exam is set in the early stages of prosecution, while the government is deciding whether there is enough evidence—and if that evidence is credible enough and persuasive enough—to proceed to trial. Therefore, this performance test provides a good opportunity for you to look at facts when they are most malleable: before trial, when they are not yet proven "evidence."

Instructions/Assignment

In *Burke*, you play the role of an assistant district attorney; in other words, you are a government prosecutor. The case is realistic, especially compared with typical law school essays and MBE exams, both because of the uncertainty about the facts and because it brings in political concerns as well as legal concerns. You might think it is not realistic that a new lawyer would be asked to make such an important determination, but a former student of mine, when she was still in law school, was clerking for a district attorney's office when a recession hit; due to budget constraints and attorneys being tied up with other cases, research assignments just like this one regarding *Burke* were regularly given to law clerks.

Doctrinal classes in law school look at whether a party will likely prevail on the merits of a lawsuit, but they generally avoid discussion of why parties bring or fail to bring lawsuits, or resolve actions prior to trial. I raise this topic because a big part of law practice is advising clients on whether to file lawsuits in the first place, how to solve their problems without litigation, and/or whether to settle (civil cases) or plea bargain (in criminal cases) prior to trial. (According to a 2012 *New York Times* article, more than 94% of state criminal cases and more than 97% of federal criminal cases end in plea bargains.[1]) These questions involve assessment far beyond simply whether the elements of each cause of action or crime can be established.

As far as facts go, both in performance tests (and in this one in particular) and in the real world, witnesses are not always credible. Certain versions of "the facts" may not always be reliable. This is radically different from law school or bar exam essay questions on which you must accept facts as given. On law essay exams, you are being tested precisely on your ability to apply the facts, as stated, to the law you know. On essays, you must not question whether the facts are believable. In contrast, in this PT and in most day-to-day lawyering, you *must* question facts.

I use a criminal law example to explain why *not* to question facts in essays. In this particular essay, the facts say that the defendant "shot at the victim" from a "very far distance away," in a "dark alley," and "aimed at the victim's toe." Students frequently

---

[1] Erica Goode, *Stronger Hand for Judges in the "Bazaar" of Plea Deals*, N.Y. Times, March 22, 2012, http://www.nytimes.com/2012/03/23/us/stronger-hand-for-judges-after-rulings-on-plea-deals .html.

will argue: "But, Professor, there is no way a person could aim at the toe, especially from that far away in the dark." My reply? "So what?! These are the facts. Use them." I then urge my students to ask why exam drafters might have included the fact that the defendant "aimed at the victim's toe." Readers, you will likely see this! These facts allow the test taker to argue that the defendant did not intend to kill but merely to injure the victim, thus potentially affecting the determination of whether the defendant acted with malice aforethought. (Aiming at the toe negates the intent-to-kill presumption raised by the use of a deadly weapon because, generally, one who intends to kill aims at a vital area, such as the head or chest.) Note that malice might nonetheless be established here, but only through intent to seriously injure or reckless disregard for human life rather than intent to kill (which in turn affects whether the resulting crime might be murder in the first or second degree). Do you see how many discussable issues (and points) stem from the test taker's thorough use of the facts presented? Do you also see that a reader who told himself or herself "No one could possibly aim at the toe in this situation, so I'm going to ignore this silly fact" may well fail the essay!

The point is that, unlike in essays where you must use even implausible facts, in PTs you can and often must question the facts. In *State v. Burke*, there were many potential factual problems. Did you see them? There are witnesses whose vantage points were such that they may not have gotten a good look at what happened between Burke and Passon. Other witnesses had motives to exaggerate (i.e., they were biased). Yes, this skeptical thinking goes beyond the "four corners" of the exam, but it is highly relevant to what is being asked of you on this PT, which is to determine if the prosecution (your office) has sufficient evidence to prove guilt beyond a reasonable doubt of each element of each crime. To respond effectively on this PT, you *had* to question the "facts."

Let's walk through the File and make some observations about what you saw or should have seen as you were reading.

The General Instructions

The first thing that you should have noticed was the percentage split, telling you how much each of the two required tasks was worth. On this exam, the only place to find this information was in these General Instructions; it was not repeated anywhere else in the exam. It would be helpful to transfer such information immediately to either the Task Memo or your scratch paper.

Here, Task A is worth 50% to 60% and Task B is worth 40% to 50%. That is close to equal, with Task A being weighted slightly more heavily than Task B. Your takeaway? You needed to allocate slightly more time to complete Task A than Task B. But, given that Task B was worth up to 50%, you had to give it almost equal attention, and clearly a poor job on Task B could sink your final score. (Many students who failed this exam made the mistake of spending too much time on Task A and running short on Task B.)

TIP: COMPLETE PT TASKS IN ORDER

When a PT includes more than one task, complete them in order. Finishing the first task often helps you complete the second one. Also, if you happen to run short on time as you are finishing the second task (which should *not* happen if you have trained thoroughly and practiced with all the exams in this book), others may also be rushing to finish that second task, so your answer will be comparable in thoroughness. Generally, write the documents out of order only if you freeze or have writer's block against the first task and are able to begin the second task more easily. In that case, do what it takes to get your brain and fingers moving.

In *Burke*, the General Instructions tell you that you are an assistant district attorney. Thus, you know—and should keep in mind as you read through the File and Library—that you have certain additional ethical obligations required of prosecutors.

The Instructions also tell you, and you see this again in the Library, that all four cases are Supreme Court of Columbia cases. The pending matter, the prosecution of Burke, is set in state court in the State of Columbia. What do you know from this? That unless one case overrules another, all of the Library case law is binding.

The Task Memo

The next File document is the Task Memo. (The Task Memo has historically always followed the General Instructions.) The Task Memo explains some of the complicating factors in our case, namely:

- The prior history between defendant and victim
- The victim's and even the police's alleged ties to one of the entities in the case, and the money that is generated from the racetrack
- That this case is what D.A. Boland describes as a political "hot potato." (Note that the politics are underscored in the article at the end of the File. Pay attention when information is repeated by bar examiners, on PTs and essays!)

In the Task Memo, D.A. Boland gives you background on and a nice summary of the case, then requests that you complete two tasks. The first task he calls a "second assessment of the case." That term always throws students. They think, "I have never done this; I have no idea what a 'second assessment' is." Then they panic. But you need not be rattled, and I hope you weren't. Read beyond the name of the task to see what they really want, and you discover that the "second assessment" is simply an internal memorandum with a special name. Specifically, in this "second assessment" memo, you are to:

- Advise the DA whether, based on evidence you currently have in the File, there is sufficient proof of each element of each crime to support a conviction (i.e., whether each element is established beyond a reasonable doubt)
- Consider potential defenses and credibility or proof problems
- Conclude with a recommendation of whether to proceed to trial or not

How should you organize your answer? The instructions make it clear: element-by-element, under each respective count. The fact that these instructions were so specific was a gift.

While reading the instructions, you might have helped yourself by writing exactly what is being asked of you in your notes. Pull components out of the Task Memo and get them either on your scratch paper or typed into your first "draft" of your answer. As you complete your final answer, look back at the Task Memo and be sure you included all parts of what was requested. In other words, confirm the task to be sure that your answer was responsive and complete. For example, did you write about the proof that exists to establish each element beyond a reasonable doubt *and* about defenses and credibility concerns, but forget to conclude with a final recommendation on whether to prosecute? That final recommendation on each count was critical. Failing to make such a recommendation would show the grader that you did not read the directions and possibly make it look like you did not finish analyzing that particular count. (The examiners put a premium on *completing* PT tasks.) Re-reading the Task Memo several times (before, during, and after you draft your final answer) will prevent your uploading an incomplete answer.

In the second document, you are again asked to proceed element by element on each charge, but here you are to determine what *additional evidence* might be gathered. For the second task, you are given a Format Memo on how to set up the assignment, which they call a "Follow-Up Investigation Plan." (Again, the name threw people who did not read carefully and see that everything requested was spelled out explicitly.)

The first page of this office procedure memo tells you what a "Follow-Up Investigation Plan" is; the second page gives an example. The first page says, among other important points: "Each charge is to be stated separately, and the additional evidence related thereto listed under the element … to which it applies, with a notation of the possible source from which the evidence may be obtained."

If you are a visual person, you might actually "see" this language in a tiered outline format such as this:

Charge 1

  Element 1

    Additional evidence proving element 1 (and where to find that evidence). Note here that you may have several pieces of evidence that you could investigate or discover that might prove element 1. List everything you can think of and note where and how you might *ethically* find it.

  Element 2

    Additional evidence proving element 2

Charge 2

  Element 1

    Additional evidence proving element 1

  Element 2

    Additional evidence proving element 2

You are role-playing a lawyer for the government. Pay close attention to the ethical obligations of prosecutors. Also, no matter who you represent on any PT, *never* suggest an illegal or unethical means for discovering evidence, no matter how much it might help prove your case.

The sample you are given on the next page of the Format Memo illustrates this format: the first count, "robbery," under which elements are listed: (1) the identity of the perpetrator; and (2) the force or fear element. Under each element is a brainstorming list of all the evidence that might prove that element, and, where applicable, how one might obtain such evidence. (For example, under force or fear, it is suggested that there may be a weapon; to get that weapon, we may need a warrant to search the house.)

A key part of PT success is following directions; where they are specific about a format, such as here, you must follow it. Such specificity is a gift. It takes all the guesswork out of how to respond. You just need to follow the sample precisely. You may have to read that sample two or three times to fully understand it and see how to translate the elements of your case into that format, but the organization is given to you.

Remainder of the File

The next document you see, the "Information" or criminal complaint, clearly sets forth the elements of the two charges: criminal trespass and assault with a deadly weapon. Remember, you were told in the Task Memo that these were the two charges, so you should have been expecting to see them in this charging document.

TIP: USE FILE DOCUMENTS AS SAMPLES FOR DRAFTING PT TASKS

When working through practice PT Files, take a step back and look at the various documents in the File for ideas on how you would draft this sort of document if it were your task. Looking at this Information, you can see what goes into a criminal complaint: just a plain and simple statement of the defendant's having committed the elements of each charged offense. (Would you have been comfortable if you had been asked to draft a criminal complaint? I hope that after completing this practice PT and studying this chapter, you would!)

Now, the Library will also provide the relevant Criminal Code sections, but this Information tells you which particular sections the defendant is charged under, and you can begin separating them out into elements:

Under § 18-602(D), that the defendant:

(1) entered the property,
(2) with the intent to interfere or obstruct.

OR, under § 18-602(F), that the defendant:

(1) entered the property which was enclosed by a fence, **AND**,
(2) refused **OR** failed to leave when requested to do so.

Notice that in the previous outline I bolded and wrote my "OR" and "AND" in all caps. Whenever I read a statute, I circle or put a box around the words "and" and "or" so that I know if elements or provisions must all be proven (if they are conjunctive), or if only one or the other must be proven (if they are disjunctive). Use this technique when reading statutes on PTs.

In the second charge, the assault, you see two elements: (1) the assault to the victim's person, **AND** (2) with a deadly weapon or instrument **AND/OR** with force likely to produce great bodily injury.

> **Note:** Do not rely on the Information alone to determine the elements. These code sections are in the Library. Read them carefully there as well to see if this Information document has stated the law correctly. (A document drafted by someone in your office may be correct, but it is also possible that the document contains errors and thus should be amended.) Also, as you can tell by the sample with the Robbery charge in the Format Memo, "identity of the perpetrator" must necessarily be established in order to charge that particular person with the crime. So, we also may need to add that, especially if it becomes unclear as we read whether the defendant in question committed the criminal acts in question. (You might make a note to yourself as soon as you think of this to add "identity of the perpetrator" as an element in both the second assessment and follow-up investigation plan.)

The following is my continued debriefing of the File, which I wrote in the first person, telling you what I would say to myself while reading each document. (It often helps to talk to yourself as you read PTs—it keeps you awake and focused!) Print a copy of the File (from the Online Question and Answer Bank at **http://ambar.org/barexamprep**) and refer to it as you read the following.

> My next File document is the sheriff's arrest report. Before I even start reading this document, I remember that my boss, the DA giving me this

assignment, told me that these sheriffs may be biased. I know generally that an arrest report may be impeached. And, I know one of my tasks is to see if there is enough evidence right now, based on what we have, to convict. But I also know my other task is to write a plan about getting additional evidence. So, I skim the police report with those thoughts in mind.

The police report, signed by a deputy named Angel Coderra, includes a great deal of information about where the picketers allegedly were and what exactly they were doing, and specifically where the defendant allegedly was and what he allegedly did or failed to do.

For this first read-through of the File, my plan is to skim each document, just to see what it is, who wrote it, and basically what sort of factual information it contains. I know that I will not yet know what specifically to look for in the File documents until I read the Library. So I know I will return to these File documents once I know the law that governs. (It's an open-book test. The File will be there for me when I need it.)

I keep the word "allegedly" in my mind as I'm reading the police report because, as the prosecutor, I have to be certain I can prove the requisite facts in court, establishing each element beyond a reasonable doubt. A police officer may be biased, mistaken, or lying; and, again, here I know from the Task Memo that there are at least suggestions of sheriff bias.

The next document is a statement of the alleged victim, Joe Passon. This is Passon's account of events. Again, only after reading the Library will I know exactly what I am searching for in this document. At that time, I definitely will want to compare what Passon said happened to other witnesses' versions of events.

The next document is a report from the chief county investigator, the same man District Attorney Boland directed to interview witnesses. The investigator indicates that each of the five witnesses' statements is "summarized." In other words, this document is what the investigator says they said, not necessarily in their own words, so we are not certain that these witnesses will testify exactly as these summaries indicate. (We may immediately note in our second task that this is information we will need to confirm.)

Be skeptical. The hint that you should question "facts" in the File was in the Task Memo when you were told to take into account witness credibility. Were you thinking that these summaries may or may not be completely accurate? Were you telling yourself we may need to double-check certain points? If so, great! You should be skeptical and thinking about getting more information, because you know your second task is precisely about conducting further investigation.

The investigator's first witness (Pentivo) clearly was not present at the scene; he was at the north gate of the property and the alleged incidents occurred at the south gate. You may want to draw a diagram of the property where the incident occurred to try to keep straight what allegedly happened where.

The Memo tells you more than once that Pentivo does not have firsthand knowledge of the events but just heard about them from others. What Pentivo does give is background on both Passon (the alleged victim) and Burke (the defendant and alleged perpetrator), and about the "bad blood" (as Boland described it in the Task Memo) or past history between the two.

The investigator's second witness (Joey Culmone) was present at the scene of the alleged incident but does not seem eager to testify about what he knew. (Why might he be reluctant to testify? Think about how that affects our case, if at all.) Culmone's version of events also differs drastically from both the police report and Passon's account. If Culmone were to be believed, this would cast significant doubt on our ability to prove either the trespass or the assault charges beyond a reasonable doubt.

Note: You may not have seen all this until your re-read of the File.

The investigator's next witness (Jack Beta) was allegedly present, but could not see clearly because of the crowds surrounding the car in which Passon claimed to have been assaulted. Jack Beta may therefore easily be impeached, because he did not have a clear line of sight at the time.

The investigator's next witness was Joseph Passon, the alleged victim. Interestingly, the investigator notes that Passon's statement was identical to the statement included earlier in the File (that the deputy attached to the police report), with certain exceptions the investigator enumerates. The investigator's report fleshes out further information about bad blood between Passon and Burke, but also notes these inconsistencies in Passon's statements. These will be critical in efforts that defense counsel might make to discredit the victim.

The investigator's final witness is Junior Harwood, the alleged passenger in Joseph Passon's car at the time of the incident. The investigator notes that Harwood is both a friend and neighbor of Passon's, so there is great room for bias. It also notes that Harwood himself says he did not clearly see what happened or whose stick hit Passon.

The last item in the File is a newspaper editorial. Even newspaper articles written by respected journalists are not fact, but this is especially true here because this is an *editorial* piece. Including this sort of document in the File is a classic PT move; you must be able to see that what is stated in such a document is not fact but someone's opinion. It does, however, provide a great deal of food for thought on bias.

If at all possible, you should try to weave in mention of this editorial somewhere in your memo. This document highlights the political pressure that the DA is under from opposing constituencies to bring or drop the charges against Burke, and you may want to underscore that your office is obligated to follow the law, not public opinion.

> **Note:** Many students avoid referring to this newspaper piece altogether because they do not know what to say about it. Here, because your task is to draft an internal memo to the DA, rather than a document meant for someone outside your office, you can easily weave this in either in an introduction or a conclusion if you do not see another spot for it, to reiterate that despite political pressures the DA should hold firm in prosecuting or not, per your recommendations.

Bottom line: Try to make at least some mention of every document in the File and make every effort to reference all the main cases in the Library. (You do not have to mention every case within the main cases, but try to mention every main case, meaning every case listed in the table of contents.)

Library

The Library (your closed legal universe) includes a few code sections (Columbia Criminal Code) and four cases (Columbia Supreme Court). This case was filed in state court in Columbia, so everything in the Library appears to be binding authority.

NOTE-TAKING TIPS

As suggested in Chapter 2, you may want to take notes about the cases directly on the Library table of contents. Experiment with this note-taking system while completing practice tests. You will not have space for detailed case briefs, just a holding and maybe a key fact or two—but that is all you really need. The exam is open book. You can always and at any time look up any additional details you want to reference. Still, it can be very useful to have all the main rules on one page. You can also "book brief" on the actual cases, noting the issue, holding, key facts, rationale, and dicta. Then "key" your book briefing to page numbers that you jot down on the table of contents page. For example, write something like "H at p. 3" next to the printed case name to indicate that you have marked the holding of that case on page 3 of the Library.

The Code Sections

Note that here you are provided only selected relevant statutes, so you must read them carefully. Compare this with a PT Library in which you are given a block of a particular code, with sections numbered sequentially, and where only certain sections apply to your case. Examples of this latter "reference Library" are in the PTs in the contracts (Chapter 6), evidence (Chapter 8), and professional responsibility (Chapter 10) chapters of this book.

Here, you have the criminal trespass and the assault with a deadly weapon statutes under which Burke was charged, and an exemption for union activity. If that exemption is applicable, it would serve as a defense and would negate Burke's guilt with respect to the criminal trespass. You will need to study each provision; as you read, circle every "and" and "or" and underline elements to learn exactly what is required under each statute.

Cases

Here I highlight just a few points about each case. I have noted the years only because the instructions told us they were all Columbia Supreme Court cases, so you must keep track of whether a case might be older and no longer applicable for some reason. (The *Burke* matter took place in 1987.)

Wallace and *Zerbe* both relate to the criminal trespass, whereas *Lathus* and *Polin* both relate to the assault. The Library will not always divide that neatly, but here it does, and seeing that would be helpful to your organization.

Note: You will not organize your PT answer in a case-by-case fashion. Rather, you will weave important points from the cases, as relevant, into your answer, and organize your answer using an element-by-element approach, under each charge. (An answer organized case-by-case would likely have failed. The instructions told you how to organize your answer, so you had to do what was asked to pass.)

TIP: SAVING TIME WITH CASE CITES

The Instructions tell you that you may abbreviate cases. You score no additional "points" with the grader by providing full cites, and it wastes your time to do so. On PTs, typically you reference civil cases by the plaintiff's or appellant's name. In criminal cases, you reference using the defendant's name because the other party is typically the "state" or the "people" in every case. You can see, in my debriefing of the cases, that I use short cites just as you would have wanted to do in your answer to this PT.

Wallace (1970)

In this case, the court (the Supreme Court of Columbia) reversed a conviction for criminal trespass, holding that some actual "obstruction" (actual physical interference) is required for a conviction of criminal trespass. The court found that the activity of the protestors in the case did not amount to an actual obstruction because members of the public were still free to do what they wished despite protestors' presence, and that the protestors were exercising their lawful rights to convey information.

Zerbe (1981)

The defendant was found not guilty of criminal trespass, even though his actions violated statute § 18-602(F), because of the exception for lawful labor union activities provided by § 18-603. The case suggests that the labor exemption to the trespass statute for lawful union activities should be construed liberally to protect union activity, when there is no violence. *Zerbe* cited *Northwestern*, distinguishing it as a case in which the activity resulted in physical obstruction of traffic and was "accompanied by threats of violence to employees … ."

> **Note:** If you wanted to cite *Northwestern* in your answer, you would do so as follows: "*Northwestern* as cited in *Zerbe.*" Why? Because the grader's "point sheet" or grading rubric will likely expect to see references to all the main cases (which, again, are those listed in the Library table of contents), so the grader will be looking to see that you cited *Zerbe* in your answer.

If Burke's activities are deemed unlawful, the union exemption will not apply. However, if his activities are deemed lawful, his engaging in union activity, even if he was trespassing, will negate the criminality of the trespass.

After reading this case, you know exactly what you are looking for when you go back to re-read the File. You want to know if Burke was actually obstructing people. If he gave them information and they turned away on their own, that may not amount to an unlawful obstruction. Armed with what you learned in the Library, you would be able to go back to the File and easily figure out what your office can prove Burke did or did not do.

You also want to know if Burke either committed acts of violence or threatened violence. We know some people said he did, but did all the witnesses' accounts match up? Can we prove this in court? Taken together, *Zerbe* and *Wallace* underscore the difficulty we may have in proving beyond a reasonable doubt that Burke had the requisite criminal intent for the trespass.

Polin (1981)

From the *Polin* case, we learn that "great bodily injury" need not be permanent or visible, but must be more than "slight, trivial, or minor." In *Polin*, the victim suffered burns, lesions, a ruptured eardrum, and an eye hemorrhage. The court cites other cases involving examples of serious injuries that all amount to great bodily injury (*Wells, James,* and *Grigsby*).

Clearly, after reading *Polin*, you want to go back to the File to see what harm Passon allegedly suffered and determine if the injuries clearly amount to "great bodily injury." If you did not see this on first read, when you go back to re-read the File, it will be very obviously troubling that Passon just plain forgot the details of some of his alleged injuries. ("How serious could they be if he forgot about them?," you must have wondered.)

Lathus (1983)

This case informs readers about two issues: what is a deadly weapon, and whether recklessness or a general intent may be sufficient for this assault crime. About the first issue, the court cites a number of other cases where objects were found to be deadly weapons, including a nail file. The court stressed that it is not just the inherent nature of the instrument but the manner in which it is used. It seems likely that a wooden stake such as that used by Burke and the other picketers would qualify, if Burke indeed used it in a deadly manner (which is still a big question).

On the second issue, the *Lathus* court found that assault with a deadly weapon is essentially a general intent crime, meaning that the intent required is only that the defendant "willfully commit" an act that has the "probable consequence" of resulting in injury to another. There is no requirement that the defendant have the specific intent to actually cause great bodily harm or death or to seriously injure this victim.

Summary of Case Work

After reading *Polin* and *Lathus*, you should have been able to zoom right in to certain facts in the File and much more readily see their significance in relation to whether or not Burke can likely be convicted on the assault charge. It was very obvious, in *State v. Burke,* that skimming the File before reading these cases just gave you general background information. In re-reading the File, after studying the Library cases, you could see much more clearly whether we now have sufficient evidence establishing that Burke actually obstructed customers and, accordingly, whether his picketing actions were lawful, and whether he possessed the requisite intent to and actually caused injuries amounting to great bodily harm. You also likely saw much more easily what additional evidence to investigate.

PULLING IT ALL TOGETHER

Once you have the law in mind, go back through the File and you will see what evidence is critical. It also becomes much clearer where evidence may be contradictory (here, different stories from different witnesses).

An organizing tip: Because both memos were organized charge-by-charge and, under each charge, element-by-element, you could actually set up one outline, copy it, and then work simultaneously to flesh out both outlines. How would that work? Well, as you are reading to insert what will have to be proven in the first memo (whether we have sufficient evidence to prove each element beyond a reasonable doubt), if a "more facts needed" question pops into your head (such as "I wonder where the property line actually ended and if Burke crossed the boundary?" or "I wonder how sharp the stick actually was?"), you could immediately scroll down and insert those questions (asking for more detail or to fill in missing information) in the appropriate place in Memo Two.

This approach—writing the two memos at the same time—will not work for every PT, but the key is always to read the instructions carefully enough that you know exactly what your job is. Here, if you scrutinized the Task Memo before writing, it might well have jumped out at you that the organization was the same in both memos, prompting you to ask yourself if there was any way to take advantage of that.

Affirmative Defenses, Failing to Prove One's Case, and Credibility Problems

On PTs, I generally find that many students fall short in giving enough weight to the defense perspective. Perhaps this results from the sort of automatic IRAC training where students take fact patterns and organize them by potential causes of action or crimes. In fact, one trick that I remind students about when memorizing elements of causes of action is to put right into the laundry list "lack of defenses." I know that is not an element per se, and you know that is not an element, but if a defendant can assert a valid affirmative defense, then the plaintiff will not prevail just as surely as if the plaintiff had not proven all the elements of his or her case-in-chief to begin with.

In the *Burke* PT, most people recognize the statutory defense because the Library included a case on it. However, many downplay the credibility, bias, and other problems that are rampant throughout the *Burke* File. Think about the big picture: Why is the DA asking for a second assessment on whether to take this case to trial? He does not want surprises. He does not want to lose. You must let the DA know, as explicitly and specifically as possible, what problems he will face at trial. Of course, on the surface it looks like Burke may have committed both crimes (the trespass and the assault), but if surface analysis were all that was needed here, you would not have been given this assignment. Identifying the proof problems in this case was critical to doing well on this PT. That is what shows the grader you can think like a lawyer, not just a law student.

In addition to not always recognizing how biased witnesses were, some of the other challenges students often have with *Burke* are spending so much time on the first task that they run out of time on the second task, and wasting time writing a statement of facts (and other parts of a traditional law school memo) that was not requested in the Task Memo instructions. Study the sample answers in the Online Question and Answer Bank and compare them to the answer you wrote. Look for any places where you might improve.

SPIN-OFF EXERCISES

Spin-off exercises provide a way to gain exposure to drafting different types of documents using the same facts and law as on the PT you just completed. Spend a few minutes, now that you have completed *State v. Burke*, to think of other tasks you could have been given and how you would have handled them. Here are a few suggestions:

- Draft a letter to the defendant's (Burke's) counsel to propose a plea bargain.
- Draft a memo outlining the pros and cons of entering into a plea-bargain arrangement with Burke in this instance.
- Draft an anticipated cross-examination plan of Joe Passon, the alleged victim, showing how he may be discredited if we end up relying on his testimony.
- Draft an anticipated cross-examination plan of Deputy Coderra, the arresting officer, showing how he may be discredited if we end up relying on his testimony.
- Pretend that you represent the defendant, Mr. Burke, instead of working for the DA in this PT. Would you look at the evidence against Burke differently?

Note: In a sense, because you were asked to analyze the evidence thoroughly and look at all information that might be used to support Burke and impeach our witnesses, you really should not suddenly see the case in a new light if you were defense counsel. Nevertheless, if my simply asking you to *pretend* you are wearing the defense hat causes you to view any facts or law in a different light, great! This may be a technique (pretending you are counsel for the other side) that you want to employ more often when working on PTs, to ensure that you see the whole picture.

PRACTICE AND LAW SCHOOL AND PTs:
COMPARE AND CONTRAST

This PT provides a wonderful exercise in factual analysis, and, if you get "into" it, it is very exciting. Although it may seem unrealistic that as a lawyer just out of law school you would be asked to give an assessment about whether or not to prosecute a matter that is so politically charged, it is a far more realistic assignment than a typical law school or bar exam essay question. (Precisely because a case is politically charged, new lawyers in the office or even law clerks may be asked to research and give second opinions, to have a few extra eyes look at the case before proceeding to trial.) This exam also allowed you a chance to see yourself as a prosecutor and assume a prosecutor's ethical responsibilities.

This exam forces you to look at facts in a very different manner than you look at an essay fact pattern. What do I mean? Well, in essays, as in appellate work, the facts are essentially frozen. (On appeal, you must work with the facts that were proven at trial; on a law school or bar exam essay, you must work with the fact pattern as written.) Here, though, in *Burke*, we basically only have informal statements from witnesses. Nothing has yet been proven, so no fact is set in stone. We have a victim who contradicts himself, or at least "forgets" key details. We also have witnesses who are extremely biased. This is real-world stuff!

In working through this PT with my students, I have found that many are uncomfortable with, and take time getting used to, the idea that the sources of information may be so biased. We have sheriffs who are moonlighting for the racetrack that is pressing for the defendant to be prosecuted; we have witnesses who have clearly taken sides and have a lot at stake, financially and personally; we have a victim who has a negative personal history with the defendant and thus a possible motive to fabricate testimony. However, after really understanding the assignments, students embrace this exercise and usually enjoy looking closely into credibility and bias.

Working through a practice PT exam like *Burke* helps you as a law student in many ways and even may give you an edge if you end up with some sort of criminal law–related job or internship.

KEY TAKEAWAYS

- Be skeptical on PTs. Sources of "facts" may be biased, and "facts" are not firm until they have been proven in court. (Even then, remember that a witness may be cross-examined.)
- Crimes often lend themselves to element-based analysis. Be sure to know the exact elements of each offense, and the elements of any possible defenses.
- Think about evidence you currently have and whether it is sufficient to prove each element beyond a reasonable doubt. Think also about evidence or information you may still need to discover.

4

CRIMINAL PROCEDURE

OVERVIEW OF CRIMINAL PROCEDURE*

In law school, criminal law and criminal procedure are very different courses. On bar exams, they are often considered one subject, as they are on the Multistate Bar Examination (MBE) portion of the exam.

Typically, criminal law is a 1L course where you study the elements of crimes: the actus reus and mens rea requirements of homicidal offenses such as murder and manslaughter, and defenses to those crimes such as self-defense, intoxication, and insanity. You might also study structure crimes such as burglary and arson, theft crimes such as larceny and embezzlement, and preliminary (or "inchoate") crimes such as solicitation, attempt, and conspiracy.

Most often, you study these various crimes by reading appellate court cases where the defendants have argued that the prosecution did not meet its burden of proving one or more elements of a particular crime or crimes (or of a defense theory). This helps you understand the law in a certain jurisdiction. You may read a number of cases about the same crime or crimes from different jurisdictions to see how older law has evolved and/or how present law differs in different states or in the federal courts. For example, you will likely study several different tests employed in varying jurisdictions dealing with how close to the completion of the target offense a defendant's actions must be in order for that defendant to be guilty of an attempt crime. This area makes for fascinating discussion in law school, especially because we know that just thinking even the most evil of thoughts is not a crime, but action taken toward completing a crime with the intent to complete the crime may amount to a criminal act.

---

*Readers interested in this field who want an overview of the criminal justice system, from arrest to appeal, see *The Criminal Law Handbook*, by Bergman and Berman, 15th ed. 2017, published by Nolo.com.

By contrast, criminal procedure courses in law school are often 2L courses in which you study the constitutional law that affects the rights of the accused, and the obligations and responsibilities of police and prosecutors. In most criminal procedure courses, students read cases dealing with the Fourth, Fifth, and Sixth Amendments to the United States Constitution, looking at the defendant's rights during police stops, arrests, and searches and seizures of evidence. You also typically study the rights of an accused when the police are questioning a suspect or defendant, including due process rights, the right to receive *Miranda* warnings, and the right to counsel.

Criminal procedure courses also often look into the history and evolution of these rights, how they have been guaranteed, when and where exceptions have been carved out, and where the courts are likely to expand or curtail these rights in the future. (You study mostly Supreme Court cases in law school criminal procedure courses.)

In bar review, you will fill in gaps in both criminal law and criminal procedure. Your law school professors typically cover fewer areas than you are responsible for on the bar exam, but in much more detail. (One of my colleagues says the bar exam is 1 foot deep and 6 feet wide, whereas law school courses are 6 feet deep and 1 foot wide.[1] Another colleague likens law school to scuba diving and the bar exam to snorkeling.[2])

On the bar exam, you will not typically have to have the depth of knowledge that law school courses require, but you will have to have a wide breadth of knowledge, including knowing rules that many basic law school criminal procedure courses skip. For example, you must know rules about bail, the rights to a jury trial and a speedy trial, sentencing, and double jeopardy. For a list of the topics covered on the MBE in both criminal law and criminal procedure, consult the most recent MBE Subject Matter Outlines published by the National Conference of Bar Examiners on their website at ncbex.org/exams/mbe/preparing.

> **Note:** It is a good thing that many law school courses spend so much time on arrests, searches, and seizures, as those tend to be the most heavily tested areas on bar exam criminal procedure questions.

Performance tests that are set in criminal law and procedure contexts may take a number of different forms. You might be asked to role-play as a government attorney (a prosecutor) or a defense lawyer. In one of those roles, you may be asked to determine whether the law and evidence support charging the defendant (or dropping charges if criminal charges have been filed) or convicting the defendant of particular crimes. You may be given statutory and/or case law that specifies what must be proven beyond a reasonable doubt, and you may have to study testimony or documentary evidence to determine what the likelihood of conviction is. You may be analyzing

---

[1] Credit to Bob Hull, Esq.
[2] Credit to Tina Schindler, Esq.

possible defense theories, or you may be drafting a discovery plan to determine how evidence may be obtained to defend against a conviction. You may be asked to draft an argument to a judge to suppress evidence before a trial, or to draft a closing argument to a judge or jury urging that your client should prevail at the close of a criminal trial. You may be asked to draft a trial brief or an appellate brief. You could be asked to negotiate a plea bargain, or advise a client on whether or not to plead guilty.

SIMULATED CRIMINAL PROCEDURE–BASED PERFORMANCE TEST

Take three hours, go to the Online Question and Answer Bank at **http://ambar.org/ barexamprep**, and complete the *People v. Duncan* test ("*Duncan*").

TIME CRUNCH TIPS

If you still want to write the *Duncan* exam but cannot take three hours now, here are a couple of suggestions: (1) Read the entire *Duncan* File and Library and thoroughly outline your answer, but do not write it out in full. This will likely take you about 90 minutes. (2) Read through all of *Duncan*, but in drafting your opposition to the defendant's motion to dismiss, only address the first few of the eight factors of the balancing test you will find (in your Library reading) that the courts consider when determining whether there was "custody" for purposes of *Miranda*. If you address all eight factors, you will need the full 180 minutes to complete the test, but you can shave off substantial time if you practice by addressing only some of the factors. Note that certain factors will be easier to establish than others, so in the best of circumstances, you would take the time and write out the answer in full.

INSIDE THIS TEST: TIPS AND STRATEGIES

Read the following only after you have completed the *Duncan* practice exam. You may want to print a copy of the File and Library and have it with you to reference as you read through the information in the rest of this chapter.

Inside the File, Starting with the Instructions

I love this exam. It drills down into *Miranda*, one of the most heavily tested areas on bar exam criminal procedure questions, and it reminds us of the fundamentals: *Miranda* protects people in situations involving custodial interrogation. That means it focuses on those who are **both** *in custody* **and** being *interrogated*.

You probably did lots of studying in law school about what constitutes *interrogation*. (You might recall that it involves not just explicit questioning but also words or actions designed to elicit a response.) In this question, however, your work centered on whether this defendant, Mr. Duncan, was in *custody*. It was clear that he was being interrogated: He was questioned for nearly six hours! However, Mr. Duncan says he was also in custody, and the prosecution (us in this PT) disagrees.

Now, let's plunge in and walk through the exam. As far as Instructions, remember there are three potential documents that typically provide directions: (1) the General Instructions, (2) the Task Memo, and possibly (3) a Format Page. Here there are only two; there is no Format Page.

The General Instructions are essentially boilerplate in this exam. They tell you that you have a File and a Library—nothing unusual. They say you have three hours to complete it. The Instructions note that you are in state court, in the State of Columbia. There is only one document to draft, so you need not worry about allocating time between tasks. With nothing unusual, you only need to take a very quick glance at the General Instructions, and because there are no Format Pages, you know that all the real "directions" will come from the Task Memo.

So, on to the Task Memo! Despite being only two paragraphs long, the Task Memo is full of important detail. The first critical pieces of information you want to pull out are who you are and whom you represent. How do you find that here? First things first, look at the letterhead: "Warren County Prosecutor" in the office of "Alicia Ouelette, District Attorney" from "Averil Park, Columbia."

Next, the assignment comes from Laurie Shanks, who is the "Deputy District Attorney." Laurie Shanks jumps in, saying "*We* have indicted Raymond Duncan for the murder of Jennifer Clark" (emphasis added). You know from this first sentence that this PT is set in a criminal law context and that it involves a murder trial.

Laurie Shanks continues using the word "we" in the next few sentences, eventually saying that the defense has filed a motion to suppress and that she wants "You" (that's you, bar exam applicant) to draft the brief arguing to the court that the defense motion should be denied. Clearly, "you" are part of the "we" that is the office of the District Attorney. Thus, you work for the prosecutor's office, and Laurie Shanks is giving you your assignment, so she is likely your supervisor.

The last sentence of the first paragraph clearly requests the document you are to produce in this PT: "Please prepare a draft of a Persuasive Memorandum of Points and Authorities that argues the motion should be denied." The entire second paragraph of the Task Memo serves the same purpose as a Format Page would, telling you what your answer should contain.

Now, just because Ms. Shanks uses the word "Memorandum" does not mean you are to draft an "analytical memorandum." No. This is not a "Memorandum of Law" like the document you drafted in first-year legal research and writing. Ms. Shanks says it is a "*Persuasive* Memorandum of Points and Authorities" (emphasis added).

In some jurisdictions, and here in the fictional State of Columbia, "Memorandum of Points and Authorities" is a term of art that is essentially synonymous with the word *brief*. Even if you were unfamiliar with the term, you would know it was a persuasive document for two reasons: (1) Laurie Shanks says so, using the descriptive term "persuasive" in front of the word "Memorandum"; and (2) you know who decides what evidence should come in and what evidence should be suppressed: the judge. So, obviously a document intended ultimately for the judge (or the court) would be a persuasive document, with your job being to help the judge make the decision that favors your client, here the State of Columbia.

As we discussed earlier in this book, documents intended for someone on your "side" in litigation (for example, an attorney in your office, your investigator, or your own client) are typically analytical. In such documents, you will generally look at both sides neutrally and evaluate pros and cons. By contrast, documents that are ultimately intended for the court or the opposing side are typically persuasive in nature. In zealously representing your client, you are arguing for your client's position; you want your client's version of events, and your conclusions as to how matters should be decided, to win the day.

Notice that Ms. Shanks, your boss, asks you to prepare a "draft" of this brief that your office will be filing with the court. That is simply a way of indicating that the document will first go to Ms. Shanks, although it is ultimately intended for the court. There is nothing to suggest that it is a rough or preliminary draft. You should write the document so that it is as close as possible to being ready to file with the court.

After reading just this part of the Task Memo, even before beginning to skim the rest of the File, I might type a header and title, such as the following, in my draft answer document:

To: Ms. Shanks (or "Laurie Shanks")

From: Applicant

Re: People v. Duncan

Date: [The date of your bar exam]

Please find the Memorandum of Points and Authorities that you requested below. If you have any further questions or follow-up queries, please do not hesitate to contact me.

Memorandum of Points and Authorities in Opposition to
Defense Motion to Suppress Evidence

You will be able to flesh out your outline as you read, but why not get started now writing some of what you know you will eventually need?

ETHICS CONCERNS

As noted earlier in the book, bar examiners may include ethics issues in PTs. Here, Laurie Shanks specifically rules out what could have been an issue by saying, "We have, of course, turned the recording and transcript of the interview over to defense counsel." I immediately noted in the margin next to this, *"Good! No ethical issue!!"* This is just a note to remind myself that the examiners made this a nonissue. (In the Professional Responsibility chapter of this book [Chapter 10], an attorney took and inappropriately retained possession of physical evidence that we had to indicate must be turned over to the prosecution.)

What if Laurie Shanks had not said this? What if she had not mentioned it at all, and you thought about the question? How do you write about that (and perhaps get some credit for your thinking) when it is not directly related to your assignment? You might have simply added a caveat note to Shanks in your introduction: "We must be sure to turn over to defense counsel any and all documents or evidence we are required to turn over."

The examiners could have planted an even more explicit ethical issue by writing in the Task Memo, "I know we are obligated to turn over the recording and transcript but I am going to hold them for a while just to make it more difficult for Duncan's counsel." Then you would have had a serious ethical issue to deal with. (Note that if this were a discussable issue they expected almost all students to see, they might even have repeated that they were holding onto the evidence. If the issue was one that only some students saw, it might have counted as a bonus point.) Assuming they had included this sort of an issue, how would you have addressed this in your answer? Well, you would not mention this to the court in your draft brief. Instead, you would address it in an introductory note to Laurie Shanks, perhaps in brackets; for example:

> ["Below please find the brief you requested. Before you read that document, however, I must bring a critical matter to your attention. We have an obligation to turn over evidence such as the recording and transcript of the police interview to the defense, and I urge you to do so immediately. We must not withhold anything we are required to provide to defense counsel, especially not for strategic purposes."]

In real life, should such a violation occur, you would want to do the same, and if necessary go over Shanks's head to Alicia Ouelette (the head prosecutor) to see that the rules are followed. It is not worth being disbarred to please or get along with any one boss or client. Better to lose your job than your license. Your license is a lifetime license: protect it as such.

One more note for now about the task: the last sentence of the Task Memo says not to write a statement of facts. So, do not write one. You will not get any extra points for drafting a statement of facts when the directions tell you not to; in fact, you may cause the grader to become biased against you from the outset for failure to follow instructions. You will also take precious time away from the argument portion of this persuasive brief, time you need to complete that critical part of your assignment.

If you are uncomfortable with the idea of omitting a statement of facts because you fear the grader will think you do not know that one will be needed, you can include the following in brackets: [The statement of facts to be inserted here.] That tells the grader that you would have written a statement of facts had you not been specifically instructed to omit it. It succinctly tells the grader that you followed directions.

Skim the File

The first thing I do when approaching the File is to look at the table of contents. I want to see what my factual world is before I start skimming. Here I have four documents in addition to the Task Memo: (1) excerpts of the interview with the defendant and two detectives, which I see is 10 pages, clearly the bulk of the File; (2) the Notice of Motion to Suppress Evidence; (3) the defendant's Affidavit in Support of Motion to Suppress Evidence; and (4) a transcript of the interview of Detective Timothy James (one of the two detectives in the first interview of the defendant), conducted by my boss, Laurie Shanks. Let's take a look at each of those four documents in turn, and walk through the read/skim step.

Excerpts of the Police Interview with the Defendant

Just glancing at this document, you can see it is very long. You know, based on what we said in Chapter 2, that you would waste precious time if you read all of this carefully now, before you understand the law in the Library. Once you have that law, the facts that are critical will pop out, and you will easily be able to weed out those facts that are irrelevant or duplicative. If you try to read this entire transcript word-for-word now, you are likely to get mired in details you do not need to write this assignment. So, for now, at this stage, before you read the Library, just flip through this excerpted transcript to see what general background you can pick up by skimming.

Here is what I might say to myself as I skim:

> *OK, I see that these are "excerpts." (I wonder what is left out?) They are thus just parts of an interview with Raymond Duncan (the defendant) with two detectives:*

Detective James and Detective Mandel. I remember from the table of contents that there is also a transcript of an interview with this same Detective James and my boss, Laurie Shanks.

I see that these detectives ask Duncan's permission to record, and they start developing a timeline. I remind myself not to read all of this now, because I don't know what's important yet. I just skim. I see that Detective James starts asking all the questions, and then, three pages in, the second detective, Mandel, starts questioning Duncan.

On the fifth page of the transcript I see asterisks and again, I remember that this document was called "Excerpts of Interview" with the defendant. I wonder what was said, if anything, in those "breaks." What if anything was omitted from this transcript? Is there anything that was said that would undermine our position?

I always tell students that if something is bothering you, make a quick note if you can say something intelligent about it, and then move on. It is not an essential part of the assignment, but might be a bonus point. Also, if it is distracting you, it might prevent you from getting on to what you are required to write.

Here, I decide to add a quick note to Laurie Shanks (in brackets), before the argument portion of my answer:

["Ms. Shanks: Before we file the Memorandum of Points and Authorities below, we should ask Detectives James and Mandel what if anything was said and what transpired where the transcript shows breaks in the record. We want to rule out any undocumented coercion, to avoid surprises. Breaks on pages 64 and 66 seem to be 20-minute breaks in the interview. But the asterisks on page 62 indicate something is missing from the transcript but for no reason. We should find out why there was a break in recording."]

Again, I'm not reading every word of this 10-page interview now, because I don't know what I'm looking for yet. I am just glancing at each page. I will come back to this after the Library. Skimming, I see a lot of polite back-and-forth, question and answer, with a number of breaks. I notice the detectives readily agree to every break and ask, as Detective James does on the bottom of page 66, "Do you still want to talk to us?" Toward the end I see Duncan confessing and the detectives placing him under arrest and reading him his Miranda *rights. I flip back to the beginning of the transcript and see that the interview starts at 12:25 pm and ends at 6:03 pm.*

I have repeatedly suggested that you skim the documents in the File, and then go back to the File after you read the Library. That is especially true of long or complicated documents that you do not readily see the significance of.

> *The next two documents in the File are short and simple. I can read those in full, now, without wasting any time.*
>
> *The Notice of Motion to Suppress. OK, that is the defense's document that, along with the defendant's affidavit, are the documents that provide the information I will be opposing. This notice is really short. All it says is that the defendant wants the judge to suppress all the statements made in the January 2nd interview, and on one sole legal basis: an alleged* Miranda *violation. That's it.*
>
> *The next document is the affidavit. I will skim this now, though I know I will have to return to it and read it carefully because I expect what Duncan says will be contradicted by what the detectives say. Also, this is the only document that provides Duncan's version. We are opposing his motion, so it will be critical to understand what he says happened.*
>
> *I remind myself that, based on my general knowledge of the law,* Miranda *requires custodial interrogation. No one could deny there was interrogation here, so I am preparing myself that the "fight" will be about whether there was custody. When I get to the Library, I expect the law will center on that issue. (And, when ultimately I see it does, I am reassured!)*
>
> *I know that whatever other details of the law are in the Library will help me see which facts support or refute the defense claims. So, I read this affidavit now, just to see what the defendant's story is. A few things pop out even now.*
>
> *In the second paragraph, Duncan says he was arrested and taken into custody at 12:30 pm. I recall from just the last page of the interview that the detectives arrest him and read him his* Miranda *rights at the end of the interview, closer to 6:00 pm. This is a huge discrepancy. I make a note on my scratch paper and in the margins to come back to this later. (I actually take my notes on the table of contents page in the File. Next to the Affidavit, I write "Timing of arrest?" That is enough to jog my memory later.)*
>
> *I look quickly at the other paragraphs in the affidavit. Paragraph 3 says that the detectives never tried to question him at his home. I immediately want to know (a) Did they? What do they say? And, (b) Is that important? Does it matter where the questioning took place?*
>
> *The next paragraphs seem to follow the same theme: the detectives allegedly never told Duncan he could refuse to go to the station or that he could leave the police*

station. Again, my lawyering instincts are wondering about the significance of where the questioning took place.

Next, Duncan talks about the room unlocking only from the inside. I don't know if that's true, or if it's important. I underline and make a note to return to it when I have read the law.

Next, Duncan says he was questioned for five hours. This appears to be true.

Next, paragraph 8 is about the cigarette breaks—I'll have to go back and look and see if they left him alone or not, or why that may be important. (I cannot really know if that is even relevant until I read the Library.)

Paragraphs 9 and 10 deal with police accusing Duncan of the crime, communicating their subjective belief that he committed it, and thus making it "objectively reasonable" for him to believe he would not be allowed to leave the station. I am now dying to have my recollection refreshed about what exactly the law requires for someone to be considered "in custody" for purposes of Miranda. *I am itching to get to the Library, which I know will have law on this, so that I can compare Duncan's statements to the legal standard. But, even without reading the law, I am sort of shaking my head and thinking, "Well, just because the police subjectively believe I am guilty does not mean I am not free to go."*

Paragraph 11 again seems like another "so what?" to me. Who cares if the detectives say it is to the defendant's advantage to cooperate. Even without reading the Library, I don't see how that relates to whether he is in custody or not. (I remind myself that is the sole issue in the document I must draft.)

In Paragraph 12 Duncan says that the detectives claimed they had evidence against him, and it would therefore be useless to deny guilt. Again, I can't know for sure without reading the Library, but it seems that is irrelevant to the issue of custody. (Note that I am not letting myself get taken in by the "side streets," interesting facts that don't relate directly to my task; I stay focused and look for "highways": main principles and relevant facts.)

Paragraph 13 appears factual and may be important. I will know after I read the cases. It discusses how Duncan was placed in handcuffs after five hours of interrogation, left alone in the locked room, and then taken to jail.

The last paragraph notes that Duncan was advised of his Miranda *rights after the five hours of interrogation, which we knew from our quick glance at the last page of the interview document.*

I again make my mental note that I will come back to this affidavit after reading the Library, and I move on to the next and final document in the File, a five-page interview with Detective James. This one is not an "excerpt," so no worries about what may be missing. Here, James provides extra information about what happened (or at least what the detective says happened!) before, during, and after the January 2nd interview with Duncan.

I remind myself that at this stage of litigation, before trial, nothing has been proven. Every bit of information is just one side's story. The defendant has his version, presented here in the affidavit. The police have their version, presented in the two interviews. I have to draft a motion opposing the defense arguments. In doing so, I'll have to learn what the law is. I will also have to make sense of the facts, especially when it appears that facts may be contradictory. More on this later. For now I keep reading.

Laurie Shanks starts her questioning of Detective James by saying she read the interview and has questions. I can see, just by quickly flipping through, that Detective James talks about how Duncan got to the station, and that at first he was only a "subject" and not a "suspect" because he was not yet suspected of doing anything wrong. (I will make a note to figure out the difference between these terms.) I see James mentioning that Duncan was not under arrest until the end of the interview. James notes at the end of his talk with Shanks that Duncan was not restrained at any point before he was read his Miranda *rights.*

I know I will have to read this interview very carefully later, and that it will make much more sense after I read the Library.

Briefly Review Task Memo

After skimming the File and "talking to yourself" as you read, as illustrated by the preceding, you want to check back quickly with the Task Memo before going on to study the Library. This helps focus you, so that your reading of the Library becomes that precision mission we talked about in Chapter 2 (rather than the "fishing expedition" of reading cases for class). You always keep in mind what you are to produce, so that you pick up the specific information you need to draft your answer. This focus is critical to passing. You cannot write around the task: You must answer specifically and directly.

The second paragraph of the Task Memo mentions twice that the courts have identified "specific factors" that will help them decide motions to suppress evidence. Re-reading this should help you see that you want to proceed into the Library in search of "factors."

I have repeatedly noted that lists (such as of elements or factors) are often "gifts" from the examiners, providing a key for how to logically organize your answer. This exam is a great example of where the list of factors serves as a perfect organizational tool.

It may also be that where there is a lot to discuss or argue, the organization is more obvious. In exams requiring students to think much more about how to organize, the actual analysis or argument may not be as time-consuming. Bottom line: The examiners do make these PTs doable!

The Library

First thing in the Library, study the table of contents. PTs are closed-universe problems. You want to know what your universe consists of. Here our universe holds only three cases: You can quickly see that they are from the U.S. Supreme Court, the Fifteenth Circuit, and the Columbia Supreme Court, respectively (and, here, we are in the State of Columbia). Be sure to note the dates as well, as it might be significant if one or another decision is outdated.

As you read, quickly brief each of the three cases, pulling out the holdings, and determining if they are good for us (meaning they support the prosecution) or not and why.

Mathiason

Mathiason is a 1977 Supreme Court case (obviously binding because this involves federally guaranteed rights). It is good for us in that the Court ultimately found there was no custody.

> **Note:** The very first thing I do when I read a case in a PT Library is look at the bottom line and determine if the holding is good for my client or not. Why? Typically, in a PT, you must spend more time carefully reading those cases that are *not* good for you so that you can factually distinguish them. You may simply use the ones that support your client for referencing legal rules.

Mathiason tells us that *Miranda* applies to "custodial interrogation" and defines that as "questioning initiated by law enforcement officers after a person has been taken into custody or otherwise deprived of his freedom of action in any significant way." The Supreme Court also found in this case that the defendant's freedom to leave was not restricted, despite the fact that the questioning took place in a police station. The operative facts that swayed the court were: (1) the defendant came voluntarily to the police offices in response to the police request, and (2) he was told he was not under arrest. The Court also stressed that the interview only lasted 30 minutes, and that the defendant did in fact leave after the interview.

When you go back in the File, you will want to compare these *Mathiason* facts with your case. You will have to go back to double-check both the defendant Duncan's version of events and the police officers' stories. When you do, you will see that both seem to agree that Duncan came to the station voluntarily. (Top of page 64, Duncan says "when I offered to come in for questioning"; Detective James tells Laurie Shanks, at page 71, that Duncan preferred talking at the police station to talking at his home.)

The detectives say they told Duncan at the outset that he was not under arrest; Detective James says at page 72 that he advised Duncan that "he was going to a voluntary interview and was free to leave at any time." Also, despite the fact that in his affidavit Duncan says he was arrested earlier, Duncan *asks* the detectives, well into the interview, at page 66, "if they are going to process" him. (Why would he "ask" if he believed he was under arrest?)

The Duncan interview did last much longer than the one in *Mathiason* (5 hours versus 30 minutes), and, unlike in *Mathiason* where the defendant did in fact leave after the interview, Duncan was jailed at the close of his interview.

So, although the *Mathiason* holding is good for our client, some of the key facts are distinguishable, so the case may not end up being that helpful after all. (Remember, as discussed in Chapter 2, we always want to try to find a way to use all the main cases in the Library, whether they are good for our client or not.)

WRITING TIP: USE EVERY MAIN CASE IN THE LIBRARY

You should use every case that is listed in the Library table of contents. If some of those cases cite other cases, you may—but do not have to—cite to those other cases within the main cases. Students always ask, "Will I fail if I don't cite every main case?" As I mentioned earlier, I liken PTs to the television cooking show *Chopped*, in which contestants are to use each of the ingredients in the basket provided to prepare each course of their meal. Will a contestant who omits a basket ingredient automatically be eliminated? No, but the burden weighs very heavily against that chef. Everything else must be spectacular for that chef to remain in the contest after failing to use one of the key ingredients. Think of the main cases in your Library as ingredients you must use. If you cannot use them for their holdings, cite a rule or dicta from the case, or cite the case within that case. (To get "credit" for that, be sure to cite both cases; for example, "*Jones* as cited in *Cray*.") Try as hard as possible to cite every main case in the Library.

We may want to use *Mathiason* to cite the general rules about when *Miranda* warnings are required. We also may want to refer to some of the language in the case, even if it is not the holding. *Mathiason* includes some very helpful language, ideas we may want to quote or restate in our own words in certain parts of our answer. First, *Mathiason* makes clear at page 80 that just because a person is questioned in a police station does not mean that the person is "in custody" for purposes of *Miranda*. Second, *Mathiason* adds by way of dicta (at page 80) that an officer's false statement about possessing evidence that the defendant committed the crime is not relevant to the question of "custody" for *Miranda* purposes. You might remember that Duncan was concerned that the detectives thought he had committed the crime and that they made up evidence of his being at the scene, perhaps just to determine if he would contradict himself.

If you are taking notes as I suggest on the table of contents of the Library, next to where *Mathiason* is listed, write: "**Helpful language at page 80." On page 80, put double asterisks next to those helpful quotes and underline them. This double-asterisk method, or some other sort of note-taking system, will be very useful for you!

Cray

Cray is also good for us, in that the appellate court overturned the lower court's finding of custody and concluded that defendant Cray was not in custody for purposes of *Miranda*. A few pages into *Cray* you should notice factors. Gold! You hit the PT jackpot.

Remember that the Task Memo repeatedly mentioned factors. Such lists are often organizational gifts. *Cray* cites *Jones* on pages 82–83 and lists eight factors that courts have identified in determining whether a defendant is in custody for purposes of *Miranda*.

This is your precise issue. This is exactly what the defense Motion to Suppress, the document you are drafting an opposition to, rests on. This is what you must battle. You must show how these eight factors stack up in the People's favor. (Remember, the "People" of the "State of Columbia" are your clients.) You may logically organize your entire opposition motion around the factors. This is it. You have your "plan" on how to structure your answer. (You will find a sample outline later in this chapter.)

Once you see these factors, which you know you will use in your answer, you also need to look through and compare and contrast the facts in *Cray* to see if the court we are writing our motion to will likely find our situation parallel enough with Cray's as to also conclude that Duncan was not in custody. You should see that there are some facts that are helpful but others that hurt. For example, in *Cray*, the defendant was questioned for seven hours, and by three officers. If that was not deemed "custody," then it is arguable (and we will make the argument) that the five hours for which two detectives questioned Duncan do not necessarily amount to custody. However, the court stresses that Mr. Cray was repeatedly told ("at least eight times") that the interview was voluntary and he was free to leave. Was Duncan ever told he was free to leave?

There are a number of other differences and similarities between the facts in *Cray* and in Duncan's case. Your work, when you go back to the File, will be to pick up on these quickly, and formulate arguments to try to make Duncan's situation look as much as possible like the parts of Cray's questioning that the court found noncoercive and thus noncustodial.

Something else you want to be sure you get out of *Cray* is that the *Jones* factors are not to be followed "ritualistically." Factors are not elements. Each one need not be established. Rather, they are to be balanced. That language guides you to exactly what you will be doing in your answer. You will take each factor, one at a time, and you will try to present the evidence that establishes that factor in the light most favorable to our clients (meaning that it tends to show there was no custody). You may have to concede certain factors, but you will have wonderful ammunition to conclude your argument with: this language from *Cray* that the factors are guiding tools rather than exhaustive elements.

Adams

The last case, *Adams*, also cited the *Jones* factors, so if you missed them in *Cray* I hope you saw them in *Adams*. Any time bar examiners repeat something within a question (a PT or essay), pay special attention, as it may be a hint. I also hope that you remembered that the person giving you the assignment in the Task Memo repeatedly referred to "specific factors" in the cases. *Adams* thus reinforces what the legal standard will be, and in turn how you will organize your answer.

Adams, however, is bad for us. It is the one out of the three cases in this Library in which the court found that the defendant was in custody. So, your job will be to look carefully at the facts in *Adams* and then go back into the File and see how we can distinguish it from Duncan's case.

What stands out without even returning to the File is that the questioning of Adams was much more aggressive and threatening than that of Duncan, and that Adams was essentially told that he was not free to leave unless he confessed. (Recall how polite the two detectives in our case were with Duncan. Go back and look at that when you review the transcript.) The *Adams* court also found it important that the defendant was never told he could stop the questioning and leave.

Again, you can refer back to the Library for any details you need. Your first read of the Library is done to see what the legal framework is so that you can then go into the File and read in an efficient manner. Before you run back into the File, though, stop and spend a few minutes thinking about what you just read. Ask yourself: How does the Library fit together, and how can I begin structuring my answer?

How Does the Library Fit Together?

This step—taking time to stop and think about how the law in the Library fits together and how best to produce the task(s) you were asked to draft—is arguably the most important strategic step for success on the PT. If you are racing through the exam and never stop to think about your client and your task(s), your answer may well be off the mark. Examiners repeatedly say that the reason many fail the PT is because they fail to be fully responsive to the instructions.

In this PT, all three cases address whether particular defendants were "in custody" for purposes of *Miranda*. Reviewing your Task Memo, you know that the defendant Duncan has moved to suppress all his statements made in the January 2nd police interview; your "answer" is the argument portion of the state's Opposition Motion.

You know, based on the defense's Notice of Motion, that Duncan's sole basis for his motion is *Miranda*. All the Library cases remind you, in case you had forgotten, that *Miranda* warnings are required when the police question a defendant who is in custody.

With your first File document being a transcript detailing five hours of questioning and no Library cases about the meaning of the term *interrogation*, you know the issue is *not* whether Duncan was interrogated. All three cases deal with whether and when a defendant is "in custody" for purposes of *Miranda*, so you should begin to see your world (and how you will approach formulating your answer) crystallizing. The issue should be clear and you should now be on a very precise mission: to argue that the defendant, Mr. Duncan, was not in custody when questioned by police.

Further, based on the *Jones* factors cited in *Cray* and *Adams*, you know exactly how you will organize your answer: factor-by-factor. Now is the fun part! You get to go back into the File with purpose, with direction, and with the *Jones* factors in mind.

One quick point, though, before looking back at the File: now that you have the basic legal framework, you can begin to flesh out your "outline." Your outline may serve as a rough draft of your answer.

SAMPLE UPDATED OUTLINE

To: Ms. Shanks

From: Applicant

Re: People v. Duncan

Date: [The date of your bar exam]

Please find the Memorandum of Points and Authorities that you requested below. If you have any further questions or follow-up queries, please do not hesitate to contact me.

Memorandum of Points and Authorities
in Opposition to Defense Motion to Suppress Evidence

[After reading the Library, you can flesh out the introductory portion of your opposition, perhaps as follows here.]

Defendant Duncan has moved that all of the statements he made during a January 2nd interview with police detectives be suppressed based on allegations that he was questioned in violation of *Miranda v. Arizona*. The People oppose said motion, as *Miranda* warnings are only required where the police engage in custodial interrogation, and, when these statements were made, Defendant was not "in custody" for purposes of *Miranda*. Therefore, the People urge that the Defense motion be denied.

[You might go on to add a paragraph such as the following with a bit more law and setting up the factors as your organizational scheme.]

Mathiason makes clear that "custodial interrogation" means "questioning initiated by law enforcement officers after a person has been taken into custody or otherwise deprived of his freedom of action in any significant way." *Cray* and *Adams* make clear that courts have "identified at least eight factors for consideration in making the custody determination" (*Cray* at page 82). Looking closely at those factors, as the People argue below, it is clear that the Defendant was not in "custody" for purposes of *Miranda*.

[Next, quickly list the factors, in your own words or copied from the case. In your final answer, you will want to turn these factors into persuasive headings or mini-arguments that advocate your client's position. There is more on how to draft persuasive headings in Chapter 2.]

Factor 1: WHETHER SUSPECT WAS INFORMED THAT QUESTION-ING WAS VOLUNTARY, THAT HE COULD ASK TO LEAVE, OR THAT HE WAS NOT UNDER ARREST, AND THAT HIS CONDUCT INDICATED AN AWARENESS OF SUCH FREEDOM

Factor 2: WHETHER SUSPECT POSSESSED UNRESTRAINED FREEDOM OF MOVEMENT DURING QUESTIONING

Factor 3: WHETHER SUSPECT VOLUNTARILY AGREED TO QUESTIONING OR INITIATED CONTACT WITH AUTHORITIES

Factor 4: WHETHER STRONG-ARM TACTICS WERE USED: DID POLICE MANIFEST A BELIEF THAT PERSON WAS GUILTY AND HAVE EVIDENCE TO PROVE IT? WERE POLICE AGGRESSIVE, CONFRONTATIONAL, OR THREATENING?

Factor 5: WHETHER THERE WAS POLICE-DOMINATED ATMOSPHERE DURING QUESTIONING

Factor 6: WHETHER SUSPECT WAS PLACED UNDER ARREST AT THE END OF THE QUESTIOINING

Factor 7: WHETHER THE EXPRESS PURPOSE OF THE INTERVIEW WAS TO QUESTION PERSON AS A WITNESS OR A SUSPECT

Factor 8: HOW LONG THE INTERROGATION LASTED

Conclusion

At this point you are still in note-taking mode. By listing the factors in your draft outline, you can take notes when you re-read the File, placing support for each factor right in this draft underneath the corresponding heading. When you begin writing, you will want to turn these factors, here stated as questions, into persuasive headings. (See examples of this later in this chapter.) Headings in your final draft serve as a roadmap and help the court see why it should rule in your favor. (As discussed in Chapter 2 of this book, in persuasive briefs to the court, headings are typically more detailed than in analytical (in-house) assignments, serving as mini-arguments in addition to being a roadmap.) Equally important, for exam purposes, headings show the grader that you followed directions, and that you read and understood the law in the Library.

TIP

If you are writing by hand, you will want to list all eight factors on scratch paper and then, as you go back to the File, jot down on your notes facts that support or refute each factor. If you are typing, you can just type rough notes underneath each heading as you read and edit those into final language before you submit your answer. In other words, for typists, your outline may actually serve as a rough draft of your answer. (Even some typists feel more confident hand-writing their outlines; experiment with what works best for you on practice tests before your real bar exam.)

File Re-Read

Now, with these eight factors in mind, return to the File to re-read and pick up the relevant facts. What pops out? It should be much clearer now what is and what is not significant. You are essentially on an "Easter egg" hunt, searching for evidence to show that under the *Jones* factors there was no "custody." As you find points that relate, either type the point itself under the factor in your draft, or use a shorthand system to underline the point in the transcript and type the page number where you have underlined key information under the relevant factor in your draft outline.

Here are just some of the selected points that might pop out at you in a File re-read:

- The interview starts with police politely asking if it is OK to record the interview. This potentially relates to Factor 3 (defendant voluntarily agreeing to talk) and does relate to Factor 4 (police don't usually politely request permission to record in situations where they are threatening, coercing, and using other strong-arm tactics).

- The first couple of pages of the transcript appear to be about the police getting a timeline of what happened. At the bottom of page 59, Detective James does say he needs to assess how truthful Duncan is, but does not do so in an accusatory manner (no Factor 4).
- Next and critical, on page 60, Duncan says *he* "called [the police] back and agreed to come down to this interview." The first time you skimmed this, before you read the Library and knew about the *Jones* factors, you likely would not have seen this as significant. Now, it should just scream out at you as direct evidence from the defendant's mouth of Factor 3, that Duncan voluntarily agreed to the questioning, and, in calling them back, that he initiated contact with police.
- The fact that Duncan refers to the questioning as an "interview" seems to be further proof that he does not see this as an arrest but as more of a discussion (Factor 1). He is a suspect only because he has "a record."
- Also on page 60, when the defendant hesitates after being asked if he is sure, he begins to sound like he is contradicting himself. This is exactly what the detectives said: that he was not initially a suspect but became so only after he began contradicting himself during the interview (Factor 7).
- At page 61, Duncan asks for water and the officers say "Sure" (Factor 4). More water and a cigarette break were offered on page 63. The interrogation lasted five hours, likely to be deemed a long time under Factor 8, though not as long as in *Cray* where ultimately no custody was found. However, there were several water and cigarette breaks, so the questioning was not continuous.
- At page 63, when they take a cigarette break, they went to the roof, so they left the interrogation room. There wasn't unrestrained freedom of movement per se (Factor 2), in that the detectives accompanied Duncan, but he was allowed to move. Also, there is no indication that he was handcuffed or restrained in any way during the questioning, at least not until the very end when they did read him the *Miranda* warnings.
- At page 66, Duncan indicates that he does not know whether he is under arrest (Factor 1) and he says that they have been polite (Factor 4) in his comments: "I appreciate the fact that you guys have been patient with me. What are you guys going to do? I mean, are you guys going to process me or what?" That is not the language of someone who is certain he is under arrest.
- Further, at the bottom of page 66, Detective James asks Duncan, "Do you still want to talk to us?" to which Duncan responds, on page 67, "Sure, I'll talk." That is clear proof of Factor 1, that the questioning was voluntary.

Now, let's look at the second transcript that we also skimmed on the first walk through the File. It should also now be clear what is and is not relevant in this document.

- At page 71, Detective James describes how it was that the interview took place at the police station, that it was at Duncan's request, and that he asked the police to drive him there (Factor 3). Also, even though the interview was at the station (a police-dominated atmosphere under Factor 5), if James is believed, the location was at the defendant's request. We know from clear language in *Mathiason* that just because questioning occurs at a police station does not make it custodial.
- At page 72, Detective James says that Duncan was driven in an unmarked police car, not handcuffed, and the police were not in uniform (again, diffusing the police-dominated atmosphere of Factor 5).
- Also on page 72, Detective James says he "did advise [Duncan] that he was going to a voluntary interview and he was free to leave at any time" (Factor 1). This would not have popped out at you as critical before reading the Library, but you likely see now, after reading *Cray*, that this "advising the defendant that he is free to leave" is a sort of superfactor, to be weighed more heavily in the balancing of factors than the other factors. The *Cray* court found this factor so powerful "that no governing precedent ... holds that a person was in custody after being clearly advised of his freedom to leave or terminate questioning" (*Cray* at page 83).
- If Detective James is to be believed (and James again says the same thing on page 73, "I repeatedly told him that he was not under arrest and that he was free to leave"), this is very strong evidence in our favor.
- It may be somewhat of a problem that Duncan, in his affidavit, at paragraphs 4 and 5, says he was never told he did not have to go to the station or that he was free to leave. However, there are several points in the interview transcript, as we noted earlier, where Duncan indicates that he voluntarily came down for the interview, supporting the detective's version of events.
- At page 72, James indicated that Duncan was at the outset only a subject, not a suspect (Factor 7).
- At page 73, James says Duncan never asked to leave, and that Duncan's requests for breaks, including with fresh air, were readily provided (Factors 1, 2, 4).
- At page 73, James notes that Duncan was never restrained physically, something that would have been done had he been "in custody" (Factor 2). On pages 74 and 75, James compares interviews with other subjects who were questioned in the same manner as Duncan, did ask to leave, and were allowed to do so.

PUT IT ALL TOGETHER AND DRAFT YOUR ANSWER

Now, armed with details relating to each factor, you want to take stock of what you have in your notes and begin turning them into the answer you will upload. The task is a persuasive brief, so you want to try to show as much as possible that each and every factor weighs toward lack of custody. But, you are also under an obligation of candor to the tribunal. Accordingly, you may have to concede certain factors.

Note that there are full sample answers in the Online Question and Answer Bank. The following are steps to take before drafting your final answer: turning the factors into persuasive headings, and marshalling supportive facts (plugging in each fact under the relevant factor). Each of the eight factors is listed in question form and then in persuasive heading form, and there are a few thoughts on how to develop the argument relating to that heading.

QUESTION FORM: 1. WHETHER SUSPECT WAS INFORMED THAT QUESTIONING WAS VOLUNTARY, THAT HE COULD ASK TO LEAVE, OR THAT HE WAS NOT UNDER ARREST, AND THAT HIS CONDUCT INDICATED AN AWARENESS OF SUCH FREEDOM

HEADING FORM:

1. **The Defendant was repeatedly informed by police detectives that questioning was voluntary and that he was not under arrest; his asking several times what detectives planned to do with him indicated clearly that he did not yet believe during the interview that he was under arrest.**

This is a strong factor to start with. To fill in what you will write under this heading, look up every place we noted that something in the File supported Factor 1. For example, you want to pick up what we wrote about Detective James indicating repeatedly having told Duncan that the interview was voluntary and that he was "free to leave at any time."

You will want to argue here, relying on *Cray*, that this factor, "advising the defendant that he is free to leave" should be weighed more heavily in the balancing than the other factors. (You may even want to quote *Cray* that this factor is so powerful "that no governing precedent … holds that a person was in custody after being clearly advised of his freedom to leave or terminate questioning." *Cray* at page 83).

QUESTION FORM: 2. WHETHER THE SUSPECT POSSESSED UNRESTRAINED FREEDOM OF MOVEMENT DURING QUESTIONING

HEADING FORM:

2. **Defendant was never handcuffed or chained, and he was free to move about at all times during the police interview.**

Here pick up the points where you mentioned Factor 2, stressing the number of times they went on breaks. (You may want to note that the fact that the detectives accompanied him on these breaks does not make the situation "custodial," comparing *Cray*, in which the defendant was not left alone at all during the seven hours of questioning and the Court still found no custody.)

QUESTION FORM: 3. WHETHER THE SUSPECT VOLUNTARILY AGREED TO QUESTIONING OR INITIATED CONTACT WITH AUTHORITIES

HEADING FORM:

3. **As evidenced by his calling the police back and agreeing to come to the interview, Defendant voluntarily agreed to be questioned.**

Here you will pick up any facts noted earlier in support of Factor 3; there are many from Detective James detailing how they first went to Duncan's house, then left, then Duncan called them back and asked that they talk at the station rather than his house. You will also want to quote Duncan himself, as noted earlier, where Duncan admits that *he* "called [the police] back and agreed" to come down to this interview.

QUESTION FORM: 4. WHETHER STRONG-ARM TACTICS WERE USED: DID POLICE MANIFEST A BELIEF THAT PERSON WAS GUILTY AND HAVE EVIDENCE TO PROVE IT? WERE POLICE AGGRESSIVE, CONFRONTATIONAL, OR THREATENING?

HEADING FORM:

4. **At no time did police engage in strong-arm tactics, and while they began to believe that the Defendant committed the crime after he repeatedly contradicted himself, they were never aggressive, confrontational, or threatening.**

Here you have a lot to write about, indicating the polite language and conduct of the police questioning, including their readily agreeing to any breaks he wanted. Duncan even thanks them for being so "patient." Just look for the places where you noted references to "Factor 4," and cut and paste those in to form your argument.

QUESTION FORM: 5. WHETHER THERE WAS POLICE-DOMINATED ATMOSPHERE DURING QUESTIONING

HEADING FORM:

> **5. Though the questioning took place in the police station, that, in and of itself, does not create "custody" for purposes of *Miranda*, and much of the way in which the interview was conducted diluted what might otherwise have been a "police-dominated" atmosphere.**

You must concede that the questioning took place at the police station, and that the station is a police-dominated place/atmosphere. However, you can start by saying that the detectives tried to talk with the defendant at his home and he is the one who requested that they talk at the police station. You also have great language from *Mathiason* that you can quote to show that being at a police station alone does not equate with custody. You might also stress that the police were not in uniform, and that they did not brandish weapons, use handcuffs, or manifest any other form of police domination. Lastly, they took Duncan for several breaks, including ones on the rooftop where they got fresh air.

You might note that here there were only two officers and in *Cray*, where there were three officers questioning the suspect, no custody was found. (Then again, this may not be helpful, as Cray was questioned in his home, obviously a less police-dominated atmosphere than the police station.)

QUESTION FORM: 6. WHETHER SUSPECT WAS PLACED UNDER ARREST AT THE END OF THE QUESTIONING

HEADING FORM:

> **6. The suspect was placed under arrest at the end of the questioning.**

This is a fact you must concede. Hence, you do not have a lengthy persuasive heading. However, you can stress that the arrest came only *after* the defendant confessed, and that the detectives had no plan to arrest him when they began talking with him.

QUESTION FORM: 7. WHETHER THE EXPRESS PURPOSE OF THE INTERVIEW WAS TO QUESTION PERSON AS A WITNESS OR A SUSPECT

HEADING FORM:

> **7. The Defendant was interviewed as a subject or person with possible information relating to the crime and only became a suspect as he began contradicting himself during the course of the questioning.**

Plug in here every place you noted facts that support Factor 7. There were several, especially what Detective James said about why they questioned Duncan initially, that they questioned several other people initially, and so on.

QUESTION FORM: 8. HOW LONG THE INTERROGATION LASTED

HEADING FORM:

8.   The questioning, although it lasted about five hours, was peppered with breaks and was very polite, and at no time did the Defendant request that the questioning stop.

Again, you must concede this factor; the time is what it is. However, you can stress the breaks. You can stress the relaxed and polite tenor of the discussion. You can point to Cray's questioning lasting for seven hours and not amounting to custody and argue therefore that neither should the five-hour interview here.

You will then want to conclude by reminding the court that these factors need not be applied "ritualistically" (per *Cray*) and that the overwhelming majority of them weigh in the People's favor, such that Mr. Duncan should not be found to have been in custody prior to the time he was given *Miranda* warnings.

For examples of a passing opposition motion for this PT, study the sample answers located in the Online Question and Answer Bank at http://ambar.org/barexamprep.

SPIN-OFF EXERCISES

Spin-off exercises are a way to gain exposure to drafting different types of documents without as much of a time commitment as it would require to complete a whole new performance test. I often suggest to my students that after writing any PT, they spend a few minutes thinking about other documents they might have been asked to draft based on the same law and facts. Then, take a minute to outline or write out in full (time permitting) those "spin-off" tasks. Pay particular attention to how your tone and approach might differ depending on the goal of your assignment and your audience.

Writing for the Other Side

A great thing to do is force yourself to turn around now and write the entire motion to suppress as if you were Duncan's counsel. You have his affidavit and you now know the law and are well versed in the facts from the police side. Doing this will help you see where the major holes are in your own (original) client's case. (For example, there are certain points you will simply have to concede.)

Memo to Laurie Shanks

Pretend that instead of writing the opposition motion, you were to draft a memo providing Shanks with the pros and cons of filing a suppression motion. This would probably help you focus more neutrally on where your weak spots in the original document were.

Letter to Mary Lynch, Attorney for Defendant Raymond Duncan

Assume that Laurie Shanks authorized you to propose a plea bargain to defense counsel. How would you write it at this point? Assume that Duncan has filed his notice of motion but you have not filed your opposition brief. You know where the holes in his case are, but you also know that this is not a "slam dunk" for either side. How will you urge Duncan's side to accept a deal?

Statement of Facts

You were asked not to draft a statement of facts here, but it may be a good exercise, time permitting, to at least ask yourself what you would have included in a fact statement if one had been assigned.

PRACTICE, LAW SCHOOL, AND PTs: COMPARE AND CONTRAST

Most criminal cases do not go to trial, but instead are resolved by way of plea bargain. The motion to suppress evidence is a great vehicle for creating test questions because it can be used to test either constitutional criminal procedure knowledge or knowledge of rules of evidence, both potential grounds for keeping out evidence that should not be admitted or considered at trial.

Miranda rights are very important—in law school, on bar essays, and in the real world. This *Duncan* PT is an excellent vehicle for both practical training and for reviewing a critically important area of substantive criminal procedure law (one that will also be tested on the MBE and possibly the essay portion of your bar exam).

For students interested in learning more about the practical aspects of the criminal justice system, from arrest to appeal, you might enjoy reading a book I co-authored with one of my former law professors: Bergman and Berman, *The Criminal Law Handbook: Know Your Rights, Survive the System* (15th ed., Nolo.com, 2017).

KEY TAKEAWAYS

- When writing to a court, adopt a more formal tone than you would in writing an in-house memorandum to someone in your own law firm.
- In a persuasive brief to a court, you will often want to set up your argument portion so that each main point is written in a persuasive manner. (An example

of this from *Duncan* was adapting the issue as to whether the suspect was informed that the questioning was voluntary into a carefully crafted persuasive heading that might have read something like: "The Defendant was repeatedly informed by police detectives that questioning was voluntary and that he was not under arrest; his asking several times what detectives planned to do with him indicated clearly that he did not yet believe during the interview that he was under arrest.") Such headings are much more than labels; they are actually mini-arguments that provide the bar grader a way to see that you not only understand the law but also know what critical facts will prove or disprove the legal element or factor in question.

- A PT can "read" very differently depending on which side you represent. A great way to ensure that you are making all reasonable arguments is to first approach the exam from the perspective of the client you represent (here, the government), and then "switch hats" and see if facts pop out as significant when you consider the situation as if you were representing the other side.

5

TORTS

OVERVIEW OF TORTS

Most law schools start you off taking torts in 1L. That is good. Torts is a fairly straightforward and accessible subject. In a sense it is even easier on the bar exam, because bar essays and multiple-choice questions tend to test in less depth and certainly with fewer policy considerations than your typical law school professor.

If you are studying torts now or took it earlier in law school, you know that torts are civil wrongs. The most typical tort cases are personal injury matters. Who is bringing the lawsuit? A private party. (The government brings criminal cases.) What will the plaintiff receive if the plaintiff wins in a tort action? Typically, monetary relief called *damages*. (In criminal law cases, the defendant may be incarcerated if the government prevails.) Some plaintiffs in tort actions seek equitable relief; for example, where a plaintiff wants the defendant to stop repeatedly invading the plaintiff's land and asks the court for a court order called an *injunction*. In most tort actions that you study in 1L, though, the plaintiffs are seeking damages.

Many torts classes start with intentional torts (battery, assault, false imprisonment, trespass to land and trespass to chattel, nuisance, and intentional infliction of emotional distress), and then move on to negligence. Most courses cover negligence in great detail, often for many months. This too is good because negligence is typically the most heavily tested tort on bar exams.

Tort law also includes what is called *strict liability* or *absolute liability* (otherwise called *liability without fault*) in certain types of actions, such as those involving wild animals or ultrahazardous activities. (For example, if your pet lion mauls the plaintiff, you will be liable regardless of whether or not you took reasonable precautions to keep your lion caged.)

You may also spend time studying an area of tort law known as *products liability*, reviewing cases in which people were injured while using products. For instance, you step on a ladder (a product) to climb onto your roof and the ladder suddenly snaps; you fall off and are injured; in a more colorful example, you open a soda bottle, and drink half of the contents before you notice the floating decomposed snail in the bottle. Products liability cases may be based on five separate legal theories: intentional tort, strict liability in tort, negligence, warranty, and/or misrepresentation.

Torts courses sometimes finish with economic- and privacy-related torts such as fraud, interference with contractual relations, defamation, and causes of action relating to invasion of privacy. However, many 1L professors never get to discussing this wide a variety of tort actions, choosing instead to focus on the more heavily tested negligence and intentional torts. Some classes rush through or skip entirely torts such as malicious prosecution or malicious institution of civil proceedings, and often there is no time to cover important concepts relating to damages, such as joint tortfeasor liability, and indemnification.

Do not be too concerned with law school coverage. Every torts class covers negligence, the most heavily tested area on the bar exam. It is also likely that whatever you did cover, you studied in great depth and have a strong understanding of. That knowledge will benefit you in the long run. Just be aware of the range of topics that could be tested on your bar exam, and commit to learning, before or during bar review, whatever you either did not study or did not understand well in law school.

The following main areas in torts are typically tested on bar exams:

- Intentional torts
- Negligence
- Strict liability-based causes of action
- Products liability
- Economic- and privacy-related torts
- Defenses (there are different defense theories that may be applicable to different tort causes of action; for example, in defending a negligence action, the defendant might claim that the plaintiff assumed the risk, or was contributorily or comparatively negligent)
- General principles such as those that arise when more than one party commits a tort, including joint and several liability

For a comprehensive list of torts topics covered on the Multistate Bar Examination (MBE), consult the most recent MBE Subject Matter Outlines published by the National Conference of Bar Examiners on their website at ncbex.org/exams/mbe/preparing.

SIMULATED TORTS-BASED PERFORMANCE TEST

For your practice PT, I chose a torts-based performance test that centers around landowner liability in a negligence setting: a commonly tested area and one on which many law school classes spend significant time. Set aside a three-hour block of time and complete the PT, called *Carelton v. Mid-Central Shipping*, in the Online Question and Answer Bank at **http://ambar.org/barexamprep**. Then, read the following sections to see how you did on the exam and gain further insight into what you can learn from this practice test going forward.

TIME-CRUNCH TIPS

To complete *Carelton* in two hours, if your time is simply too crunched to afford three hours, read the entire File and Library, and only answer the first part of the requested memorandum. Skip the multiple-choice questions and the second part of the memorandum. As always, if you can make the three-hour time commitment, it will be worth your while. In particular, completing the multiple-choice questions will help you assess your case briefing and analysis skills, critical components of success on the PT and in law practice.

INSIDE THIS TEST: TIPS AND STRATEGIES

Read this section only *after* you have completed the *Carelton v. Mid-Central Shipping* PT.

Overall Comments

One of the first things you may have noticed is that the *Carelton* File has 12 pages and the Library has 17 pages. That in and of itself suggests that the exam is "law heavy." When you get into the Instructions and see that your primary task is to draft a memorandum of law setting forth the theories of liability upon which your client might bring suit, you know for sure that the exam is "law heavy."

Did you see that you also had to complete a second part of the task: a fact-gathering assignment? The legal memo could have taken up all your time and you had to budget carefully to leave enough time to complete that second task as well.

Note: This exam did not specify what percentage of your total points that second task was worth. If this exam were given percentage-point allocations, likely the fact-gathering assignment would have accounted for about 20% to 25% and the legal memo for about 75% of your written score.

The other very unusual part of this exam is that it includes multiple-choice questions along with the written tasks. *Carelton* is the only PT in this book that includes multiple-choice questions. The MPT and state-specific PTs today do not include multiple-choice questions. But when the performance test was first introduced, the examiners used multiple-choice questions along with drafting assignments as a diagnostic to determine applicants' accuracy and thoroughness in briefing cases. (You saw, if you completed these multiple-choice questions, that they focused on the holdings and facts of the Library cases. Accordingly, these questions provide a helpful tool to test yourself on your own case briefing skills.)

Instructions

The general or so-called boilerplate Instructions, the first pages, tell you the basics: this is a performance test, you have three hours to complete it, and so forth. The Instructions also state that the case is set in the fictitious state of Columbia, and that the Library includes six cases that are all from the Supreme Court of Columbia. This tells you that the cases will all serve as binding precedent, unless a later Library case overturned an earlier one. (The opposite happened here in this Library; as discussed later, the *Wiseguy* case impliedly accepted a Restatement section that had been explicitly rejected in a previous Library case. We discuss this further later in this chapter.)

From the Instructions, you learn that you are role-playing an associate in a private law firm, and that you represent an individual named Henry Carelton who is suing a business, Mid-Central Shipping Company. You know the case involves personal injury, so even before you get to the Library, you can put on your "torts hat" with respect to your general knowledge of the law. As noted in Chapter 2 of this book, in your PT answers you will only apply the specific law from the Library; you will not cite outside case law. However, you *will* use your general familiarity with legal reasoning and general knowledge of the law. Here, because this is a tort action and thus a subject you would know well before the bar exam, you might approach the exam by asking yourself which of the main liability theories the suit will be based on: negligence, strict liability, or intentional tort theory. Furthermore, as on *every PT*, you always want to keep on your "professional responsibility hat," and be prepared to comment appropriately on matters that may raise ethical issues.

HOW WIDE IS YOUR PT UNIVERSE?

The *Carelton* Instructions say that your "universe" consists of two sets of materials: a File and a Library. Reading this, you simply nod and say to yourself, "Great, this is a regular PT. No unusual materials to work with." PTs are closed-universe assignments that almost always consist of a File (which includes Instructions) and a Library. On rare occasions, though, examiners have provided a third set of materials, such as draft trust instruments in an estate planning exam, or have omitted the Library and provided jury instructions as the law to work with. You always want to confirm your universe before you begin. Again, almost always there will be a File and a Library, but the seconds it will take to verify this by carefully reading the Instructions are well worth your while. (When a third set of materials was included, many students mistook it for extra scratch paper, because they had failed to carefully read the Instructions.)

Task Memo

The document following the Instructions is the Task Memo. First, notice the language the Senior Partner uses: he wants your help in "thinking through" the case. What does that indicate? Neutral analysis. Your job is to analyze, not to persuade. You must set forth the relevant and appropriate legal theories, but you will point out the arguments both for and against the firm's client.

Note the context in which this matter arises. Mid-Central has filed a pretrial motion to dismiss for failure to state a claim, which we must prepare to defend against. That is a fairly low threshold. In most jurisdictions, all that is needed at this stage is a showing that Henry (our client) has some legally cognizable claim. All the complaint requires is a short, plain statement of the ultimate facts that make up the plaintiff's cause(s) of action. This is not yet the trial stage where those facts must be proven by a preponderance of the evidence.

The Task Memo next provides a preview of each File document. From this overview you can get a sense of the relative importance of each document. The most critical part of the Task Memo is usually at the end, where the specific tasks that you are to complete are spelled out. This is crystal clear as the assignment is prefaced with: "In your memorandum to me, please address the following." I would star that, put a paper clip on the page, and read it several times over to be certain I understood the assignment.

After reading the Task Memo, especially these last paragraphs that Mr. Brown writes to you, you have enough information to start sketching a basic template for your answer. Before even reading the File and Library, you might have typed something like the following in your answer document:

START OF DRAFT OUTLINE FROM TASK MEMO

To: Edward Brown

From: Applicant

Re: Henry Carelton v. Mid-Central Shipping: Preparation for Response to Pretrial Motion to Dismiss

You have asked me to think through this case and discuss the theories of liability under which we can contend that Mid-Central is liable for Henry's injuries, and additionally to let you know what more evidence we should begin to gather to build our case. Please find my analysis below. I am available at your convenience if you have further questions.

PART I—Theories of Liability

    Theory A _____

    Theory B _____

    Theory C _____

PART II—Additional Evidence to Be Gathered

Note: You can complete this fact-gathering section of the memo when you finish the first memo, or, to save time, you could have dropped points in here as you thought of them. In this sort of case, where you have both a legal analysis memo task and a fact-gathering assignment, you may be well served by multitasking; if you note points as they come to you, you are less likely to forget them later on.

File

Let's walk through the rest of the File now. I will highlight selected points along the way, starting with the judge's letter. Compare my thoughts to what you saw as you were reading the exam.

The Senior Partner, Mr. Brown, author of the Task Memo and the person you are writing to, told you that the judge is "an esteemed member of the retired judiciary." That is a hint that what Brown says may be particularly credible. Contrast that with the repeated warnings in the last paragraph of the first page of the Task Memo that the complaint is deficient. Brown characterizes the complaint as "slapped-together," notes that the lawyer who drafted it is no longer with the firm, and says "I am not at all sure it is good enough," indicating that we may need to amend it.

Note: Any time the bar examiners repeat something within an exam (whether a PT or an essay), *pay attention.* This is usually a suggestion that whatever is repeated is important and not to be missed.

Abner Goodfellow's letter tells you a bit more about the facts, how the injury occurred, where the plank and electrical wires ran, and what happened to Henry.

Goodfellow also stated firmly that Mid-Central put up and maintained the wires and "[t]he power company has nothing to do with this case." That is probably a hint

NOTE-TAKING TIPS

As you read, sketch a picture of the property on your scratch paper to help visualize the scene of Henry's injuries. Draw where the plank was, where the wires were, where the river was, and where Henry was. (My Real Property professor in law school, the late great Jesse Dukeminier, taught us always to diagram property problems, and to this day I cannot read a property question without a pencil in hand.) This can be equally helpful in any subject where you have to picture a scene, such as here in *Carelton* with a torts problem. In addition to whatever other notes and sketches I make, I also write a cast of characters to keep everyone straight. For example, here in my notes I wrote:

EBB: Edward Brown, senior partner in our firm, person we are drafting assignment for.

Henry Carelton: Our client, injured in accident at M-C.

M-C (Mid-Central Shipping Co.): the defendant, on/near whose property Henry was hurt.

Abner Goodfellow: Retired judge. Gave facts about case.

Martha Carelton: Henry's mother.

to focus on liability of Mid-Central alone and not waste time with a discussion of possibly amending the complaint to add the power company. But: were you skeptical? Did you ask yourself, "Is Goodfellow certain? How does he know the power company has nothing to do with this? He may be a good fellow, but what if he is wrong, and our client missed out on recovery from a potentially 'deep pocket'?" If you had such thoughts, here is how to address them on a PT. In a note to your senior partner (Mr. Brown), suggest that your firm do some investigating and confirm that the utility in no way shares liability with Mid-Central. Here, the perfect place to make such a note is in the second part of your memo about factual or proof problems. You may well get credit for your thinking. Also, getting this thought out quickly (and in a place that might even help you score points) will free your mind to let the issue go and focus only on Mid-Central's potential liability, clearly the central aspect of this assignment.

As we discussed at length in Chapter 3 on criminal law, on PT exams it is appropriate to question the credibility of certain facts. That is a key distinction between bar exam essays and PTs. On essays, you accept the facts as true and work with them. If an essay question stated, "Do not address liability of the power company," you would never waste even a second thinking, "Well, but what if the power company really were liable?" You certainly would not take time to write about it. On a PT, though, you may consider the sources of facts and assess their credibility. As in the real world, facts are not evidence until they are proven in court. Just because Goodfellow *says* the power company has nothing to do with this, I would still wonder, and I would take 20 seconds to jot down somewhere in my answer that our firm should verify this information. (Again, I would not take more than 20 seconds, because likely this is a hint, but our notation that we should follow up with this, could indicate to a grader that we are thinking like lawyers.)

There are a couple of other interesting points in Goodfellow's letter: First, he likens the Muddy River to a public street. This is incredibly important, but you do not see why until you read the cases about landowner liability where private land is adjacent to or indistinguishable from public property. *This is precisely the kind of fact that will likely not have significance to you until you read the Library, but will jump out at you after studying the cases!* This is exactly why I urge you to skim the File and then go back to read it again *after* you have briefed the Library authorities.

Second, Goodfellow states a conclusion about "causation," declaring that the wires fell as a result of the rotten pole. That too is a fact I would suggest we note should confirmed as soon as possible. (The place to note this is in the second part of the memo that focuses on fact-gathering.) As part of your general knowledge, you know that causation must be established as part of any of the applicable liability theories. Our client loses if we cannot establish causation!

Next in the File, after Goodfellow's letter, you find the Senior Partner's notes from his interviews with our client and his mother. At a quick glance, you might have seen that several questions are underlined. If you did not notice that as you were reading, look back at those interviews now. Much of what is underlined focuses on factual or proof problems—your second task! If you noticed these questions Brown posed, and if you happened to be running out of time in writing your answer, you could have turned back to these interview notes, and quickly and easily picked up enough information to write something intelligent and complete the second part of your memo in probably about five minutes.

Examiners don't always give away pieces of the puzzle, but often they give hints. Take the time to think carefully about what your assignment really asks of you, and keep that front and center as you review each of the File documents. You too might find such "hidden gold" on your bar exam, and you are much more likely to notice hints when you are clear on all aspects of your assignment.

As a professional responsibility note, you may have noticed that Brown asks Henry's mother to leave the room when he talks to Henry. Why? If you have already taken any classes in professional responsibility, you will readily see that this makes perfect sense, because Henry is the client, and even if Henry's mother is paying the bills, the attorney must respect the client's wishes. The mother might pressure or influence him if she were present. For example, he might not want to admit it if he was ditching school at the time of the injury, or was somehow at fault. Also, confidentiality may be breached if the lawyer talks with the client in the presence of a nonclient (though there may be exceptions for the parent of a minor client).

Many facts emerge from Brown's notes that are critical to your analogizing and distinguishing the cases and establishing which legal theories Henry may likely sue on. I won't list them all, but some include:

- Henry accessed the Muddy River through an open gate. On days the gate was locked, the boys did not swim there.
- The plank came from Mid-Central's warehouse and had been there "a long time."
- One of the workers admitted that the injury occurred because of the rotten pole.

These facts may have hit you as significant on the first read of the File because of your good lawyering instincts. But they definitely would have popped out as critical after reading the cases.

The next document is an internal memo from Mid-Central. (Did you wonder how our firm came into possession of this document? It could have triggered thoughts for the fact-gathering portion of your memo about subpoenaing or requesting production of other internal security documents. If you had that thought while reading, you could note it right away in your second memo.) It was important to look at the entire page of the document. Some students miss the note above the letterhead stating that the memo was posted at the warehouse *prior to* the injury. If you missed this, go back and look at it now. It is so critical! It makes clear that Mid-Central was aware of intruders on its property, before Henry was injured there. This sets up one of our arguments for Henry that even if he were a trespasser, he was a "known trespasser," which might well give rise to a higher duty on the part of Mid-Central.

As to the complaint, it alleges negligence and sets forth facts that would help show certain elements of the claim, but not all of them. Again, you know from the Task Memo that your firm plans to amend the complaint. So, at this stage, you read the draft complaint simply to pick up any helpful additional facts.

The last File document you see is the motion to dismiss. It is interesting in that it only denies intentional or willful misconduct; it does not deny liability based on negligence. Did you wonder: "Does Mid-Central think they ruled out negligence by characterizing the plaintiff as a trespasser?" After reading the Library, you see that many exceptions have been carved out to the general rule that no duty is owed to trespassers. Also, it is quite likely that your entire memo will focus on theories of negligence under which Henry can sue. Again, you would not see those theories until you read the cases. However, you likely noticed that nowhere in the File do you see evidence of intentional or willful acts on the part of Mid-Central.

Library

Before you even begin reading the Library, based just on your general knowledge of tort law, you may have a sense of what to expect in the Library. What do I mean? Well, there are no facts supporting willful action by Mid-Central, and Mid-Central was not engaged in ultrahazardous activity that might give rise to a strict liability claim. So, what is left? Negligence. Further, based on clear facts from the File (albeit facts we may seek to confirm), you know that causation and damages are not in dispute. So, what should the Library logically contain? Cases that focus on the duty and breach (of duty) elements of negligence—and that is precisely what you do find in the Library: one case asserting a general rule of no duty to trespassers and all the other cases regarding potential exceptions to that rule.

Now, I am *not* suggesting that you waste time trying to "guess" what's in the Library. After all, this is an open-book test! I am simply urging you to *think* as you read, and continuously put the PT puzzle pieces together. Keep the big picture in mind. Think about who your client is and what he wants. Think about your assignment and what the Senior Partner has told you. Think about what facts you have and what facts are missing. As you read the Library authorities, ask yourself how the cases (and/or statutes) fit together.

As discussed earlier in this book, facts are generally not relevant in a vacuum; facts are relevant as they prove or disprove elements of rules of law. Thus, it makes sense that the Library forms the organizational structure (the "tree trunk" or cause of action, and "branches" or elements, here theories proving a particular disputed element); and that the facts ("leaves") hang on or flesh out that law. The logical organization of most PT answers thus comes from some combination of the Task Memo and the law. The Task Memo tells you what to write; here it details the two parts of your memo (legal analysis and additional facts). Synthesizing the law in the Library will help you see how to organize your thoughts within the legal memo portion of your answer.

Now, let's highlight selected aspects of the Library cases. Again, they are all Columbia Supreme Court cases (which means they are all binding), so we need to pay special attention to the date on which each case was decided. As we discussed in Chapter 2, you may want to take notes on the table of contents page that lists the cases and the dates they were decided. Your goal is to cite to all the main cases in your answer, so it can be very helpful to organize all the main rules on one page. Next to each case, in addition to citing its holding (or noting the page number in the Library where you have "book-briefed" the holding), you might note whether each case supports Henry or Mid-Central. Ironically, you will likely have to spend more time carefully reading cases that seem *not* to support your client, typically because you will be searching for ways to factually distinguish them. With the cases that support your client's position, you may not have time to extensively reference analogous facts; it may be sufficient to simply pull out a helpful rule to cite.

Sample answers located in the Online Question and Answer Bank provide a sense of how thorough an answer one might produce in the allotted time. They also help you pull the law together. In addition, I have highlighted some points of interest from each of the cases in the rest of this chapter.

> **Note:** You do *not* want to organize your answer case-by-case. An effective *Carelton* answer would determine the legal theories that can be distilled from the cases and analyze them theory by theory. Brown did not ask you to summarize the cases, but rather to see how they help Henry in developing legal theories upon which he may bring suit. I am running through them case-by-case here simply as a way of helping you see what you learned from reading the Library.

Scoundrel

Scoundrel was the first and oldest case in the Library. This case set forth the general rule that a landowner does not owe a duty to trespassers. This is "bad" for Henry's case because Henry most likely was a trespasser on Mid-Central's property. What to do? You cannot ignore unhelpful law: not on PTs and not in law practice. You want to strive to use every main Library case in your PT answer. When cases are bad for your client, try to distinguish them factually.

Here, the *Scoundrel* facts are distinguishable from Henry's situation in that the plaintiff in *Scoundrel* climbed a five-foot fence, whereas Henry walked through an open gate. Further, the *Scoundrel* plaintiff was in the defendant's yard at the time of the injury, whereas Henry was poised to dive into the Muddy River, a public waterway. (You may not have seen this point as essential until you read some of the later cases. Just as you want to get into the habit of skimming File facts and returning to them once you have more context, in a Library such as this, with so many cases, it can help to skim each case, then re-read them to pull out rules and distinguish facts once you have a better picture of the Library as a whole.)

Scoundrel also noted that the defendant in that case gave no license or invitation to trespassers, either express or implied. We will likely argue that Mid-Central impliedly consented, and certain employees may have even expressly consented, to the boys' use of its property to access the river. Further, the *Scoundrel* court observed that the defendant in question had no reason to suspect or anticipate the plaintiff's trespass. As a great deal of evidence in *Carelton*, including Mid-Central's own internal memo, indicates, Mid-Central had every reason to anticipate Henry's trespass.

Again, these are just some points in *Scoundrel* you might have noticed.

Wanderer

In *Wanderer* the plaintiff, who was lawfully using a public street, suddenly had to get out of the way of an oncoming cyclist, and did so by going onto the defendant's front steps. There, a loose brick from the defendant's property fell and injured the plaintiff. The court found for the plaintiff. This is a very good case for Henry, especially if the Muddy River is analogous to a street, as Mid-Central's wires fell on him while he was poised to dive.

The court articulated the rule as requiring an obstruction in the road by fault of the defendant and no negligence on the part of the plaintiff. The obstruction in our case (the plank) may be Mid-Central's fault if they left it out, or it may be Henry's fault if he put it there. (This is something we will have to determine.) The obstruction might also be the wiring which M-C controlled. Assuming we can get over the obstruction argument, and the second hurdle (that Henry is not deemed to have lacked due care himself in diving/swimming under electrical wiring), then this case may well support Henry's claim.

Poorsoul

This is another case that appears helpful to Henry. Here, the court found that the defendant had a duty to maintain a boardwalk that was essentially a "sidewalk" which, because of its placement, made ambiguous the line dividing the private property and public property. Based on this case, Mid-Central will likely be found to have had a duty to maintain the banks of the river.

Child

This case is likely not helpful to Henry because it found for the defendant against a child who was injured on a chain-link fence that formed the border between the public alley and the defendant's private property. The court used a two-part test: (1) whether the defendant should have known the post could break or fall when kids swung on it; or (2) whether the defendant had reasonable grounds to apprehend an accident from the placement of the post in the alley. The court in *Child* found that the injury was not foreseeable and therefore found that no duty was owed to the plaintiff in question.

Did you see the dicta in *Child* in the footnote that sets forth a Restatement section upon which liability might be established? The court declares, however, that the jurisdiction does not recognize this Restatement section as good law. Did you wonder why the court bothered to reproduce the section in full if it was not useful in answering the question? The answer becomes clear in the *Wiseguy* case, decided some 12 years later, which references the Restatement, suggesting that by that time the section has indeed been recognized in Columbia.

Fall

Fall is one of the best cases for Henry, as it makes clear that a duty is owed to trespassers where the owner has permitted trespassers to use the land, thus giving them an implied license to trespass. The facts appear very similar to those in Henry's case. In *Fall,* the court found that the defendant could not make a dangerous pit and leave it unprotected without bearing some responsibility to those who were accustomed to (and permitted to) use the defendant's lot as part of their way, and who, while exercising due care, were injured falling into that pit. Similarly, we would argue that Mid-Central should not be allowed to fail to maintain poles that held electrical wires directly over an area where they allowed the public to come swim.

> **Note:** We will need to explore whether Henry himself was negligent in his diving/swimming. Other than the fact that he was likely skipping school, and that his mother said, "Everyone knows the shipping yard is dangerous," it does not appear from the facts in the File that Henry failed to use due care.

Wiseguy

Wiseguy, the last and most recent of the Library cases (decided just eight years before Henry's accident), is also not very helpful to Henry. Although it established a duty similar to that found in *Child,* the *Wiseguy* court found: (1) that no injury was foreseeable because the flagpole was not in obvious disrepair; and (2) the plaintiff (a 15-year-old, one year younger than Henry) should have been able to appreciate the danger of jumping on a flagpole.

You need to read this case carefully and distinguish it factually. For instance, you might note that while the plaintiff in *Wiseguy* admitted he knew it was foreseeable that he could be injured and simply did not know the possible seriousness of that injury, Henry seems to have had no clue at all that there was even a danger. It may well be that it takes much more sophistication to appreciate the possible danger of overhead electrical wiring randomly falling than to realize the fairly obvious danger of swinging on a pole designed to hold only the weight of a flag. Also, Henry likely had no way of knowing the poles were rotten from the inside out.

Lastly, as noted earlier, *Wiseguy* references the Restatement section, so assuming that the Restatement is now good law in Columbia, it too may provide a basis for liability against Mid-Central. You could also have written in your answer about that section as a theory Henry might assert.

YOUR OUTLINE AND ANSWERS

Once you have made quick notes on the rules from and key facts in all the cases, you should think about how they logically fit together, and update the draft outline of your answer accordingly. Again, do not summarize the cases one by one. That might be something a partner would ask a law clerk to do, but not a lawyer. As a lawyer, you need to think through the case law and figure out how the authorities in the Library as a whole fit together. Library authorities in PTs are like puzzle pieces. Once you see how they fit, you can begin to sketch out an outline of your answer.

Here, the first case (*Scoundrel*) established a general rule and the subsequent cases established a number of exceptions to that rule. Each exception may form a liability theory upon which Henry may argue that Mid-Central owed him a duty.

Notice that all the cases were about the duty element of negligence. Thus, there is only one cause of action here, but several theories upon which a duty might be established. That may have confused you at first. Students read the Task Memo and initially assume that the theories of liability that Henry will assert will be negligence, intentional tort, and strict liability. However, the only viable cause of action here was based on negligence. Unless we find more evidence, there appears to have been no intentional action on Mid-Central's part, nor are there grounds for strict liability. (Merely maintaining electrical wiring would not be deemed an ultrahazardous activity.) So, after reading the Library and File and thinking carefully, you would see that what Brown (the senior partner) had to have meant in terms of liability theories was theories under which *duty* can be established in order to bring a negligence cause of action.

Here is how you could have updated your outline after briefing the cases.

UPDATED SAMPLE OUTLINE

To: Edward Brown

From: Applicant

Re: *Henry Carelton v. Mid-Central Shipping*, Preparation for Response to Pretrial Motion to Dismiss

Introduction

You have asked me to think through this case and discuss the theories of liability under which we can contend that Mid-Central is liable for Henry's injuries, and additionally, to let you know what more evidence we should begin to gather to build our case. Please find my analysis below. I am available at your convenience if you have further questions.

    PART I—Landowner Liability Theories re: Duty Element of Negligence

A. General Rule is that there is no duty to trespassers.

[Discuss. Try to distinguish *Scoundrel* factually to show why it should not apply; for instance, in that case the trespasser scaled a five-foot wall whereas Henry walked through an open gate.]

Exceptions to General Rule

1. Public necessity (where obstruction is fault of defendant [D] and plaintiff [P] was not negligent). Cite to *Wanderer* and *Poorsoul*. Provide your analysis here of how the case law supports Henry's claim that Mid-Central owes Henry a duty under a public necessity theory.

2. Implied consent (landowner knew that public regularly used its land and impliedly consented to that use). Cite to *Fall*. Provide your analysis here of how the case law supports Henry's claim that Mid-Central owes Henry a duty under an implied consent theory.

3. Child trespassers (landowner knew of danger and had reason to apprehend accident). Cite to *Child:* Children not likely to appreciate danger under case law. Cite to *Wiseguy:* Liability also under Restatement, rejected by earlier cases but impliedly endorsed in *Wiseguy*. Provide your analysis here of how the case law supports Henry's claim that Mid-Central owes Henry a duty under a child trespass theory.

Conclude as to legal theories available to prove duty.

PART II—Additional Evidence to Be Gathered

Write a quick introductory sentence saying something like: "Here below, per your request, is a list of some of the additional evidence we will need to prove Henry's claims."

Pick up all the questions from File documents, such as E.B.B.'s Rough Notes Interview with Henry Carelton and with Martha Carelton (Mother), and add any other questions you can think of. Because this is an internal memo and thus a less formal document than one written to the court or opposing counsel, and because of the nature of this type of assignment, it would be fine to just list in bullet points any additional evidence to be gathered. To maximize points here, however, you would want to note why you want any evidence you suggest gathering (what it would help prove or disprove and why).

Conclude with one line here to show the grader that you completed the assignment, and that you followed directions. For example, "If you have any additional questions about the legal theories or factual/proof problems discussed above, or any other aspects of Henry's case, please let me know and I will address them.

It is critical to outline performance test answers *before* writing. One of the main criteria you are being graded on is your ability to draft a well-organized answer that is responsive to the specific requests in the Task Memo. Again, the graders do not want to see you listing and summarizing cases, but rather pulling holdings from cases and using them to craft a thoughtful response that will be helpful given the context of the case.

You will find sample passing answers to *Carelton* in the Online Question and Answer Bank. They are provided to give you an idea of what a successful student answer might look like. As you read through them, do not judge yourself harshly, but rather look to see how you might improve on your next practice exam. Here too is a list of mistakes that students most frequently make on this exam:

1. Not finishing. Many students do not get to the second task on factual or proof problems within the allotted time.
2. Organizing case-by-case instead of theory-by-theory.
3. Including questions presented, a statement of facts, and/or other parts of a traditional law school memo that were not specifically requested in the Task Memo and would have taken precious time away from what you were directed to write about.

TIP: REVERSE ENGINEERING— WORKING FROM THE ANSWERS BACK TO THE QUESTION

A helpful exercise is to outline the sample answers. Then, look back from the answers into the question and ask yourself: What would you have needed in an outline of your own to draft these answers? Where is the most helpful information in the Library and File? How much information do you have to pull out before writing? This reverse engineering will help you become more efficient in your own organizing, outlining, and writing.

SPIN-OFF EXERCISES

Spin-off exercises are a great way to gain exposure to drafting different types of documents without as much of a time commitment as it would take to complete a whole new performance test. I often suggest to my students that they spend a few minutes, after writing any PT, thinking about other documents they might have been asked to draft based on the same law and facts. Then, take a minute to outline or write out in full (time permitting) those "spin-off" tasks. Pay particular attention to how your tone and approach might differ depending on the goal of your assignment and your audience.

In *Carelton*, your task was to draft a memo to the senior partner. As spin-off exercises, using the same facts and law, try drafting a:

- Letter to Henry explaining the likelihood of success in suing Mid-Central (this would involve breaking down the law into simple and easy-to-understand language) and describing what Henry will need to go through during the process (what bringing a lawsuit really entails)
- Letter to Henry's mother about the likelihood of success in suing Mid-Central and what she, Henry, and their family will go through in this process
- Memo to a private investigator to get more facts to support Henry's case
- Questions to ask in depositions of Mid-Central employees
- Discovery plan
- Settlement proposal to Mid-Central

The following are just a few thoughts on the drafting of such assignments for a bar exam performance test. Note that these are just tips; they are not sample answers and do not cover everything you might need for a top score on these tasks. Rather, they are designed to get you thinking. Also be aware that the comments do not necessarily mirror the exact concerns you would have in the "real world" litigating such a matter, but rather issues to highlight in the context of a bar exam PT.

Letter to Henry

Remember, Henry is a boy; he obviously has no legal training. Therefore, you must keep your language simple and straightforward. However, you can tell him that Mid-Central will likely try to argue that they are not responsible for his injuries because he went onto their land without permission.

You may go on to explain that based on what Henry told you, you will try to dispute Mid-Central by arguing that: (1) Henry did not realize there was a danger from wires falling, (2) Mid-Central knew kids regularly used their land to swim, and (3) Mid-Central's allowing its plank and wires to extend into the Muddy River gave Mid-Central an obligation to keep the area safe for people lawfully using the river.

You will want to explain confidentiality and attorney-client privilege and make sure Henry knows that he can and should tell you everything he knows, but that he must not talk with anyone else about the case without your knowledge, permission, or presence. You will then need to tell Henry that Mid-Central will want to talk with him, and that likely they will want to take his "deposition." You may explain simply that during a deposition, they will ask him a series of questions under oath, in their office or your office, but also reassure him that you will be there to help him. You may need to warn Henry that they are likely to ask all about his "ditching" school, and other things that he may be uncomfortable answering, but that he will have to answer the questions honestly. You can tell him you will prepare him for anything like that, but that he should know it might occur and should expect that it may well happen. You might also go on to tell him that if the case goes to trial, he may have to appear in court, and explain what that entails.

You can tell Henry that you believe you will win, but that there is always a likelihood that you will not, especially if they are able to show that he's a sophisticated 16-year-old who should have known better. You can also say that it is very likely the case will not go all the way to trial, but will settle instead (and explain what that means).

In this sort of an assignment, the graders would not be looking for everything that could possibly be said to Henry. Also, there are many ways such a letter could be organized. What they will want to see is that you have written in plain English that your client Henry can clearly understand. They will want to verify that you know that Henry, and not his mother, is the client. They will also want to see that you touched on most of the basics mentioned earlier.

Letter to Henry's Mother

Most of what was noted with respect to the letter to Henry would also be appropriate to include in a letter to Henry's mother. She is also likely to want to know about costs and timing, and she must understand the fee arrangement. You must prepare her for what happens both if he wins or if he loses, and you must warn her that litigation sometimes takes a long time. You will need to let her know that they may try to tarnish Henry's reputation, though you can suggest that they probably have more to lose by bad publicity and may want to settle (and you would explain what *settlement* means). You need her to understand that even though she is paying your bills, she is not the client, and she must not be offended when you tell her she may not be present in all your meetings with Henry, and that Henry must not discuss the case with her.

What else do you think you would include in a letter to Henry's mother? Remember, because his mother is not a professional, and definitely not a lawyer, you want to use plain, simple English. You also want to convey empathy in your tone, as she has undergone a traumatic event and likely is still dealing with many problems stemming from Henry's injuries.

Memo to a Private Investigator

On a performance test, the best way to set up a memo to a private investigator is often to organize by legal theories, noting what you (the plaintiff) have to prove and what types of facts might be helpful to establish each element of each liability theory. You will likely also want to suggest that the investigator ask about information that could be damaging to your case: best that you know it now, before continuing too far into the litigation.

Successful PT answers must be well-organized. (Drafting well-organized PT answers is one of the great challenges in mastering PTs because time flies!) A first-year law student or paralegal could provide a list of the holdings of each of the cases, but thinking like a lawyer requires synthesizing the case law and presenting the legal theories in an order showing that you see how the cases relate to one another; that is, how the body of law "fits" together.

Part of what you are doing in the first half of your allotted time, while you are reading and thinking and outlining, is trying to determine what the relevant pieces of the puzzle are and how they fit together. Only after figuring out that part can you truly write an effective answer. When you work on fact-gathering documents on a performance test, the key is really to make explicit why facts you want to obtain would be relevant. That is what proves you are thinking like a lawyer! A nonlawyer might just randomly list facts. (Being organized and thinking logically are the hallmarks of a skilled lawyer.)

If you are given this sort of an assignment, the examiners will likely set it up in such a way that information you disclose to the investigator working for your firm will be privileged. Remember, though, your investigator cannot just go and talk freely with Mid-Central employees, because the company is represented by counsel. However, the investigator can likely talk with any of the other school kids who were swimming, and/or ask questions of witnesses who are not Mid-Central employees (perhaps other people who run barges or boats up the Muddy River who might have seen kids swimming regularly). The investigator can pull up public records of property boundaries, and possibly school records showing how often and when Henry missed class, and many other things.

What can you think of that you would want to know to help prepare for trial? What pieces of that information could a private investigator help you find out informally, and what might have to be determined in formal discovery?

Discovery Plan

Similar to the letter or memo to a private investigator, you will likely organize a discovery plan by elements or legal theories. For each of the applicable theories, you would likely want to discuss evidence that may be obtainable using discovery tools such as depositions, interrogatories, requests for admission, and requests for production of evidence.

You may note that, strategically, it would be helpful to get the documents, admissions, and answers to interrogatories before you take depositions so that you have further information on what questions to ask. Also, obtaining these is generally less expensive than taking depositions.

Starting with the negligence theory based on implied consent allowing outsiders to freely use the property, here are a few points you might include for each discovery device:

Negligence Based on Implied Consent

Deposition

We may want to depose the foreman and a number of employees who were working at the Mid-Central shipyard when Henry was injured. We will ask them questions to find out (among other things):

- How often they locked the gate
- Whether they knew kids came onto the property to swim
- Whether each person being deposed spoke to any of the kids swimming and to relate the details of any such conversations
- Whether there were "No Trespassing" signs
- How often they serviced the poles and wiring

What else can you think of?

This sort of assignment may require you to specifically say why you want the particular information you are seeking; for example, what theories would be supported depending on which answers the people questioned provide.

Requests for production of documents

We will want to ask for any internal memoranda, email, or other correspondence relating to intruders and security. We will want the repair logs for any maintenance or repair of the electrical wiring, including the posts.

What else?

Requests for admission

We will want Mid-Central to admit that the gate was frequently left unlocked and that they knew the pole was rotted.

What else can you think of?

Settlement proposal to Mid-Central

You could well be asked to draft a letter to Mid-Central's attorney urging the defendant to settle. What are some of the points that you would make in that sort of a document?

- That Mid-Central will very likely be found liable based on one or more landowner liability theories
- That it would cause bad publicity for Mid-Central to go to trial when they were at fault for injuring a local 16-year-old boy
- That it will cost Mid-Central far more in protracted litigation than to settle now

What else would you include in a settlement letter?

PRACTICE, LAW SCHOOL, AND PTs:
COMPARE AND CONTRAST

In the real world, a case like this would be all about settlement. It is possible, though doubtful, that such a case would ever make it to trial. Mid-Central undoubtedly has far more resources than Henry to mount a protracted fight, and that too might push the Carletons to want to settle. However, Henry might well make a very sympathetic plaintiff, and Mid-Central may not be able to afford bad press.

On this practice PT, none of this was your concern. You were instructed to draft documents to prepare for trial. (In other words, do not "write yourself out of the question" by suggesting that we settle and not even amend the complaint, and therefore skip drafting what was requested in your answer.) Give the bar examiners what they want and ask for!

Nevertheless, you should remember that even in the real world, the better prepared you are for trial, the stronger your negotiating position will be when working out a settlement agreement with opposing counsel. We typically do not spend a lot of time in law school talking about settlement. Traditional law exams are written in such a way that we immediately think in terms of elements of causes of action and whether the parties will or will not prevail in litigation. This PT makes a great springboard for discussion with classmates about settlement, and your role as a future lawyer in both litigating and negotiating.

KEY TAKEAWAYS

- When briefing cases in a PT Library, pull out the holding, and then try to find at least one or two key facts that distinguish the case from your client's situation (especially if the case holding does not support your client's position). Determine at least one or two facts from the cases that are analogous to the facts in your client's situation (especially if the case holding does support your client's position).
- The multiple-choice questions in *Carelton* helped you test yourself on your case-briefing skills, but your bar exam PT will likely **not** include multiple-choice testing.
- Think both about facts you know and can prove (and how they will be proven), and facts that may still have to be gathered.
- Do not just list or summarize cases case-by-case from the Library in your PT answers. Rather, strive to see how the law in the Library fits together, and organize your answer logically in a way that synthesizes the rules and shows the grader that you see how it all fits together and makes sense. In *Carelton*, you had one older case (that was decidedly bad for your client), and then a number of other cases establishing theories that were exceptions to the rule in that first case. As you studied the sample answers, you undoubtedly saw that those memoranda were organized theory by theory.

6

CONTRACTS

OVERVIEW OF CONTRACTS

When dealing with contract law, you find yourself in the world of civil litigation and/ or transactional matters. Parties are making deals with one another every day in the real world. They may come to you to plan, to draft or edit contracts, or to seek relief (usually in the form of money damages) when promises made as part of a deal are broken.

A homeowner might sue a contractor for breach of contract if her home was not built as specified under their agreement. An employee might sue an employer for breach of contract if the employee is fired without good cause. A seller might sue a buyer if the buyer suddenly refuses to purchase goods that the seller delivered. These are all typical scenarios in contracts essay questions in law school and on the bar exam. They are also things that happen in everyday real life.

Breach of contract is not a crime. In fact, in many commercial aspects of society, it is considered a routine part of business to get out of agreements that are not profitable and move on to other arrangements. Damages are often thought of simply as the cost of doing business. Watch your terminology on bar exams: one may be "liable" for, but is not "guilty" of, breaching a contract.

1L contracts courses are almost always based on casebook study. In the appellate cases you read, the parties have already litigated and are now appealing lower-court decisions about contracts that typically:

- Were never properly formed
- Include conditions that were never satisfied
- Were breached, or
- Spawned disputes as to the appropriate remedies for breaches

You also may study situations where third parties are litigating about their respective rights, studying assignments, delegations, and the rights of third-party beneficiaries.

Performance tests, like typical law school or bar exam essays, may look at contract problems from that same perspective: hindsight, after a deal has fallen apart. However, PTs also may be forward-looking, in the context of a time when the parties are negotiating deals and want to draft contracts that will avoid or prevent future disputes. We will look at just such a drafting/revision problem in the practice PT in this chapter.

On the bar exam, major contract issues typically arise in the following areas:

- Applicable law (common law or Uniform Commercial Code [UCC])
- Contract formation (offer, acceptance, consideration, defenses)
- Contract modification
- Conditions, discharge, breach
- Remedies (including damages, restitution, and equitable remedies)
- Third-party issues (third-party beneficiaries, assignments, and delegations)

Law school contracts courses sometimes may get to all of these areas of law, but typically do not. Many spend much of the semester on contract formation. Do not worry; contract formation is the most heavily tested area of contracts on bar exam essays and even on MBE questions. If you understand contract formation very well, you can likely learn all the other pieces of the contracts puzzle fairly easily before or during your bar review course.

In law school, you will read many cases about what it takes to make a valid offer, to accept that offer, and to then have a deal that is legally binding; in legalese, this means that along with a valid offer and acceptance, there is "consideration" or a consideration substitute such as promissory estoppel. We also study defenses to formation. Even after there is a "deal," it may be that the deal is not valid because it was oral and should have been in writing, for example; or because one of the parties did not have the capacity to enter into the deal in the first place. There are other contract formation defenses you will need to know as well, including illegality, fraud, duress, and mistake.

SO MUCH TIME ON OFFER AND ACCEPTANCE!

It shocks some first-year students just how many cases they might be required to read on the very opening piece of contract formation: what it takes just to make a valid offer. I am reminded of *Lucy v. Zehmer*, a classic contract formation case that appears in a number of contracts casebooks. I love the court's colorful language noting that Mr. Zehmer's drinking left him "high as a Georgia pine." The Zehmers had allegedly offered to sell their farm for $50,000. Lucy wanted to hold the Zehmers to the deal, but the Zehmers claimed it was all a joke.

We study the case to determine how we look at the parties' intent to enter a contract. Specifically, do we consider what these particular people were actually thinking (subjective intent)? Or do we look at whether a reasonable person would consider this an offer to contract (objective intent)? The court looks at all the facts in the case (though they all were drinking, among other key facts they wrote the deal on a napkin and rewrote it so Mrs. Zehmer could sign it), and concludes by saying that only if Lucy knew (subjectively) or should have known (objectively) that the Zehmers were joking, then no contract was formed. An offer will be judged by how a reasonable person would understand the offeror's words and conduct.

Your professor may engage in hours of hypotheticals about just this sort of situation, changing the facts to see how each shifting scenario might be analyzed. (What if they hadn't been drinking? What if they only had one drink? What if they hadn't written the deal on a napkin? What if these parties had negotiated prior deals?) If your professor plays with "what if" hypotheticals and asks probing questions that you feel certain there is no right answer to, embrace this. This is learning to think like a lawyer! Even if your head starts to hurt, enjoy the process. Listen carefully to every word that is exchanged. Engaging in this sort of intellectual sparring will serve you well: all this time spent on excruciating details about offer, acceptance, and consideration is critical to gaining a fundamental understanding of contracts and contractual relations, and will help you do well on many bar exam contracts questions.

Most classes do eventually move on from contract formation to contract performance and breach. You may read cases about what constitutes a "material breach" and what might be deemed simply a "minor breach," and the effect of concluding either way. You will also learn about damages in the event of a breach, including the requirement to mitigate damages.

Your class may move quickly through contract remedies and only get to money damages. Some professors skip certain areas, assuming that you will either pick them up in bar review or in an upper-division course such as remedies, where you would learn not only more about damages but also about equitable remedies such as specific performance (where a party seeks a court order enforcing the actual terms of the contract rather than money because of a contract breach) and restitution (returning money or property so as to prevent unjust enrichment).

A WORD ON CONTRACTS REMEDIES

Legal remedies (money damages), restitution, and equitable remedies are all important for bar exams. Some professors skip these because they are covered in other classes, such as UCC or remedies courses. Other professors assume that you will get to them in bar review. It is important, especially if you do not take a remedies course in law school, that you take time, well before bar review begins, to be sure that you understand all applicable contract remedies as well as contract claims. Know how damages are calculated in typical agreements such as buyer-seller, employer-employee, homeowner-homebuilder; understand different types of damages such as expectation damages, consequential damages, and liquidated damages; and understand equitable contract remedies such as specific performance.

For a more complete list of the topics covered on the MBE in contracts, consult the most recent MBE Subject Matter Outlines published by the National Conference of Bar Examiners on their website at ncbex.org/exams/mbe/preparing.

SIMULATED CONTRACTS-BASED PERFORMANCE TEST

Take three hours and complete the performance test in the Online Question and Answer Bank at **http://ambar.org/barexamprep** called *Southwest Health Center v. Computech* ("*Computech*"), an exam set, as you will see, in the contract drafting stage.

One quick historical context note will be useful before you start: *Computech* was given in July 1986 when the technology described in the problem (hardware and software) was cutting edge. You may be shocked to read about the size and costs of computer equipment then. And, as we all know, today's cell phones are enormously more sophisticated than the machines in *Computech*. That said, the lawyering work you must do to complete this task is wholly consistent with both more recent exams and real-life contract negotiating. Ignore the outdated machines, and focus on determining (as the instructions direct) which contract provisions pose problems for your client such that they have to be revised, and why. You will see that concerns such as when equipment is installed, who pays shipping costs, whether warranties are sufficient, and so forth would be very similar today. (As you complete this practice test, if you happen to note something that would radically differ today, mention it. It won't appear in the sample answers, but I may have noted it in my debriefing later in this chapter.)

TIME-CRUNCH TIPS

If you do not have three hours and must save time completing this practice PT, outline it thoroughly rather than writing it out in full. There is only one task to be completed on this PT, so it does not break naturally into parts; thus, one of the key challenges is determining how best to organize your answer, and highlighting some key suggestions or additions to the agreement in question. You can read all the materials and complete a thorough outline in about 90 to 100 minutes.

INSIDE THIS TEST: TIPS AND STRATEGIES

Congratulations on finishing *Computech*! One unusual part of this case, which you likely noticed, is that the entire Library is comprised of UCC provisions. There are no cases. I chose this exam for three reasons. First, it provides an excellent example of a drafting/editing/document review task. Second, it gives you a chance to study certain UCC rules. Contracts is tested with both common law and UCC law on the MBE and frequently in bar exam essays, so you will know this entire area well by the time of your bar exam. Third, I wanted you to see that not all PT Libraries contain the same types of legal authorities. Most include cases, but occasionally you will have a Library such as this with different types of authorities: here, only statutes.

General Instructions

The first thing you might have noticed, in a twist on the standard PT, is that this problem is set in two different states, Columbia and Franklin. You learn later that our client, Southwest Health Center (SHC) is in Columbia (as is our law firm, which you see from the Task Memo letterhead). SHC wants to buy a computer system from Computech, a company based in Franklin. (From correspondence later in the File, you learn that Columbia is on the West Coast and Franklin is on the East Coast, an important fact with regard to several contract provisions such as shipping costs and on-site training.)

The minute you saw two states, you may have thought: Which state's law will apply? If so, great lawyering instincts! That is the exact topic in Provision 16 of the Agreement, one you may well want to suggest revising (but we are getting ahead of ourselves here!).

The Task Memo, as always, gives background information as well as detailing your specific assignment. Sometimes it also gives hints. This Task Memo stresses the date on which the computer system should be ready. (The fact that the system should be fully operational when SHC opens its doors on December 1 is noted repeatedly. Any time bar examiners repeat a fact, it is likely critical.) Thus, timing will be an important term to look out for in the contract. You might not have seen this on a first read, but you would not miss this if you re-read the Task Memo after reviewing the other File information, before writing.

You find your exact assignment on the second page of the Task Memo. Notice that before Jim Hagelund (the partner giving the assignment) details the task, he says, "I would like your help in preparing for the meeting," referring to talks he will have the next day with the administrative director of SHC, Laura Sauer. He also tells you not to go into attack mode and rip apart every provision; he acknowledges that we will not get everything our client wants, that there will be negotiation and compromise.

From this paragraph, you should already have an understanding of the appropriate writing tone for this task. You are writing to a lawyer on your team, a partner in your law firm, to help him prepare for a meeting that will discuss how SHC might negotiate with Computech about the proposed contract provisions. Helping him prepare involves thinking things through so as to inform him. This is not a persuasive assignment. You will be writing in a neutral manner, analyzing whether each provision complies or not and why, helping Hagelund see what parts of this proposed deal may have to be rewritten. (Again, his underscoring that you are not to rewrite every provision shows that your job is not to argue, but rather to inform and determine where we must protect our client.)

Your tone is also affected by the fact that you are writing to a lawyer, Jim Hagelund. Jim may need to explain certain concepts to Sauer (presumably a lay person). However, in this document you do not have to define every legal term. For example, when you mention that Computech has expressly disclaimed the warranties of fitness and merchantability, you do not have to tell Jim in plain English what these warranties are, as you would if your task were to draft a letter to SHC. As a lawyer, Jim would understand these terms. Hence, your focus will be on why Computech's attempts to get out of warranting its goods and services may hurt your client.

Hagelund details exactly what you are to draft in the next-to-last paragraph of the Task Memo: "Please read the correspondence and review the Agreement ... ." The paragraph is full of important detail, including directing you to:

- Analyze the Agreement in light of SHC's goals
- Focus discussion on the most problematic provisions (this is also a hint on how to save time; it provides a way of avoiding perfectionist tendencies so that you can finish within the allotted time)
- State why each problem provision is troubling, identify exactly what the problem is, and give suggestions on how to resolve it, and move on to the next provision

- Assess the importance of any revisions you suggest, noting which are merely desirable changes and which are musts for the client
- Be aware that some provisions need not be revised; even where you do urge revisions, you do not have to suggest specific language; just say what is problematic and why, and note how to resolve the problem

Again, this last part (freeing you from having to propose specific new terms) is critical to helping you finish. Examiners design PTs so that they can be finished within the allotted time. They test and retest that timing. On many PTs with drafting/editing tasks, you do have to propose specific new language. However, where the examiners realize that it will be difficult for applicants to finish in time, they either explicitly restrict the assignment or provide hints to rein it in. You must be alert to these hints, though, noticing and heeding them. (On that note, I hope you did not waste time writing a statement of facts or other things that were not requested. To finish these PTs in time, give the examiners what they want and *only* what they want.)

Read the Task Memo several times before you begin drafting your answer. Seeing exactly what to write and what not to write is essential to producing a responsive, passing-quality answer within the allotted time frame.

The last paragraph of the Task Memo is also interesting. It essentially tells you that your Library is what we called earlier in this book a "reference library": a set of authorities you are already familiar with by the time of the bar exam but that are there for your reference in case you need to look things up.

Note the last line of the Task Memo, which says, "most of [these UCC provisions] may not be relevant to your review, but where they are the basis for your recommendations, please cite to specific UCC sections." This is very helpful. First, it tells you that many of the statutes in the Library will not help you to evaluate the Computech Agreement, so (hint hint) do not pore over each provision. You could easily spend a (wasted) hour reading every word of every UCC provision—but Hagelund tells you not to. Instead, read the Library table of contents and note generally which provisions are included. Then, as you read corresponding sections of the Agreement, consult the Library selectively.

Also, though generally you do not have to cite to specific cases or code sections by number on bar exam essays, here you do: (1) because the examiners are giving you the provisions (and thus not testing your memory), and (2) because Hagelund tells you to cite to any specific sections that are the basis for your recommendations. So, for example, where you see a provision that is directly implicated, such as § 2-314 and § 2-315 (warranties that Computech expressly disclaims in Provision 12.7 of the Agreement), you will want to look those up in the Library and cite to them by code section in your answer.

Moving on to the rest of the File, the next document after the Task Memo is fascinating. These are internal notes that Laura Sauer wrote to herself after reading articles about computer systems. This is a critical list of concerns. As you read the Agreement, make sure that none of these are problematic. You may need to come back to this, though, after you have read through the Agreement. At that time, you would really see how helpful this list is for focusing in on problem areas that may require revision, such as price, warranty, getting the system operational in a timely manner, software compatibility, and training. Looking back at this list before you started writing (or even at some point during your writing) may have helped you spot some problematic provisions that you would not otherwise have thought to write about.

The next letter is from Ed Pinkney (SHC Head Nurse) to Laura Sauer. (This is in-house correspondence from two of the SHC staff.) Pinkney points out potential problems with the computer system. Like the previous document, this too helps flag certain concerns that we want to be alert to when we read the Agreement. Among Pinkney's concerns are:

1. How will SHC be protected in the event the computer malfunctions?
2. Will malpractice insurance cover errors in patient records because of computer problems?
3. How will rules requiring nurses to maintain medical records be satisfied by use of the computer system?
4. Will the system work going forward not just when it is first installed?

Like Sauer's notes to herself, this Pinkney letter also helps us focus on potential problem areas. Nevertheless, some of these are not problems with the computer system itself, but rather with the way SHC implements computer usage in its practice. So, some of these concerns are points you might address in either your introduction or conclusion to Jim Hagelund, rather than in your provision-by-provision analysis of the Agreement. (One sample answer in the Online Question and Answer Bank does just that; the other addresses Pinkney's concerns by suggesting that new provisions be added to the Agreement.) This is a great example of how much creative leeway you have in how and where to incorporate certain points in PT answers. The key here is to have seen that Pinkney raised some important concerns and to have addressed them somewhere in your answer.

WHO IS SHE AGAIN? TAKE NOTES USING A "CAST LIST"

Did you find yourself halfway into the File seeing the name "Laura Sauer" and wondering, "Who is she again?" As suggested in earlier chapters, it can be helpful to start a "cast of characters" list when you first read the Task Memo, and add to it as you read other File documents.

Sample Cast of Characters (compiled piecemeal as you come across names)

Jim Hagelund: Our senior partner, person to whom we are writing, who is helping client negotiate deal.

Southwest Health Center (SHC): Our client. New medical center set to open on 12/1.

Computech: Computer business from which SHC wants to buy computer system.

Columbia: Our state and state where SHC is located (West Coast).

Franklin: State where Computech is located (East Coast).

Laura Sauer: SHC administrative director.

Ed Pinkney: SHC head nurse.

Gene Minard: Computech Pacific sales representative.

The next File documents are letters between Laura Sauer and Gene Minard, a Computech sales representative. The first is an inquiry letter from SHC (written by Sauer). This provides important background about SHC, stressing its initial and expected needs and goals, and asks if Computech can provide the "equipment, software, and services" that SHC needs. Yet again, Sauer stresses the importance of the December 1 opening, and the corresponding need for the system to be operational at that time. Sauer also notes the importance of support services and other things SHC will need. You must re-read this letter after you read the Agreement to effectively complete the task that Hagelund asked of you: "analyze and evaluate the Agreement in light of Southwest's goals." Pay special attention to any document that highlights your client's goals and needs.

The reply from Minard is a sales pitch, and an offer for the sale of an equipment and software package. This letter is long. Skim it the first time you see it, and then re-read it later, after you have read the Agreement. It would be much easier at that time to see that Minard "sells" a number of points that seem to have changed significantly in the proposed Agreement, including the use and compatibility of independent hardware and software, warranties, maintenance, and updates (to ensure that the system works in the future). Minard references Computech's slogan, "Computech systems are designed for today and *tomorrow*" (emphasis in Minard's letter); you may suggest that your firm use this language in negotiating with Computech to get them to offer better assurances of future performance.

The last File documents are the Agreement itself and its attached Schedule of Equipment. This is the Agreement you must analyze in your answer, so you will have to read it slowly and carefully. To complete this analysis in the most efficient manner, given your assignment, use the following sequence:

- First, glance at the headings of each UCC provision in the Library.
- Then, read the Agreement through once quickly.
- Then, re-read the other File documents, starting with the Task Memo.
- Then, read the Agreement a second time, slowly and carefully. On this re-read, read with three senses simultaneously. Touch each word of the Agreement as you read aloud but softly, under your breath. Take notes as needed while you read. Reading with sight (eyes), hearing (listening to yourself mouth each word), and touch (putting your finger or pencil on each word as you read it) ensures that you are focused and attentive to detail.

Note: This technique of reading with three senses is discussed in *Pass the Bar Exam*[1] and recommended for reading essay and MBE fact patterns. You cannot, nor should you, read every PT document in this detailed manner. You will never finish in time if you do. Nevertheless, selected documents such as one you will be working from (here the Agreement) and the Task Memo in every PT must be read precisely and thoroughly.

OUTLINING, ORGANIZING, AND WRITING YOUR ANSWER

I suggest organizing this sort of a drafting/editing assignment provision by provision. It is the easiest way to stay on track and for the grader to follow your thinking. (The Constitutional Law chapter of this book, Chapter 9, provides an example of another PT with a similar type of task, analyzing a proposed speech code; you will also organize your answer to that PT provision by provision, for the same reasons.)

Start with a simple header and introduction; then evaluate each provision in order (where you suggest no revisions, say so), then conclude. (See the following draft outline and notice that both sample answers are also organized in just this way.) Most past PTs that involve drafting or editing tasks have been best organized paragraph by paragraph. This differs greatly from legal memoranda and many other tasks that are typically best organized with something akin to a theory-by-theory approach (and then subcategorized by elements or factors).

Many students find it most efficient, in this sort of an assignment especially, to start typing a draft outline as soon as they see a logical organization/structure. They then take "notes" under the relevant provisions, which notes they later turn into their

---

[1] Sara J. Berman, *Pass the Bar Exam: A Practical Guide to Achieving Academic & Professional Goals* (American Bar Association, 2014).

final answer. You can also write notes to yourself in a draft outline; just remember to delete them in your final answer. For example, in the sample outline, see my notes "[Under each provision, note what is problematic for our client and why.]" I put them in brackets and italics to avoid forgetting to delete them in the final answer.

SAMPLE DRAFT OUTLINE

Header/Intro

To: Jim Hagelund

From: Bar Applicant

Re: Analysis of Proposed Agreement from Computech

Date: [exam date]

Mr. Hagelund,

You will find my evaluation of each provision of the Agreement from Computech below. As requested, I have addressed the most problematic concerns, especially considering how they help (or as written do not help) our client achieve its goals. Please let me know if you have any further concerns or follow-up questions.

[Under each provision, I must note what is problematic for our client and why.]

Provision 1: Purchase and Sale

Provision 2: Prices, Payment, and Security Terms

Provision 3: Price Protection Period

Provision 4: Taxes

Provision 5: Shipment Terms and Charges

Provision 6: Title and Risk of Loss

Provision 7: Installation

Provision 8: Acceptance of Computer Products

Provision 9: Manuals and Documentation

Provision 10: Upgrade Policy

Provision 11: Copyrighted Materials

Provision 12: Warranties

Provision 13: Limitation of Remedies and Liability

Provision 14: Delays in Performance

Provision 15: Maintenance Service and Parts

Provision 16: Governing Law and Jurisdiction

Provision 17: Miscellaneous

Other Notes [to senior partner JIM HAGELUND]

Conclusion

Because the sample answers in the Online Question and Answer Bank provide a fairly detailed analysis of each provision, here I will only briefly touch on some that should be changed. I have put some of the following comments in italics to indicate my own internal thoughts; you may have had similar reactions as you read the Agreement. Of course, you would not write this way in your final answer, (write in a tone that is appropriate to whomever is your intended audience) but often this method can help you to stay awake and alert to "interact with the document" as you think and prepare what you actually will write.

Introduction

This could have been short, simply telling the partner that he will find the analysis that he requested in this document, though you could also have noted how you organized your evaluation and that you focused only on those provisions that were the most problematic. These introductory points remind you of what you must write, and they tell the grader that you read and understood the directions. An introduction could also preview what the main problem areas will be (the main problems could also be recapitulated in a conclusion).

Provision 1: Purchase and Sale

You likely saw problems with SHC being responsible for selecting computer equipment. *[Huh? Do they really expect my client, a medical center, to do this? Isn't that what they sought out a company like Computech for?!]*

Provision 2: Prices, Payment, and Security Terms

This was not a major point because we don't have enough factual background to fully analyze price, although Sauer's notes to herself in the File suggest there may be discounts for purchases of more than $25,000. *[I would like to get my client a discount for a large purchase and perhaps for timely payment. Ah, but on the flip side, we may want more flexibility if for some reason SHC finds itself having to make a late payment. The language here unfairly favors Computech, discharging all its duties if a payment is late (with only 10 days' written notice).]*

Provision 3: Price Protection Period

You likely saw problems here, too, in the great freedom Computech would be afforded to raise its prices up to 20 days prior to shipment (with only 5 days allowed for SHC to cancel the order). You might have suggested some limit on price increases or some other way to keep our client from having to pay more than it bargained for.

Provision 4: Taxes

These concerns must be addressed by someone else in our firm. *[I will note this quickly so my senior partner makes sure to consult the appropriate person about this provision.]*

Provision 5: Shipment Terms and Charges

These are problems. As written, the delivery is F.O.B. Computech's plant, putting all transportation costs and risks of loss on our client. (F.O.B. stands for "free on board" and indicates when and where the responsibility for shipping is incurred. "F.O.B. Computech's plant" means that SHC is responsible for every cost associated with getting the goods from Computech's door to SHC's door, including loading and unloading, transportation, and insurance.) *[We may need more information from Sauer as to whether she expected these additional shipment costs and what sort of insurance SHC has. This may well be something to negotiate, ideally for F.O.B. the Southwest Health Center, but perhaps with some compromise to share costs.]*

Perhaps even more important is clause 5.2, which, as one of the sample answers puts it, allows Computech to "ship the goods just about whenever it gets around to it." *[This must be revised, because we know how important it is to SHC to be fully operational by a time certain. We should change this to specify a date certain when all hardware and software shall be shipped. We could also add a "time is of the essence" clause here.]*

Provision 6: Title and Risk of Loss

You may have thought the language stating that "Computech will assist in all reasonable ways" was too vague. You may have wanted this specified. Also, this provision reiterates what you probably discussed under Provision 5: that all risk of loss shifts to

SHC the moment shipping begins. This repeats that the shipment is F.O.B. Computech's plant. Any time bar examiners repeat something within an exam, you can take it as a hint that this matter or fact is important, and you should notice it wherever and whenever it crops up.

Provision 7: Installation

First you may have read this and thought that SHC should get this pre-approval for the site and that more should be specified about the installation. Good instincts. Imagine how it would destroy SHC's opening if the goods arrived from Computech but could not be installed.

Some other problems also arise here: (1) The timing of the installation is too vague; again, we know how important timing is to SHC. (2) Does SHC have the expertise to unpack and position the equipment? *[Isn't this something Computech should do? And Computech should pay for this as well. If it were "F.O.B. Southwest Medical Center," then Computech could be made responsible for all of this. Maybe we negotiate installation issues hand-in-hand with shipment costs.]*

Provision 8: Acceptance of Computer Products

This provision is problematic both because of the limited time our client has to inspect the system, and because SHC may not have the expertise to determine whether the system is working properly. This may require either the use of a third party to ensure satisfaction or an allowance that gives SHC sufficient time to use the system to see that it is fully operational. One sample answer suggests that SHC might be given a trial period before it unequivocally accepts the equipment.

Provision 9: Manuals and Documentation

This provision would likely be obsolete today, as most manuals today are online and can be downloaded for free. As and when written, this provision may have been a problem, especially when read with Provision 11, which prohibits SHC from making copies of manuals. This should be rewritten to ensure that SHC has all the manuals and documentation it needs for everyone who will work with the computer system. *[It would also be nice to have assurances that any updated manuals will be sent free of charge and that SHC will be notified of any updates.]*

Provision 10: Upgrade Policy

This could be a problem and relates to Computech's assurances that it will provide for today and tomorrow. If tomorrow's upgrade causes compatibility problems, SHC needs assurances that changes or required "fixes" will be made and handled free of charge. If upgrades simply enhance the system, SHC may simply want more specificity regarding how SHC will be informed of them and what SHC would be charged for purchasing upgrades. *[Can we get some sort of good customer discount here?]*

Provision 11: Copyrighted Materials

See comments about Provision 9.

Provision 12: Warranties

This was one of the most problematic provisions. By drafting the provision with seven subparts and writing Provision 12.7 in all-capital letters, the examiners were likely hinting that this was important. (No way to miss the sudden shift to all caps!) Here are some standouts among the problems that you can study in the sample answers:

- SHC needs a longer warranty. *[Remember Sauer's notes to herself suggesting the need for three to six months to debug a system.]*
- SHC needs warranties for compatibility with independent hardware and software, as indicated in the correspondence between Sauer and Minard. *[Computech should warrant that the products it sells are not defective, even if those products are made by another company.]*
- SHC needs timely repairs, if service is required. *[Remember the nurse, Pinkney, having warned about what could happen to patients if the system were down too long.]*
- SHC may have to negotiate a better deal on the place where repairs will be done. It cannot be required to return hardware to Computech's plant in another state, nor should it have to pay each time a tech person comes out from Computech to help.
- Computech specifically disclaims the warranty of fitness and warranty of merchantability. SHC is entitled to the protection of those warranties under UCC §§ 2-315 and 2-314 respectively, and SHC should not allow Computech to get out of these.

Provision 13: Limitation of Remedies and Liability

[This seems far too one-sided favoring Computech, in that it allows SHC no recovery for incidental, special, or consequential damages. It is totally foreseeable that computer malfunctions might cause SHC to lose patients, or worse still harm the patients. Our client needs to have some protection for foreseeable consequential damages, along with other remedies that Computech is disclaiming. Anyway, what SHC would most want and most need in the event of a defect is specific performance—a new, working computer!—rather than money damages. Are injunctive remedies barred under this provision, too? This has to be rewritten.]

You may also have noticed the limited statute of limitations under this provision, something for SHC to be aware of.

Provision 14: Delays in Performance

Computech is already protected by the doctrine of impracticability, but this language seems to protect Computech even for some delays that it might be able to prevent or limit. At a minimum, the language should be tightened up and made less vague than "unforeseen circumstances" or "causes beyond its control."

Provision 15: Maintenance Service and Parts

You might have had no changes here, or you might have wanted Computech to commit to some time period during which it will ensure maintenance. Therefore, inserting a comment about continued maintenance was nice but not necessary.

Provision 16: Governing Law and Jurisdiction

Because this provision as it stands would force us to litigate in Franklin, you might have suggested that this be altered so that litigation could take place in Columbia or in either location.

Provision 17: Miscellaneous

The assignment prohibition is one-sided. *[Why should my client be prohibited from assigning but Computech could still assign or delegate its responsibilities? SHC chose Computech because of its expertise. Should SHC have to deal with "Chuck's Computer Shack" if Computech were to sell its business? I don't think so.]*

Other Notes, Additional Provisions, and Conclusion

Somewhere in your answer, either in your conclusion or in an "other notes" or additional-provisions-type section, you want to be sure to include Pinkney's concerns about responsibility for overseeing the computer data, hacking and security concerns, and so on.

> **Note:** If this problem were set in today's environment, computer security and information safety might have been given much greater emphasis than they were in 1986.

After reviewing the entire agreement and studying the sample answers located in the Online Question and Answer Bank, you can see that there were certain points that almost everyone spotted and others that only some students noted. As you review the sample answers, focus on how to improve your reading, note taking, analysis, and writing. Do not get frustrated if you did not see everything in the sample answers. Also, notice that both answers got passing grades, even though they were very different. In this assignment, there was a lot of room for differences in approach, level of detail, and creativity of analysis.

SPIN-OFF EXERCISES

Spin-off exercises provide exposure to different document types without taking time to learn new facts and law. Having completed *Computech*, spend a few minutes thinking of other tasks you could have been given (using the same facts and law), and how you would have handled them. Here are some suggestions:

1. Negotiation with Computech

Pick a few provisions that are particularly problematic, such as the delivery, training, warranties, and remedies provisions. Pretend that you will be negotiating with counsel for Computech tomorrow. Write a dialogue of what you would say, what you expect your Computech counterpart will say, and how you would respond as to each problem area.

2. Parade of horribles

Pretend that SHC signed the contract as is. Picture it being the New Year's holiday, a month after the target opening for SHC. Write a list of everything you can imagine that might have gone wrong between now (negotiating the deal) and January 1. Some examples might be that Computech is late in delivering the computer equipment, they deliver the wrong equipment, the equipment breaks down, some of the SHC staff were not trained well enough and are having problems using the computers, and so on. For everything that you can imagine might have gone wrong or could go wrong in the future, write whether SHC is protected under the proposed contract or not and why.

PRACTICE AND LAW SCHOOL: COMPARE AND CONTRAST

This is an extremely practical exam, and totally hands-on. You studied a proposed contract and advised your boss on what our client should accept and what the client must renegotiate in order to meet its needs. The perspective you had to adopt in this problem was forward thinking: acting as a "preventive" lawyer rather than a litigator. The client was smart to get counsel involved early on to see that it entered into the best deal possible, especially given how integral this computer system was to the new business the client was starting.

Many lawyers never see clients until problems are so far advanced that lawsuits seem inevitable. Many other lawyers spend most of their time handling problems just like this one, often on a much larger scale.

To finish this exam in the allotted time, you had to be selective about what you commented on and how much you said about provisions that you thought needed revision. There was certainly enough fodder for discussion that you could have

written for six hours or more, saying something intelligent about each and every provision—but three hours was the limit. So, this test was very "real world" in its content
but limited in its scope to satisfy exam conditions.

TIME CRUNCHES IN THE REAL WORLD

Sometimes the time constraints on exams appear ridiculous and far-fetched.
In fact, especially in today's fast-paced world, lawyers often get emails or texts
from clients expecting immediate answers. It would not be unusual for a client
to email an agreement to a lawyer with a note saying, "I'm going in to meet
about the deal in about an hour. Let me know if this contract seems OK for me
to sign as is or if I should suggest changing anything."

I hope you saw how different this test was from the typical contracts essay question, which usually looks at a situation after the parties' agreement has been breached
(or, sometimes, where a contract was never properly formed in the first place). In such
essay exams, you can approach them as a law student and think about issue spotting
and IRAC. You can try to see yourself as a litigator on essays, looking at the fact patterns as the attorney for each side respectively and determining what rights can effectively be asserted (and why), who will likely prevail (and why), and what remedies the
prevailing party will be entitled to (and why).

With this PT, your role was very different. No problems have occurred yet. The
parties have not even consummated their deal. They are just talking so far. This exam
required you to put on your various hats as counselor, problem solver, planner, and pre-
dictor. I hope you enjoyed this forward-thinking role. If you liked it a lot, consider doing
some work in the transactional or preventive law arena. If you are still in law school,
take some electives in contract drafting, estate planning, and other transactional areas.

I also hope you had fun with this practice exam and now feel confident that you
could effectively handle any sort of drafting or editing task you might see on your bar
exam. I also hope it helps you continue your important transition from law student
to lawyer.

KEY TAKEAWAYS

- This practice exam helped you see the difference between PTs set in the litigation context (more common) and those set in a transactional context, such as
  the *Computech* problem.

- This PT also helped test your problem-solving skills, particularly the need to analyze the agreement in light of your client's goals and needs. You had to know what those goals and needs were, and think about how each provision satisfied or failed to satisfy the client's concerns.
- In this sort of editing/document-analysis type of task, often the most logical organization is simply to proceed clause by clause (or paragraph by paragraph). You could have to draft a contract or contract provision for a PT, but more likely you will have to edit one, or analyze the provisions of a document such as this to see if it meets your client's needs and/or is lawful. You may also face similar types of tasks set in a wills or trust context, a business associations context, or some other planning/transactional area of law.

7

CIVIL PROCEDURE

OVERVIEW OF CIVIL PROCEDURE

Civil procedure issues tested on bar exams range from pretrial concerns, such as jurisdiction, joinder of parties, joinder of claims, and discovery; to posttrial matters such as issue preclusion (collateral estoppel) and claim preclusion (res judicata).

Law school civil procedure course coverage varies greatly. Many classes spend most of their time on jurisdiction: which courts may hear which cases. Students read dozens of cases on subject matter jurisdiction and personal jurisdiction, covering traditional jurisdictional bases and long-arm statutes. Venue concerns, critical in practice and tested occasionally on bar exams, may or may not be discussed in class.

Some classes start with and quickly cover pleading requirements, then highlight the professor's favorite topics (perhaps Rule 11 or class action rules). All of these are fair game on the bar exam. So too is discovery, the lifeblood of litigation, something that is often absent or rushed through in traditional law school civil procedure courses.

Bottom line: You will typically have to study and learn numerous procedural rules in bar review to be ready for the bar exam, especially because many jurisdictions test your knowledge of both federal and state-specific civil procedure.

Note: A bar exam essay may be brought in one court but include *Erie* or removal issues such that you have to discuss both federal and state court matters within the same question.

For a list of the topics covered on the MBE in civil procedure, consult the most recent MBE Subject Matter Outlines published by the National Conference of Bar Examiners on their website at http://www.ncbex.org/exams/mbe/preparing/.

SIMULATED CIVIL PROCEDURE–BASED PERFORMANCE TEST

Piccolo v. Dobbs, our civil procedure based PT, located in the Online Question and Answer Bank at **http://ambar.org/barexamprep**, is a multistate performance test (MPT) designed to be completed in 90 minutes. I recommend you make every effort to complete the exam within that time, in one sitting with no interruptions. If you do not finish, draw a red line after the 90 minutes have passed and then finish up, noting how much additional time it took to complete the assignment. If possible, set aside about two hours before you begin so that immediately after you complete the 90-minute exam, you can read the rest of this chapter to see how you did and to gain further insight into improving your work on future exams.

TIME-CRUNCH TIP

If you have a habit, something you do while studying—such as drinking coffee or checking your phone every time you get a text—wean yourself off that habit so you can focus solely on your exam for the entire testing period. Bar exams often test in several-hour blocks. You may go to the bathroom if you need to during a session, but you may not go out to eat, drink, or smoke. Students who have gotten used to sipping tea, or stopping for a cigarette, or checking a social media site on their phones, may be in for a rude shock when they are unable to indulge these habits during the bar exam. Break such habits well before the actual exam and develop your ability to concentrate for a minimum of three hours at a stretch.

It is recommended that you spend 45 minutes reading and outlining *Piccolo* and 45 minutes writing your answer. Refer back to Chapter 2 for strategies on how to approach PTs generally, if you want a refresher. Important reminder: On the actual MPT, you may *not* rip or tear any pages of the exam. Check to see if your bar exam allows you to use paper clips. If permitted, you can clip important pages such as the Task Memo or table of contents to easily refer back to them and help you stay organized.

TIME-CRUNCH TIPS

This exam is designed to be completed in 90 minutes, so it is already shorter than the previous PTs you have completed. If you are still crunched for time with this assignment, read all the materials and complete the argument portion of this task, but skip the statement of facts. If you have very little time but still want to dig in and do some quality work, read everything, write the statement of facts, and simply outline the argument section. (Be sure that your outline includes the persuasive headings you will use in the body of your argument.)

INSIDE THIS TEST: TIPS AND STRATEGIES

You will notice a Table of Contents that lists both the File contents and the Library contents or legal authorities. Here there are five items in the File and three in the Library. We will walk through both the File and Library in this section, highlighting points you may have picked up on. If you did not notice everything, do not be concerned. That is exactly why you are practicing these PT exams! Also, you may have noticed some points while re-reading that you did not notice when you first skimmed through the File. Again, this is perfectly normal; it's the reason you train extensively before actually taking the bar exam.

Debriefing the File

The first document in the File is the Task Memo, and from a close read of that document, you can develop your "cast of characters." As soon as you begin reading, you see that Alice Nagle is the first named partner. She is also the person giving you your assignment.

We represent Pat Piccolo. The defendant is Julia Dobbs. Note that the examiners have given you a plaintiff whose name begins with "P" and a defendant whose name begins with "D." Bar examiners often use this sort of naming on essays, and you really want to thank them when they do, as it will help you keep the parties straight. In any law exam, you also want to remain aware of the roles each person plays, as that drastically shapes the analysis and often the conclusions you reach.

TIP: REFER TO PARTIES BY THEIR ROLE RATHER THAN THEIR NAME

When writing bar essays and sometimes PTs, it can be helpful to rename the parties using their roles rather than their names to keep each party straight; for example, refer to a landlord and tenant as such, rather than as they might be named on the exam. (For example, the first time you mention the name, write: "Tanya, the Plaintiff and Tenant bringing this action ('Tenant') and Larry, the Defendant Landlord ('Landlord') who is being sued.") Many students use "P" and "D," which is fine and can also help; however, because it is so easy to confuse Ps and Ds after hours of typing or writing, it may be more helpful to refer to people by their roles.

The suit here is filed in federal court. The passenger in our client's car was killed in the accident in question. There are problems now with discovery. Specifically, we have had difficulties in obtaining certain statements. We will need to make a request that the court order the other side to produce the recordings and transcripts of the interviews with the defendant and the key witness.

The task is to draft an argument in support of a motion to compel. The person giving us this assignment could not be more explicit. She says: "Your brief should argue that, under the facts of our case, we are entitled to get the transcripts and tapes." What do you get from this? Within the first few minutes of starting this PT, you understand that your job will be to persuade the court to order the other side to give us the transcripts and tapes.

What about the format of that argument? How do we know how to set up our argument? In the document after the Task Memo, the examiners give you a format page for persuasive briefs and memoranda. This is a gift, letting you know exactly how to set up your answer: simply follow the format provided in that memorandum.

Here, you are told to provide a statement of facts and an argument. You are further instructed that the argument section should be broken down by the main reasons supporting your position and that each of these should start with a proper and carefully crafted persuasive heading. The examiners describe such persuasive headings as a "specific application of a rule of law to the facts of the case and not a bare legal or factual conclusion or a statement of an abstract principle." They then provide an example of improper and proper headings.

In this type of persuasive assignment, your carefully crafted headings may be the most important part of your assignment: They essentially provide a roadmap of your entire argument. Once you study the Library and understand the main reasons that support your argument—in other words, the reasons why the plaintiff should be entitled to the tapes and transcripts—draft your headings using this format. Mirror the tone and structure of the proper heading examples.

PERSUASIVE HEADINGS ARE ESSENTIAL IN TASKS THAT ARE BRIEFS TO THE COURT

Here are additional examples of proper and improper headings, reproduced from past California PTs. (All credit for this language to the California Committee of Bar Examiners.) Study these examples and review the information in Chapter 2 on how to draft persuasive arguments to the court.

Improper: Defendant had sufficient minimum contacts to establish personal jurisdiction.

Proper: A radio station located in the State of Franklin that broadcasts into the State of Columbia, receives revenue from advertisers located in the

State of Columbia, and holds its annual meeting in the State of Columbia, has sufficient minimum contacts to allow Columbia courts to assert personal jurisdiction.

Improper: The evidence is sufficient to convict the defendant.

Proper: Evidence of entry through an open window is sufficient to satisfy the "breaking" element of burglary.

Note: You are not instructed specifically to write an introduction or conclusion, but, as long as you write them quickly so they do not take time away from what was actually requested, adding these can help let the grader know you understood and completed the assigned task(s).

Based on directions in the Task Memo and your general knowledge of how to put together complete answers, minutes into reading this exam you could already have begun a rough outline of the basic format for your answer.

SAMPLE OUTLINE FROM THE TASK MEMO

TITLE—[Optional but helpful. Here, this could simply be:]

Argument in Support of Plaintiff's Motion to Compel Discovery

INTRODUCTION—[Optional but again useful. For example:]

To: Alice Nagle

From: Applicant (your name on the bar exam)

Re: *Piccolo v. Dobbs*, motion to compel discovery:

[Here you might add one sentence telling Alice Nagle that below she will find the persuasive argument requested.]

STATEMENT OF FACTS

This was specifically requested in the Task Memo, so in this PT, you must draft a statement of facts. As discussed earlier in the book, it is typically best to omit a statement of facts on PT assignments unless you are instructed to write one. When instructed to do so, as here, failure to include a statement of facts may well result in your failing the exam.

ARGUMENT

> Persuasive Heading 1
>
> > Body of argument 1
>
> Persuasive Heading 2
>
> > Body of argument 2
>
> Persuasive Heading 3
>
> > Body of argument 3
>
> CONCLUSION
>
> [Optional, but helpful.] A quick conclusion signals to the grader that you completed the assignment. In a brief to the court such as this, your conclusion could be one sentence recapping the relief you are seeking, such as: "For all the foregoing reasons, Plaintiff prays that this Court will compel production by the Defendant of the requested tapes and transcripts."

Look how much information can be gleaned from a close read of the Task Memo and Format Memo! You are only two pages into your File, and you already have a sense of how to tackle this PT, and a draft outline! Armed with this organization and structure, as you read the rest of the File and Library, you can plug relevant information directly into this template and flesh out your answer.

Let's now walk through the rest of the File. The next document is "Excerpts from Deposition of Julia Dobbs." Remember, she is the defendant, the person our client is suing. Our boss, the senior partner, Alice Nagle, took this deposition. As you skim these excerpts, contradictions in the defendant's testimony may pop out at you, but you may not yet realize what is and what is not critical. Basically, this first read/skim of the File simply allows you to get the lay of the land. When you return to these documents after studying the Library, what is important from the File will be obvious.

The next File document is "Excerpts from Deposition of Ted Wallace." Again, our boss took the deposition. Who is Ted Wallace? He is a witness. (Did you notice that in this exam, the witness's name starts with a W, the plaintiff's name starts with a P, and the defendant's name starts with a D? Thank you, bar examiners!)

Wallace was at the scene of the accident and subsequently befriended the defendant Dobbs. He also hired Dobbs's father as his lawyer in an unrelated matter. (Your antennae may have been raised here, wondering about Wallace's bias in favor of Dobbs.) These excerpts also note that this witness talked with our boss two days after the accident. There appear to be some contradictions in Wallace's statements, but again you may not have noticed these until you re-read the File, or you may have noticed but not considered them relevant or important until you had a good grasp on the law in the Library.

The last document in the File is "Excerpts from Deposition of Alan Isaacs." Note that his name starts with an "I" and he works for the insurance company that insured the defendant Dobbs. What Isaacs says will be critical to the arguments in your motion, but you cannot know that until you familiarize yourself with the law in the Library.

One thing Isaacs notes is that the only eyewitnesses were the defendant Dobbs and Ted Wallace. This tells you that Wallace and Dobbs are the only people able to give us information about the accident and why the statements they made right after the accident are so important in preparing our case. After reading the Library, you will learn that this is a major component of one of your arguments.

We also learned from the deposition excerpts that neither Dobbs nor Wallace testified at Dobbs's criminal trial. Again, you may not have seen the relevance of that point on your first skim, but why that is important becomes clear once you know the law. Let's jump in now and take a look at the law in the *Piccolo* Library.

Library

There is an excerpt from one statute, Federal Rule of Civil Procedure (FRCP) Rule 26. This is a rule you would know by the time of your bar exam, because civil procedure is tested on the MBE and on the essay portion of many bar exams as well. There are also two cases. That is the whole Library. (Didn't I tell you that 90-minute PTs would be easier after having completed 3-hour practice PTs?!)

Two subsections of FRCP Rule 26 are excerpted: FRCP Rule 26(1) and FRCP Rule 26(3). They basically state that everything that is not privileged is generally discoverable; however, documents and items prepared in anticipation of litigation may only be discoverable upon a showing "that the party seeking discovery has substantial need … and that the party is unable without undue hardship to obtain the substantial equivalent … by other means." The provision continues to note extra safeguards even when a substantial need is shown, to protect against disclosures of lawyers' or other representatives' "mental impressions, conclusions, opinions, or legal theories."

Pacamor, the first case, provides mostly law; it has sparse facts. The action was one alleging false advertising. Certain customer surveys were sought to be protected against compelled discovery. The lower court ordered them produced and the decision was affirmed in the case in our Library. A great deal of what is written in this case will be helpful to your understanding of the applicable law and to the drafting of the argument in support of the motion.

There are a couple of particular points you should have seen in *Pacamor*: the work-product doctrine must be "narrowly construed," and the "burden of proving the material was prepared in anticipation of litigation" is on the person asserting the privilege. In our case, that would be Dobbs.

Perhaps the language in *Pacamor* that will be most useful to us in this part of our argument is this: "Materials assembled in the ordinary course of business … are not protected, even if the party is aware that the documents may also be useful in the event of litigation." Why? Isaacs thought this matter might go to trial because it involved a death, but it was arguably still not prepared "in anticipation of litigation," as Isaacs was not certain there would be a lawsuit. No case had been filed at the time these recordings were made.

The next case, *Basinger*, is more closely aligned with our case in terms of facts. There is an insurance company seeking to protect accident-related documents from discovery. The first point the court made is that the documents were not prepared in anticipation of litigation—exactly what we will try to argue (though we may not prevail on this argument). However, the court's second point is that even if the subject documents were so prepared, that protection can be (and in *Basinger* was) overcome by a showing that the information could be obtained elsewhere.

We will need to distinguish the facts in our case from those in *Basinger* with a clear showing that the information from Dobbs and Wallace *cannot* be obtained elsewhere, that the reports made to Isaacs by these witnesses are the only information available, that we tried to depose Dobbs and Wallace and could not get the equivalent information by other means. Also, because Dobbs and Wallace spoke to the investigator quite soon (close in time) after the accident, their statements would be considered "unique," per *Basinger*. All of this will help us prove we have a clear need for the statements we seek.

OUTLINING YOUR ANSWER

After reading the Library, sit and think about an appropriate organization to pull all of this together. How do the puzzle pieces fit? Try to see if the law forms a "tree" with "branches" and what facts ("leaves") you need to hang on each branch in order to prove your arguments. (If you do not remember the tree metaphor for organizing PTs, this is a good time to review the sections in Chapter 2 on PT organization.)

Here, looking at a combination of FRCP Rule 26, *Pacamor*, and *Basinger*, what strikes you? Do you see the prongs you will have to set forth to make the argument that we need the tape recordings and transcriptions that Isaacs took of Dobbs and Wallace on the day after the accident? (These argument prongs are your tree "branches.") Look in the statute, and then (hint!), look at the headings and subheadings in *Pacamor*. Something like the following should emerge in your mind as you seek a logical organizing principle:

1. The tapes and transcriptions are discoverable under FRCP 26(b)(1).
2. The tapes and transcriptions are not privileged as attorney work product because they were not prepared in anticipation of litigation.

3. Even if the tapes and transcriptions are deemed attorney work product, they are discoverable because the plaintiff has a substantial need for them and is unable without undue hardship to obtain the substantial equivalent elsewhere.

If you look closely at the headings in *Pacamor*, you see that they mirror this logical organization. It is not unusual for examiners to give you such organizational hints in PTs.

As you read PTs, always be on the lookout for lists: lists of steps, headings, factors, or elements. Here, these logical analytical steps, the headings in *Pacamor*, track the rule sections FRCP 26(b)(1) and 26(b)(3), and the court's thinking in *Pacamor*. The examiners gave you this organization. You should have seen it if you looked carefully.

If you did not notice this organizational hint when you were taking this practice exam, go back in now and see if what I am saying makes sense. If it does, great! The whole purpose of completing practice tests is to learn from the process. The more practice PTs you complete, the more you will become attuned to seeing one or more logical ways to organize and outline your answer. Sometimes there is more than one sensible organizational method. If that's the case, just pick whichever makes the most sense to you. Just remember that the examiners always make PTs solvable puzzles that do fit together in some logical way.

Plugging the Legal Argument into the Format of Your Answer

You can also go back now and flesh out the outline you started drafting when you first read the Task Memo.

[Title]

> *Argument in Support of Plaintiff's Motion to Compel Discovery*

[Introduction]

To: Alice Nagle

From: Applicant

Re: *Piccolo v. Dobbs*, motion to compel discovery

Please find the argument you requested below.

Statement of Facts

Here fill in facts that you carefully select as pertinent to your argument. It may be helpful and quicker to draft this portion after you draft your argument section so you know which facts you relied on. Just be sure to save enough time for this!

Argument

You may want to start with a sentence that sets the stage: for example, "For the reasons stated below, Plaintiff seeks to compel the production of tapes and transcripts of interviews Alan Isaacs took of Julia Dobbs and Ted Wallace."

Persuasive Headings

Next come your three persuasive headings and the arguments supporting each. Here are examples:

I. Because they relate directly to the subject matter of the case at bar, the tapes and transcriptions are discoverable under FRCP 26(b)(1).
[Here insert your full argument, interweaving law and fact to persuasively prove the point in this heading.]

II. Because the tapes and transcriptions were prepared by an investigator before a case was filed and not in anticipation of litigation, they are not privileged as attorney work product.
[Here insert your full argument, interweaving law and fact to persuasively prove the point in this heading.]

III. Even if the tapes and transcriptions were considered attorney work product, they should be deemed discoverable here because the plaintiff has a substantial need for them, in that they are the only fairly contemporaneous statements made, and the plaintiff is unable without undue hardship to obtain the substantial equivalent elsewhere.
[Here insert your full argument, interweaving law and fact to persuasively prove the point in this heading.]

Conclusion

"For all the foregoing reasons, plaintiff prays that this court will compel production by the defendant of the requested tapes and transcripts."

Writing the Answer

Your next step would be to re-read the File, take notes, and write your answer. Armed with a logical organization, your job is to flesh out the facts to support each prong of your argument. Going back into the File at this point, the information you need about the circumstances surrounded the taking of information from Dobbs and Wallace should pop out because you know exactly what you are looking for.

On this re-read of the File, notice things you may not have seen initially. For example, you quickly and easily see why it matters that neither Wallace nor Dobbs testified at trial or talked to anyone else at the scene of the accident, and that they refused at the time to talk with our law firm. This bolsters the point that there is no other way for us to get the critical information provided in their statements. It also shows that what they said in those statements is unique because it was provided to Isaacs "fairly contemporaneously" with the accident.

You also readily see why it is critical to nail down what Isaacs thought about the case (because it involved a death, he "felt" that it was "virtually certain that a lawsuit would be filed"). But go back and review the facts, and you see that at that time Isaacs had not yet consulted with counsel and was not acting at the direction of counsel.

These and other facts may not have seemed important on the first read, but now, after studying the Library, they should jump out at you as critical. Do you now see why the SS-BROW system from Chapter 2 works so well? SS-BROW stands for:

- **S**tudy the Instructions
- **S**kim the File
- **B**rief the Library Authorities
- **R**e-Read Instructions, File, and Library as needed
- **O**utline
- **W**rite

You will find the Drafter's Point Sheet, which summarizes what needs to be included to pass this PT, in the Online Question and Answer Bank.

SPIN-OFF EXERCISES

As we have seen in previous chapters, spin-off exercises are your opportunity to leverage the time investment you made in reading this Library and File, and picture how you would write your answer if you had been asked to draft a different type of assignment using the same facts and law.

Representing the Opposing Party

First, before you even change the assignment, try thinking about the exact same assignment as if you were representing Dobbs rather than Piccolo. How would your argument change? Other than the result (your asking to keep the documents privileged and not compel turning them over to the plaintiff), what else would differ? How about the way you argue whether the statements were initially taken in anticipation of litigation? (Hint: This may be a much stronger argument for Dobbs than for Piccolo. Bar examiners often make you work on the PT by giving you the "weaker" side in a particular conflict.)

Offer of Settlement

Now imagine you are still representing Piccolo, but this time counsel for Dobbs sends our client a letter offering to settle. What might that letter look like? What would be a reason they might try to persuade Piccolo to settle, and what might we advise Piccolo on how to think through the offer?

Prepare for the Other Side's Deposition of Our Client, Piccolo

This assignment asks you to anticipate the questions the other side would ask our client. To think this through, you first want to look at the types of questions that our boss, the senior partner Alice Nagle, asked Dobbs, Wallace, and Isaacs in the initial depositions. Looking at documents in one PT File can help you prepare if you end up having to draft that sort of document in a later PT.

What do you think counsel for Dobbs may be looking for in deposing our client? Is there any information out there about what happened that day that might possibly place some sort of blame or some part of the fault for the accident on our client? If so, we must know that, and we must advise Piccolo on how to answer questions.

Letter to Piccolo

How would you draft a letter to Piccolo explaining what we are doing in the case: that we are going to court to compel the other side to grant our discovery request? Piccolo is a lay person. Will she even understand the word *discovery?* How will you explain it? Practice explaining this in easy-to-understand terms; the process will help you ensure that you understand the discovery process and tools, and will help you prepare for a PT where your task is to write to a lay person.

Cross-Examination of Wallace, Dobbs, and/or Isaacs

Assume that our motion was denied and we are now in trial trying to discredit these witnesses based only on the information we now have. Can you think of what you might want to ask on cross-examination to help prove our case and/or cast doubt on the credibility of these key witnesses? To draft your cross-examination plan, for each main topic of questioning, write the following:

- Your proposed question
- The witness's anticipated answer
- Opposing counsel's likely objection
- Your response to the objection
- The court's likely ruling

Note: You will find much more on cross-examination in the "Evidence" chapter of this book, Chapter 8.

PRACTICE, LAW SCHOOL, AND PTs: COMPARE AND CONTRAST

This PT provides a very realistic accident fact pattern and a plausible discovery dispute. The legal issues in the assigned task were narrow, specific to this motion to compel. Arguments about discovery are commonplace. When litigating smaller cases, it may not be cost-effective to engage in protracted discovery battles, and people may give in or settle such matters. Here, because it involved an insured motorist who killed someone, this may well be the type of case an insurance company would fight hard over.

This exam helps you to think about discovery rules—what is and what is not discoverable—from both parties' perspectives. It therefore provides great experiential training in a realistic setting.

KEY TAKEAWAYS

- This practice exam helped you master actual bar exam timing, as this PT was designed to be completed, start to finish, in 90 minutes. This is very representative of what you will see on your exam.
- This PT provided excellent exposure to a commonly tested PT task, a brief in support of a motion. You had to draft a persuasive though accurate statement of facts and a persuasive argument section (the main body of your brief) with "carefully crafted" persuasive headings. Practice writing such headings; they are the key to this sort of persuasive task.
- Like many PTs, this PT included organizational hints that, if you recognized them, were time-savers and helpful guidelines. Here, the hints were that the headings in the *Pacamor* case mirrored the same logical organization that you might well have used in setting up your answer.
- The Library here, with the hints noted earlier, reminds us not to just read and brief the cases and rush to begin writing. To succeed on PTs, sit back for a bit before taking fingers to keyboard and think carefully about how each case helps or hurts your client's position and how all the cases and statutes fit together. The examiners will want to pass you if you produce a well-organized, thoughtful answer that is responsive to the instructions.

8

EVIDENCE

OVERVIEW OF EVIDENCE

In law school evidence classes, we generally study rules and principles that govern how facts are proven in court. People may *think* that what someone tells them or what they read online is what really happened. In a lawsuit, though, unless someone's words or documents or other physical items are admitted in court as evidence (or were admitted into the record as part of pretrial discovery), these cannot really be considered "the facts." They are perhaps the alleged facts, or facts anticipated to emerge, but they are not the definitive story.

Even when "facts" are first accepted in court at the trial level, they are still only the evidence that one side presented. The other side will present its story with other evidence and/or by casting the first side's facts in a different light. Each side will poke holes in the other's evidence, by impeaching witnesses and pointing out contradictions or other reasons that evidence is unreliable.

What emerges from this litigation process is eventually "frozen" as the factual record. That record is generally the "story" an appellate court considers when making its ruling to uphold or overturn a lower court.

In law school, we study most subjects by reading appellate cases, so when an opinion discusses "the facts," those are what was proven at trial (in the lower court). Similarly, essay questions in law school and on bar exams typically include paragraphs (sometimes pages) of facts that are meant to be taken as true for purposes of the exam. You do not want to be in cross-examination mode when reading essay-question fact patterns. On bar exam essays, you never think "what if" a fact were not as it is stated. It *is* so stated, in the particular manner written, and you must use it as given. You may use the fact to support or refute the existence of an element of a cause of action or crime or defense theory, but you must not waste time wondering whether something in an essay fact pattern "really happened." Law essay exams are almost always based on hypotheticals and written to see how you *use* the facts as they are presented.

In sharp contrast, in performance tests, just as in investigating cases as a lawyer and establishing facts in court, doubt and credibility are major concerns. As you will see in the PT to be completed in this chapter, your job might well be to destroy the believability of someone's "story."

PTs such as this evidence-based PT may feel more like the "real world." It may be fun to see yourself more as an attorney than a law student. At the same time, practicing with this sort of PT is also helping you to review important rules of evidence that you will likely be tested on in your evidence class and on the bar exam.

In most law school evidence courses:

- You will study how evidence is presented (rules about which witnesses can testify about what and how) and how it is rebutted (how witnesses may be impeached).
- You learn about what is relevant and why sometimes even evidence that is logically relevant (directly on point!) can be excluded. (You all know one reason: where the prejudice outweighs the probative value.)
- You learn how some evidence can be kept out of court (for example, communications that are privileged).
- You typically spend a lot of time on the hearsay rule and exceptions to it.

For a list of the topics covered on the MBE regarding evidence, consult the most recent MBE Subject Matter Outlines published by the National Conference of Bar Examiners on their website at http://www.ncbex.org/exams/mbe/preparing/.

Several of the key points on the list of what you will likely cover in evidence class are integral parts of the PT you are about to complete, including, but not limited to, relevance issues, impeachment concerns, policy objectives achieved by restricting evidence of subsequent remedial measures, and more. *Dodson v. Canadian Equipment Company* is a great test. I hope you have fun with it!

SIMULATED EVIDENCE-BASED PERFORMANCE TEST

Complete the three-hour *Dodson v. Canadian Equipment Company* practice PT in the Online Question and Answer Bank at **http://ambar.org/barexamprep**.

TIME-CRUNCH TIPS

I suggest that you write this whole exam as one three-hour exam. However, if you prefer to complete this exam in two 90-minute sittings, that is fine too. This exam was designed to be broken into two 90-minute exams, each with one task. Here's what to read for the respective tasks: All of the File except the "Excerpt from Interrogatories to Canadian Equipment Company" is relevant to the first task. The law that relates to the first task includes most of the Federal Rules of Evidence (FRE) excerpts and the *Christmas v. Sanders* case. When you are ready to complete the second task, review the File (skipping the Format page on witness cross-examination, the report from the investigator John Ripka, the arrest record, and the "Excerpt of the Deposition of Denise"). For the second task, also be sure to read the "Excerpt from Interrogatories to Canadian Equipment Company." The law that relates to the second task is FRE Rule 407, the Columbia Products Liability Act (CPLA), and the *Moe*, *Walker*, and *Stewart* cases.

INSIDE THIS TEST: TIPS AND STRATEGIES

Welcome to evidence in action!

The General Instructions are fairly boilerplate in this exam. They tell you the basics about how much time you have, that cases are not real, that you may use short cites, and so on. The only information in the General Instructions that is unique to this problem is in the second paragraph, which tells you that you are set in the fictitious 15th Federal Circuit.

> **Note:** When you get to the Task Memo, you see that this exam involves a negligence and product liability case, and thus is not a "federal question"; but from the complaint you see that you are in federal district court under diversity jurisdiction.

Also, at the end of the Instructions, you see that each of the two tasks is weighted equally.

The Task Memo is never boilerplate, and that is where we start getting all the information that will really help us on this PT. Let's look at how the Task Memo starts: "I need your help preparing for trial." From this we know that the role-play takes place before the trial. We learn that we represent the plaintiff.

Did you notice who is giving you the assignment? Elizabeth Duke. Who is that? Well, the Task Memo is written on firm letterhead, and the firm is called "Freeman, Duke, and Woolridge," so in all likelihood the person giving us the assignment is the second named partner in your law firm, Ms. Duke.

Next in the Task Memo, we learn a little about the case. Our client is suing a company, Canadian Equipment Company (CEC), the manufacturer of her car. We are claiming that our client was seriously injured (she's a paraplegic as a result of the accident) when the car's glass sunroof shattered.

We also learn that we are in a contributory negligence jurisdiction. The Task Memo tells us, but we should also understand from our general knowledge of tort law, that means that if our client should be found to have been in any way negligent herself, her negligence claim against CEC will be barred. She is bringing two claims, though. The senior partner tells us that this contributory negligence issue makes the second claim, the strict liability claim under products liability, "all the more important." This makes sense because, as you know, claims based on strict liability would not be barred even if the plaintiff were at fault.

Now comes another interesting part, the real-world stuff. Our client's sister, Denise Johnston, was a passenger in the car at the time of the accident. The sister is a key witness whose testimony is essential to our negligence action—but our client and her sister are not talking. Ironically, they were meeting to try to reconcile on the day of the accident. Unfortunately, in part because of the accident, they are now more distant than ever. In fact, we are told that Denise is likely to sue Esther (our client).

Are you feeling a little sorry for Esther right now? She was terribly hurt, she is embroiled in litigation with the car manufacturer, and her sister Denise is likely going to sue her! It gets worse. Not only might the sister (Denise) sue our client, but your job, your first task, is to draft a cross-examination plan that will "destroy" Denise's credibility. (Even if they are estranged, it may still be very hard for Esther to be responsible for causing any further pain to her sister.)

The second assignment is a legal memo discussing whether federal or state law will apply on the question of introducing evidence of subsequent remedial measures. This is a more straightforward assignment, likely similar to memos you completed in your legal research and writing course. Most students find the law a bit complicated in the second assignment, but they find the task very clear. By contrast, many students find the law easier in the cross-examination plan, but find the format and organization of that task to be challenging.

The next page is a classic Format page. This document tells you exactly how the examiners want you to set up this cross-examination plan.

Note: If you have prepared for cross-examination in a trial advocacy course or working in a law firm, and you set up your plan differently, forget what you did before. Set up this assignment exactly the way this Format Memo tells you to. As in every PT, the Format Memo (if they give you one) and the Task Memo are the most important documents. You are being tested in large part on following directions.

After you understand the assignments, then skim the File. Read quickly just to get the main points. If you do not clearly see the significance of a document, come back to it after reading the relevant Library authorities and it will make more sense.

The next page is the accident report. There is a diagram and narrative. The narrative is simple, just a paragraph, but you likely saw that it contains a significant internal contradiction. It says at first, "Passenger, Denise Johnston, stated that she wasn't sure what had happened." She also said that her sister was driving under the speed limit. Then, in the last line, it says that an officer "spoke to Ms. Johnston after she was admitted to the hospital" and this time she said that "her sister hit the sunroof because she wasn't wearing a seatbelt."

You should ask yourself (and later on cross-examination ask Denise!), why at first she said it could have been a deer that shattered the sunroof *or* her sister's head, but then a short while later she said definitively it was her sister because she wore no seatbelt.

Now, I know I said to "skim" the File the first time you go through it, but what I am referring to in the accident report was just one paragraph. It was easy to read, and if the contradictory stories popped out at you on the first skim, great. Take note. If at first you did not see this conflicting information, you would have seen it the next time you went back through to re-read the File.

The next document is the complaint. You should glance at documents like this for two reasons:

1. It is part of this PT, of course, and it tells you what claims we (the plaintiff) are asserting. Notice, as to Claim 1, that we say the car impacting the guard rail caused the sunroof to shatter. We also say the plaintiff was wearing a seatbelt.

2. Review the complaint with an eye toward how to draft such a document if you were asked to do so on another PT. Just look at the components: (a) jurisdiction, (b) a short, plain, factual statement that shows which facts give rise to each of the claims (here there are two claims: negligence and products liability), and lastly, (c) a prayer for relief and signature. That's it. You could draft something like that if your assignment were to draft a complaint!

The next document is the answer. This is the defense reply to our complaint. No surprise: they deny everything, and assert that our client was not wearing a seatbelt. (You now know what some of the "fight" on which this lawsuit is centered is going to be about.)

The next document is an investigation report. This is a list of all of Denise Johnston's arrests. Note that there is also an arrest report. Denise, remember, is the sister of the plaintiff, Esther Dodson. Denise was a passenger in the car at the time of the accident, and now, allegedly, wants to sue her sister (our client). This document relates to the first task, the cross-examination plan. The minute you saw this report, you likely suspected that we would be attempting to impeach Denise's credibility with some of these past crimes. If you did not think about that yet, you would have immediately thought of it when you read the *Christmas* case in the Library.

Lists on PTs, whether they are fact-based or law-based lists, can often provide helpful organizational and writing hints. Here, this list of Denise's arrest record is a gift. Students completing this exam sometimes make the mistake of combining the items listed (for example, putting all the fraud charges together). By doing that, though, students may be losing points. Denise was prosecuted separately for each charge, at different times and under different circumstances, and each may form the basis of impeachment. (Recall from your study of evidence different ways to impeach someone, including felony convictions, convictions for felonies or misdemeanors that involve dishonesty, prior inconsistent statements, and more.)

The next document is an excerpt of a transcript of a deposition taken of Denise Johnston. We will want to look at this carefully to see if she contradicts herself at all, and any other information that might be valuable to us in preparing our cross-examination of her. Just reading deposition transcripts in the File will help you get in "the zone" and ready to think in a question-and-answer format, which is how you will have to draft your cross-examination plan.

The last document is excerpts from interrogatories (questions and answers) that we sent to the defendant. This relates to the second assignment, the memo. *It is absolutely critical*—but you would not necessarily see or understand why this is so important on the first skim, before you have read the Library. After you read the cases, this piece should have fallen right into place.

In these responses, the defendant is saying that the company changed the type of glass it used in sunroofs from the tempered glass that shattered in the accident to laminated glass; however, it is also saying that it is not feasible to use laminated glass for sunroofs. As you probably know already, and as you will read in the Library, evidence of subsequent remedial measures (such as changing the type of glass used in the sunroofs) is generally not admissible as evidence of negligence, but it may be used for other reasons, such as to impeach a party who denies the feasibility of the subsequent measure. The answer for Interrogatory No. 10 is about as close to a "smoking gun" as you will find in a PT-type assignment, and it provides very useful information to incorporate into your answer to the second task.

Library

As noted, this PT divides neatly into two separate 90-minute exams. In the Library, the documents separate out as follows: Most of the FRE provisions and the *Christmas* case relate to Task A. FRE Rule 407, the Columbia Products Liability Act (CPLA), and *Moe, Walker,* and *Stewart* all apply to Task B. You can likely tell, just from glancing at that allocation of authorities, that Task A is a bit more fact-heavy and Task B a bit more law-heavy.

Note: You are likely (or will be by the time of the bar exam) familiar with most or all of the FRE sections. (These will be tested on the MBE portion and on many bar exam essay portions as well.) For that reason, I would treat the FRE excerpts here as a "reference library," if I need it. I would start by skimming the titles of each section, and later go in and read the provisions in detail as needed. (As usual, the cases had to be studied and briefed as if new to you.)

If you take a step back and consider what you will be using these provisions for in Task A, discrediting Denise, you might have noticed that the titles of each section provide a sort of roadmap of the topics you will likely question her on: past crimes, character evidence, prior statements. (Not all PTs contain such hints, but where they do you must be alert and notice them. If you did not, go back and scan the rule headings in the FRE excerpts.) Some of the FRE sections may also provide reasons why the defense will object; for example, where our questions lead to evidence that is more prejudicial than probative. The *Christmas* case also provides further guidance on what can and cannot be used to impeach.

In Task B we will compare and contrast state law and federal law (here the CPLA with FRE 407), and then use the cases to determine which law our court will likely apply in this sort of diversity action. You may already be thinking state substantive law and federal procedural rules, but not so fast: Is the rule about subsequent remedial measures substantive or procedural? Reading through the Library, you see that there is not necessarily a clear answer. Should that bother you here? No, because your task is to write a memo to your senior partner about the issues. This is an in-house, analytical document, and you might well end up concluding that the law is not 100% in our client's favor. That is fine. Recall what the senior partner wrote in the Task Memo: "Write an objective memorandum for me discussing which of the statutes will be applied, the theories supporting admission of this information, and the likelihood that each theory would be successful." This necessarily means that you will objectively set forth the situation, explaining that which tends to favor our client and that which does not. Your conclusion may well be one that begins with the word "Likely."

The issue again is the policy exclusion regarding evidence of subsequent remedial measures. You all learned about this in evidence. It is the law's way of saying that we don't want the fact that people fix problems after accidents to be held against them and lead to conclusions about their liability. Let's say I am a store owner. You fall on my carpet. Assume I am certain that you fell because of your own dizziness (you were drunk at the time). However, I decide to go ahead and replace the carpet after your accident, thinking that it does have some small rips in it that someone might get hurt on eventually, even though I know those rips are not what caused your injury. If I replace the carpet and a jury hears about it, jurors might jump to the conclusion that my making the repairs means I must have been at fault. Knowing that my good deed could be used against me would discourage me from taking precautions to keep my premises safe for others. Because we don't want people to be "chilled" in taking positive actions to make the world a safer place, we limit use of such action in evidence.

You will see by studying the sample answers in the Online Question and Answer Bank what you should have pulled out of each of the cases, what would be a thorough cross-examination plan on the first task, and what would constitute enough analysis to be a passing answer on the second task.

PUTTING IT ALL TOGETHER

For the first memo, the cross-examination plan, the key is really to follow the sample in the Format Memo. It is easy to get hung up and feel the need to write long Q&A scenes as if in a movie, but that is not what the example indicated. The witness's answers need not be lengthy; in fact, that is not really very important. (In the sample, the answers are just "Yes.") It's the questions that are important: they contain the precise information we are trying to elicit, and they suggest what we want jurors to conclude. In cross-examination, we ask leading questions that contain the desired answers. All we are doing is looking for confirmation, which essentially then turns our questions into facts (unless the judge sustains an objection to our question, or strikes the witness's response).

Additionally, the key here was to separate issues. Do not ask a question that combines queries about multiple inconsistent statements and/or multiple arrests. Just the way the sample illustrates, let each Q&A set focus on one circumstance to impeach Denise, then move on to the next, and the next.

For the second memo, the law may have seemed confusing and could have thrown you. Remember, the purpose of the memo was to help your boss understand the law in the context of our case. So, what was the difference between the two laws? Which law benefits our client, and why? How do we convince the court to use the "better" law? And, if the court decides not to use that better law, how might we prevail anyway?

The Task Memo asked which statute will be applied, the theories supporting admission of the information, and the likelihood of success of each theory. Our problem is that the laws conflict. Your memo should explain the differences, noting that under state law we cannot use this evidence unless feasibility is brought up first by the other side and we are impeaching. However, the federal statute says we may assert this evidence affirmatively, in our own case, to show feasibility. Study the sample answers in the Online Question and Answer Bank for a sense of how each task should have been handled.

SPIN-OFF EXERCISES

Spin-off exercises provide a way to gain exposure to drafting different types of documents using the same facts and law as on the PT you just completed. Spend a few minutes, now that you have completed *Dodson*, to think of other tasks you might have been given and how you would have handled them. Here are a few suggestions.

Mediation between Esther and Denise

Right now, the litigation is between Esther and CEC, and Denise will likely be testifying for CEC. It appears likely that Denise may also end up bringing her own lawsuit against Esther. If so, Esther may want to propose mediation. Try drafting a dialogue of the various stages of a mediation between Esther and Denise. What might the mediator say to both sisters together? What might the mediator say in private caucus with each? What sorts of win-win agreements might be possible to help the two resolve their difficulties without litigation?

Typical stages of a mediation[1]:

Introductory—During this part of the process, the mediator helps the parties create a safe environment in which to discuss difficult topics. Depending on the parties' experience with mediation, the mediator may provide a process overview: the role of the mediator, what will happen in various mediation sessions, and confidentiality. During this phase, parties may agree to ground rules for the conduct of the mediation (e.g., ensuring that only one person speaks at a time) and a general timetable for the process. This phase includes a joint session among parties, during which opposing sides have an opportunity to state their views and desired outcomes.

Problem-Solving Stage—During this stage, parties principally focus on issues, interests, options for resolution, and criteria for evaluating those options. Parties may meet separately with the mediator to share confidences and fully consider options in private.

Closure—During this phase, parties decide whether and on what terms to resolve the dispute. The mediator may help them draft a document that reflects any commitments they wish to make. As needed, the agreement then may have to be passed to others for approval. If parties do not reach agreement, the mediator makes sure they understand why and what next steps are available to them.

Letter to Esther

Let's say that in addition to the cross-examination plan of Denise, the senior partner asked you to draft a letter to Esther explaining to her what we need to accomplish in this cross-examination and why. You might start by explaining the parts of a trial and

---

[1] Slightly adapted from U.S. Department of Health and Human Services, "Mediation," available at http://www.hhs.gov/dab/divisions/adr/mediation/process.html.

what cross-examination is, but you will want to go on to prepare Esther that this may be hard. Her own sister is going to be discredited (and, if we do our job well, her sister will look very bad when we are finished). What can you say to Esther to prepare her?

Settlement Offer to the Defendant, CEC

Why might CEC be inclined to settle? Are some of their witnesses less than credible? Might they benefit from some sort of confidential or sealed agreement? What sorts of things did their expert, Dr. Leyhe, say that might make for terrible publicity if they were to emerge at trial? Also, what if CEC loses? How much money might they have to pay to someone as severely injured as Esther? Might they cut their losses and give her sufficient damages right now to make her as whole as possible, and not drag her through an extensive and difficult trial? Try drafting an offer of settlement to present to counsel for CEC.

PRACTICE, LAW SCHOOL, AND PTs: COMPARE AND CONTRAST

This PT was evidence-based, but the underlying claim was grounded in tort. (One cause of action was based on alleged negligence, the other on strict liability in tort.) This is a reminder that while we tend to study evidence as a discrete subject, it is all about the information that comes in to prove or disprove elements of claims in other substantive areas: here torts. In other words, in this PT, as in practice, you were simultaneously "in" both the world of evidence and the world of torts. Further crossing subjects, the second task was more a civil procedure question as to which law governs, state or federal. Accordingly, some see this PT as an evidence/civil procedure cross-over.

Whereas certain bar exam essays test multiple subjects, law school courses "silo" learning into discrete buckets: You will not sit down to your evidence final in law school and see a constitutional law question. In real life, though, clients often come to you for help in one area and it quickly becomes apparent that their problems cross into numerous other areas. (Someone may come to you for a divorce and child custody matter. One or the other spouse may then have to file for bankruptcy. There may be tax consequences. Real property may be sold. Depending on how complicated things get, you may have to consult with another attorney or refer parts of the case to someone else to handle. That is reality.)

This PT also differed from a typical evidence essay in that here you were actually framing the question-and-answer courtroom dialogue. You might have felt more like a screenwriter than a law student. This is litigation prep in action. Nevertheless, even within this "realistic" drafting, the exam was still about the testing more than reality in this respect. In real life, you never want to ask a question on cross-examination that you don't know the answer to. Here, for exam purposes, it was fine to draft some questions to which you were not certain how the witness would respond. It was also fine to draft questions that you knew would be objected to (even when those objections would likely be sustained), because your purpose was to show the grader that you understood all the law and facts in the Library and File. It would have been a much more difficult assignment had you been asked only to think of questions that you believed would not be objected to.

So, in some ways, the *Dodson* PT was realistic and gave you a snapshot of the kind of lawyering you might do in practice. In other ways, it was still an exam, testing you on what you read and how to apply the law to the facts. I hope you enjoyed this work, zealously advocating on behalf of your client, and that at least for a moment you saw evidence law come to life!

KEY TAKEAWAYS

- This practice exam exposed you to a task that required a very precise format: the cross-examination plan. Not only did you have to write detailed information, but the examiners also wanted it set out in the exact way they instructed. (As is often the case on PTs, *Dodson* tested your ability and willingness to follow instructions, as well as your lawyering skills.)
- This PT was in the evidence chapter, and a great many of the issues (especially with regard to the cross-examination) were evidentiary concerns, but the underlying case was a torts cause of action; some of what was tested in the second memo (about which law applies) you may well have studied in a civil procedure course. This illustrates how PTs "cross over" from one subject to the next, rather than putting subjects in airtight boxes or silos as law school tends to do.
- This PT provided a good example of a "reference Library," in terms of the provisions that the examiners noted were from the Federal Rules of Evidence. The sections were there for your reference if you needed to review them, but you probably did not need to study each FRE section. Because evidence rules are typically something you need to know for the bar exam, these provisions would have seemed familiar by the time of the actual bar exam. The Columbia rule (the Columbia Product Liability Act), and the cases, were of course new to you (as are all cases in PT Libraries, no matter how familiar they may look!).
- This exam was divided into two 90-minute PTs, so it provided great practice in both skills and timing.

9

CONSTITUTIONAL LAW

OVERVIEW OF CONSTITUTIONAL LAW

Many law school constitutional law classes focus on due process, equal protection, and the First Amendment: freedom of speech, religion, the press, and association. (There is so much to study with the First Amendment alone that it is often broken out as a separate semester course.) On bar exam questions, you typically must be fluent in these rules and principles and also many others, including (but not limited to) standing, ripeness, and mootness; legislative powers (interstate commerce, taxing and spending, war powers and other powers relating to foreign affairs); federal preemption; eminent domain; and more. For a list of the topics covered on the MBE in constitutional law, consult the most recent MBE Subject Matter Outlines published by the National Conference of Bar Examiners on their website at ncbex.org/exams/mbe/preparing.

SIMULATED CONSTITUTIONAL LAW–BASED PERFORMANCE TEST

This multistate performance test (MPT) was designed to be completed in 90 minutes. If you want a review of how to approach PTs generally, return to Chapter 2 before tackling this question. Otherwise, please take 90 minutes, go to the Online Question and Answer Bank at **http://ambar.org/barexamprep**, download the question for *In re: Gardenton,* and draft your answer. Then return and read the rest of this chapter to see how you did and to learn from the practice test experience.

TIME-CRUNCH TIPS

This is a 90-minute exam. I would strongly urge you to find a full hour and a half and complete this exam under timed conditions. If you do not have the time at this sitting, take 45 minutes and read all the facts and law, and just outline the memorandum. Come back another time when you have an additional 45 minutes and complete the writing assignment.

INSIDE THIS TEST: TIPS AND STRATEGIES

Congratulations on finishing *Gardenton*! (Again, if you have not completed this exam, please download it from the Online Question and Answer Bank and do so now.) This is a great question. It is different from assignments you have seen before if you have been working through the chapters in this book in order. (Each chapter stands alone, so there is no need to work them in order, but for those who are doing so *Gardenton* should provide a nice change.)

This practice PT was shorter than some of the PTs in other chapters in this book. (*Gardenton* was designed to be completed in 90 minutes, so naturally your legal and factual universes were smaller than in the three-hour PTs.) The *Gardenton* Instructions and File consisted of only three documents: the Task Memo, the transcript of the meeting with Kantor, and the proposed code in question. Your Library had small sections of the U.S. Constitution, the Franklin State Constitution, and the Franklin Education Act (FEA), along with three short cases.

MPT NOTE TAKING

Unlike the three-hour PTs that we have seen in earlier chapters, which include a separate table of contents for the File and Library, this MPT has one table of contents for both. As suggested in Chapter 2, you can use the table of contents as your central note-taking page. You may *not* tear out pages from the MPT, but you may paper-clip this page so it is easy to return to it to find your notes. Especially if you are rushing to finish, it is convenient to have all your notes in one place. This is much more efficient than searching through notes you wrote on every page of the File and Library to find points you want to make. You can still "book brief" within the cases, but also note the page numbers where you wrote key points on your table of contents page.

Let's say there is language from the *Hazelwood* case that you want to quote. Underline it and put a double asterisk next to that language in the case itself. Then also place a double asterisk on the table of contents page next to the *Hazelwood* entry and jot down something like "1st A Rts of students not same as Con'l Rts @ p. 6." This note reminds you to return to page 6 to reference the exact language you underlined. And, this "book-briefing" saves you the time that it would otherwise take to write more about the case in your notes.

Try this approach. See if it helps you to make your table of contents your one-page "go-to" resource guide, to organize what you will need to write your full answer.

The key to success on this PT (as on all PTs!) is to carefully read the Task Memo and clearly understand your assignment. Here the Task Memo was from Frank Eisner. I always suggest looking at the letterhead on File documents. Here, you notice that "Eisner" is the second named partner on the firm letterhead. From this you know that the person giving you this assignment appears to be one of the senior partners in a private law firm; you are an associate at this firm. Remember, as on every PT, your name as you write it in your answer is "Applicant." (Do not ever write your real name or any identifying information other than your exam number or whatever else the examiners direct you to write.)

This Task Memo is typical. The first paragraph provides a summary of who the client is, what that client's immediate problem is, and what the client's goals are. You want to read this Task Memo slowly and carefully.

I urge you to get in the habit of reading the Task Memo aloud but under your breath. Touch each word as you read. This reading with your eyes, ears, and voice will keep you focused and attentive to detail. (This reading strategy, detailed in Chapter 6 of this book and in *Pass the Bar Exam*,[1] is especially important on bar exams where you must complete a PT in the afternoon and are tired from the morning portion of the exam.)

Re-read the Task Memo after you skim the File. Read the Task Memo again after you study the Library, before you draft your answer. Re-reading the Task Memo a few times gives further insight into the assignment. You process the information differently as you get more "into" the problem. You notice important points that may not have seemed critical at first read. Re-reading also ensures that you follow directions—the most important key to passing the PT.

IT IS EASY TO FORGET THE DIRECTIONS!

PTs contain a lot of information, and much is asked of you in a short amount of time. It is easier than you would think to forget all or part of your instructions by the time you start writing, especially if you only read the Task Memo once. A stark reminder comes every time I teach PTs where the task is to draft a closing argument. Inevitably, at least one student will write the argument for the other side. Why? The examiners often place applicants on what appears to be the unenviable side. The more you read, the more you think of arguments for the other side, and the easier it becomes for those who did not review the instructions to forget whom they represent. On one PT, applicants were to represent

---

[1] Sara J. Berman, *Pass the Bar Exam: A Practical Guide to Achieving Academic & Professional Goals* (American Bar Association, 2014).

the party that seems to have done exactly what it is being accused of: exerting undue influence over an old lady to change her will in their favor before she died. Time after time, students get so persuaded by the law and facts that there was undue influence that they end up arguing for the wrong side, all because they failed to go back and carefully re-read the instructions. Another mistake in that same problem is that students forget that the judge already concluded, early in the case, that the testator had capacity and the argument now centers on only one issue: undue influence. They end up needlessly arguing capacity issues, a colossal waste of time. Moral of the story: Re-read the Task Memo several times as you complete each PT.

What exactly do we learn from the *Gardenton* Task Memo? Frank Eisner, your boss, consulted with Dr. Edwina Kantor, who is the president of the Gardenton Board of Education. You know, again from looking at the letterhead, that your firm is situated in the city of Gardenton in the State of Franklin. Kantor was clearly consulting Eisner and your firm not as an individual but in her capacity as Board president. The Board wants to adopt a communications code for the local public high school. (You likely underlined the word *public*, because you know that rules may differ for public and private schools.)

You also learn the Board's main goal: to get a code adopted that is as restrictive as possible so that it helps the school prevent the publication of offensive material. Always pay attention to any information (in the Task Memo or other File document) that details or hints at the client's goals and needs. Such language helps you to effectively perform the problem-solving skill that is one of the main skills tested on the PT. (The skills tested on PT exams are discussed extensively in Chapter 2.) Picking up on language in the Task Memo and/or File about your client's needs also shows the graders that you are detail oriented, a critical skill for successful lawyering.

It appears that the Board must present a proposed communications code for public comment, and Kantor wants advice for herself and the other Board members for preparing to face public questioning. The Memo describes the heated emotions on both sides of this issue: the free speech advocates, irate about censorship, on the one side; and the parents and civic groups on the other side, who are equally outraged about what they see as profanity and sexually charged material coming from the school.

The last paragraph of the Task Memo gives you specifics on what you are to draft. Note that you are writing to your senior partner. We have talked in the past about using simplified plain English when writing to non lawyers and more sophisticated legal terminology when writing to lawyers. In this *Gardenton* task, you are role-playing a lawyer writing to another lawyer. Thus, you may freely cite cases and use legal terms that in a client document you would want to define, simplify, or avoid.

Note also that this is an in-house document, for this senior partner (your supervisor) to use in advising the Board of Education. The Task Memo uses the term "evaluate," so you know that this is an analytical memorandum wherein you are looking at this situation as a neutral. You are anticipating what language will help achieve the Board's goals, where those goals are achievable. You will also note where what they seek to accomplish may not be permissible. In other words, you do not want to treat this as if it were a brief and you were arguing persuasively to urge that every provision of the proposed code be adopted as written. Rather, you are studying each provision to see whether it passes constitutional muster or not, and why, and to propose edits where they would be necessary or helpful.

The Task Memo specifies that you are to evaluate the preamble and each provision of the proposed code. The word *each* is repeated several times. Any time bar examiners repeat something, pay attention. Here this repetition suggests a provision-by-provision organization for your analysis. Caution: In rushing to write, students sometimes start with Provision 1, forgetting to analyze the preamble, and thereby lose precious points.

The Memo goes on to explicitly spell out your tasks. You can highlight or underline this part of the Memo or write a note to yourself on scratch paper or as a rough outline in the document that will ultimately become your answer. (Be sure to delete any notes to yourself before uploading your answer.)

For example, after reading this Task Memo, I might write something like the following to myself:

> *In my answer, I must:*
> - Identify *the* legal issues *that can give rise to* constitutional challenges *of each of the provisions* and *analyze whether each such provision is likely to be found legally permissible.*
> - Make suggestions *to delete, modify, or add language as needed to help our client (the Board) achieve its goal (of presenting the most restrictive code permissible).*
> - Conclude as to whether each provision is or is not permissible.
> - *Also, for each conclusion about permissibility and for each editing suggestion,* explain and support my reasoning with specific references to the facts and law. *In other words, write WHY I came to particular conclusions or made specific editing suggestions.*

What I wrote for myself is not the exact verbatim words of the directions, but rather a way of breaking those directions down and putting them into words that help you tell yourself exactly what to do. (See examples following for how I use this framework to outline my answer.)

You will get points *both* for saying which provisions are permissible even without revisions, and for saying which must be rewritten, so long as in each instance you say why. Your job here is not just to jump to those provisions that may be impermissible, but to critically review each and every provision.

It helps to read the Instructions a few times over and really think carefully about who you represent and why and what your job is. Here, once you do that, you may well begin to develop an organizing structure for your answer, even before you read the rest of the File and Library. You may have even noted something like the following and put it immediately into a blank document on your computer.

FIRST ROUGH DRAFT OUTLINE

Header

To: Frank Eisner

From: Applicant

Re: Proposed Communications Code:

Date: _____ [If you write a date, use the date you are taking the exam.]

Introduction: [Even though the Task Memo did not explicitly direct you to draft an introduction, short introductions are important. Introductions tell the grader to expect to find what was requested; in other words, introductions declare that you followed the directions. They do not have to be long, and in fact long introductions waste time and sometimes make it look like you did not understand the actual assignment. Here, one sentence would be sufficient]:

"Here below is the analysis of the proposed code that you requested. Please contact me if you have any follow-up questions."

[Legal Issues Giving Rise to Constitutional Challenges]—optional

Most students completing this test identify the legal issues for each provision while analyzing the permissibility of the provision. Others interpret the directions as first requesting a short few paragraphs noting some of the major legal concerns; for example, that the FEA grants more significant rights to students than does the Constitution, and that the level of scrutiny of particular restrictions on communication will be determined in part by whether the publication in question is seen as a public forum or a limited public forum.

If you included this sort of preliminary legal analysis before your provision-by-provision analysis of the code, write your introduction as follows:

"Here below is a brief exploration of the legal issues that may give rise to constitutional challenges in this matter, followed by the provision-by-provision analysis of the proposed Code that you requested. Please contact me if you have any follow-up questions."

[Again, this tells the graders that you followed directions.]

Analysis of Proposed Code

Preamble:

    a) Legal issues raised? Permissible? Why/why not?

    b) Suggested edits and reasons for edits?

Provision 1:

    a) Legal issues raised? Permissible? Why/why not?

    b) Suggested edits and reasons for edits?

Provision 2:

    a) Legal issues raised? Permissible? Why/why not?

    b) Suggested edits and reasons for edits?

[And so on with each remaining provision.]

Conclusion [again, at most one or two sentences.]

Without even reading the Code or the rest of the law and facts, just from reading the directions, you could have come up with this sort of a logical (albeit rough-draft) structure for your answer. You could type it right into your answer document, as a sort of skeleton outline of what you will edit into your final answer.

After you read the Code (on page 4 of the File), you will be able to build on that skeletal structure, fleshing out descriptive headings with the title (subject) of each provision. Rather than referring to the first provision simply as "Provision 1," it will be clearer for graders if your heading reads: "Provision 1: Professional Standards of English and Journalism." (See the updated outline later in this section.)

Also, to help the grader easily follow your analysis, keep your numbering consistent with the Code's provisions. Some students mark the Preamble as heading 1, which requires that the analysis of provision 1 be labeled as heading 2. That can confuse graders. Instead, give your discussion of the Preamble a heading that uses the word "Preamble" so that the discussion under your first heading addresses the first code provision, the discussion under your second heading addresses the second code provision, and so on.

ORGANIZING EARLY WITH YOUR OUTLINE AS A DRAFT ANSWER

For many people, it helps to get an organizational structure started and typed into your exam-answer file document as soon as possible into your reading of each PT. That way your "notes" or outline form the first draft of your final answer. It's not always as easy as on this exam to see a logical structure. Sometimes you really have to sit and think about how the Library authorities fit together and how that structure merges with the task you have been given to settle on a logical format for answering the assignment. Nearly always, though, your organizational structure (how to set up your answer) comes from some combination of the Task Memo, Format Pages if there are any, and the Library authorities.

File Review

After the Task Memo, all the File contains is a transcript and the draft Code. Skim the transcript of the discussion with Dr. Kantor. You won't understand the legal significance of all the facts until you have read the Library, so do not waste time with a detailed reading at this stage. Here are a few things you may have seen in the Transcript, even during a skim: points that certainly would have popped out as significant when you re-read after studying the Library:

- Kantor first discusses what she calls "degenerating quality" of the subject matter and language in student publications. Then there's mention of problems with student theater.
- The next question and answer, about how wide the audience is for the paper and plays, is a perfect example of something that won't make a lot of sense until after you have read the Library. *Lopez*, the second case in the Library, explains the forum analysis, wherein public property may be divided into public, non-public, and limited public forums. The *Lopez* case equates a public forum with a "traditional soapbox" where "prior restraints are rarely permissible." A nonpublic forum such as an administrative informational bulletin is one where the school would have "full power to regulate access and content." Somewhere in the middle, is a limited forum, where "school officials must demonstrate that the particular regulation of student expression advances a compelling state interest."

After reading *Lopez*, when re-reading the File, Kantor's answers to the questions about the circulation of the student newspaper, and who attends the school theater productions, pop out. You will re-read them, after reading *Lopez*, and you will readily assess as to what sort of forums these are and how that affects what sort of expression must be allowed.

You will likely have concluded that the school newspaper is a limited public forum, as are the small school plays, but you may have seen the regular annual live theatrical productions as public forums and as such subject to greater scrutiny. This is open to interpretation. You will get points not so much for concluding one way or the other as for your analysis, so long as you explain your reasoning, support it, and follow it through to its logical conclusion.

- At the bottom of page 2, Kantor mentions several alleged problems: reporting without adequate fact checking, use of profanity, potentially defamatory statements, and stories that are not "in good taste." Kantor also talks about the "sexually charged" and "morally questionable" subject matter of theater being objectionable. Without even getting to the Library, your lawyer instincts may rise up inside you to a point where you think to yourself: "*Well, I can see how defamation might be prohibited, but it sure sounds wishy-washy to try to stop something that is 'not in good taste.'*"

If you do not have that sort of gut reaction, that is fine; the cases spell out what may and may not be prohibited. You will study them, then come back to this transcript (and of course to the proposed Code itself, which is what you need to analyze), and the relevant facts will then become clear. The point is that, for many students, it can be very reassuring to realize that you are already "thinking like a lawyer," when your eyebrows raise at certain suspect facts.

THINK LIKE A LAWYER AND
KEEP A COOL HEAD

Have you ever found yourself in a social conversation listening to someone say something abstract and think, "Void for vagueness." That's when you know law school has sunk in! It's a good thing to think like a lawyer; it's also good on PTs and in law practice, to remain calm. As you read through this PT, you may have realized that you do not want to get swept up in the community debate aspect of this situation. That is not your job. Your tasks are very clearly spelled out: analyze the constitutionality of the preamble and each provision of the proposed code. Keep your focus. (Imagining yourself thrust into the middle of a community debate may help you get "into" the role-play aspects of the PT, which is fine. It is great if you can enjoy these exams! Just do not allow your emotions or biases to sidetrack you from your task.)

PTs always include interesting detours. I like to say that on PTs you must "take the highways, not the side streets." You have to finish in 90 minutes; you cannot afford to lose sight of the narrow focus of your assignment. The time flies. If you pursue "side streets" or interesting tangents, you will not complete the main parts of what is specifically asked of you.

Page 3 of the File talks more about the politics of the situation: that the proposed Code was supposed to have been secret but that it got out and everyone is preparing for battle. This is interesting, and tells you why Kantor needs you to analyze the Code, but it doesn't really relate to producing your exam answer. Remember, there are always tangents on performance tests. They are testing you on your ability to sort relevant from irrelevant information, so there will always be some facts that do not help answer the specific questions you are asked to write about.

Nevertheless, these background facts again do help you immerse yourself in the role-play. They help you see why this matter is so important to Kantor, and so urgent. You might expect that everyone on both sides of this issue will be scrutinizing the Code, so in your analysis, you must help Kantor and the Board see exactly what is and is not permissible and why.

- One of the last points Kantor makes is to reiterate the Board's goals: "The main thing is that we be able to censor unacceptable language and morally questionable subject matter that runs counter to our educational goals, especially things that open us up to suits for libel and slander and invasion of privacy."

The word "censor" might well have hit you as a flag reminding you that, in the big picture, this is a case about prior restraints of free speech, something that even in the case of high-school-age children is not to be done lightly or without adequate justification. Nonetheless, you know that your mission, as you proceed, is to consider just how much of this "unacceptable language and morally questionable subject matter" can be curtailed. Off to the Library to find out!

MOTIVATIONAL NOTE

Try to have fun with these PTs as you work through them. You control the exam; the exam does not control you. It's open book; it's all there for you. You can read and re-read as many times as you need to. The examiners take pains in drafting these PTs to ensure that they are doable, meaning finishable, within the time limits. Assume that you will eventually "get it," and you are more likely to relax and complete your PTs skillfully. Panic, and you are more likely to be blocked and not see what is clear and relevant. Above all, remember that all you have to do is produce a passing answer. You are not writing an amicus brief for the Supreme Court!

One last document in the File, though, before you get to the Library, is the Code itself. This is the document you will work from when you get to writing, as your job is to analyze and suggest edits for the preamble and each provision of this proposed Code. You will not know whether each provision is permissible until you have read the Library, so scan them quickly now, study the Library authorities, and then return to this Code. However, after even a quick skim through the Code, you can update your outline as follows:

UPDATED DRAFT OUTLINE

To: Frank Eisner

From: Applicant

Re: Proposed Communications Code

Date: [date of exam]

Introduction

Here below is the analysis of the Code that you requested. Please contact me if you have any follow-up questions.

[Legal Issues Giving Rise to Constitutional Challenges]—optional

A few short paragraphs noting some of the major legal concerns (for example, that the FEA grants more significant rights to students than does the Constitution and that the level of scrutiny of particular restrictions on communication will be determined in part by whether the publication in question is seen as a public forum or limited public forum).

[Again, if you included this sort of preliminary legal analysis before analyzing the Code, provision by provision, I would suggest writing your introduction as follows:]

"Here below is a brief exploration of the legal issues that may give rise to constitutional challenges in this matter, followed by

---

the provision-by-provision analysis of the proposed Code that you requested. Please contact me if you have any follow-up questions."

Analysis of Proposed Code

Preamble:

a) Legal issues raised? Permissible? Why/why not?

b) Suggested edits and reasons for edits?

Provision 1: Professional standards of English and journalistic style

a) Legal issues raised? Permissible? Why/why not?

b) Suggested edits and reasons for edits?

Provision 2: [This provision refers to both language and depictions; I have addressed each separately here.]

—Language not in "good taste" and considering age, experience, and maturity

a) Legal issues raised? Permissible? Why/why not?

b) Suggested edits and reasons for edits?

—Depictions not in "good taste" and considering age, experience, and maturity

a) Legal issues raised? Permissible? Why/why not?

b) Suggested edits and reasons for edits?

Provision 3: Verification of fact and quote accuracy to "satisfaction of teacher supervising"

a) Legal issues raised? Permissible? Why/why not?

b) Suggested edits and reasons for edits?

Provision 4: Permission for quotes or photos from adult or parents if minor, with exception for group photos

a) Legal issues raised? Permissible? Why/why not?

b) Suggested edits and reasons for edits?

Provision 5: Prohibition against publications that:

a) Are libel, slander, or violate privacy rights;

b) Contain profanity (judged by local newspapers as standard);

c) Criticize or demean any public official, including school administrators and teachers;

d) Are deemed by principal not to be in school's best interests.

For each of these, assess:

a) Legal issues raised? Permissible? Why/why not?

b) Suggested edits and reasons for edits?

Provision 6: Prior approval by principal before publication/distribution.

a) Legal issues raised? Permissible? Why/why not?

b) Suggested edits and reasons for edits?

Conclusion

I hope the preceding analysis helps you prepare for your meeting with Kantor and the Board. If you have any additional questions, please let me know.

Library

The first document you find in the Library is the First Amendment, which, by the time of the bar exam, you would be very familiar with if you weren't even before that. Everything else in the Library is new.

You recall, of course, that you are located in the fictitious State of Franklin. The Franklin Constitution's provision on free speech is interesting but not terribly helpful to you in terms of guidance on what is or is not permitted speech. (What exactly does it mean to "be responsible for the abuse of" the free-speech right?)

The Franklin Education Act (FEA) section, however, is very interesting, useful, and clearly broader than the U.S. Constitution in terms of respecting student rights. Under this section, students appear to have wide-ranging free-speech rights, though expression that is "obscene, libelous, or slanderous" is prohibited. Also prohibited is speech inciting unlawful action on campus, violations of school regulations, or "substantial disruption of the orderly operation of the school."

From what Kantor said to Mr. Eisner, it does not look like these are the main concerns that the Board has, although Kantor did suggest that there were some publications bordering on defamatory. Also, the FEA clearly allows prohibition of defamatory speech. This FEA section may not prevent some of the other concerns Kantor brought to our attention, however. Thus, you should expect to find further clarification in the cases.

The last paragraphs of the FEA section deal with student editorial control. This grants students responsibility for "official school publications" (a term defined on this same page), with the limitation that "it shall be the responsibility of journalism advisers or advisers of student publications within each school to supervise the production of student staff, to maintain professional standards of English and Journalism, and to maintain the provision of this section."

The "standards of English and Journalism" language might have popped out at you, and if you flip back, you will see that this language is mirrored almost precisely in Provision 1. So, right away, you could have gone into your draft outline document and explained why, per FEA § 48, Provision 1 is likely fine as drafted.

Remember, as you read each case, that your goal is to figure out which provisions are acceptable, which are not, and why, and to make suggested edits to help the Board redraft the Code to achieve its goals. You will not simply brief the cases, but use them to help explain why certain provisions are or are not permissible. Students too often jump into PTs and start writing by just briefing (or worse still, summarizing) each case and not writing the tasks as directed in the Instructions. Throwing case-by-case summaries of law into your answer is a sure way to fail this sort of exam.

In the Online Question and Answer Bank, you will see the grader's point sheet, which give specifics on exactly what was expected in a passing answer to this assignment, so I will not detail every point. Rather, I will simply highlight some key points from each case. Be sure to study the point sheet carefully after reading this chapter.

Hazelwood is a Supreme Court case from 1988. *Lopez* and *Leeb* are both more recent and from Franklin Courts (*Lopez* was in the Franklin Supreme Court, and *Leeb* was a Franklin Court of Appeal case). Remember, states may not provide less protection than the federal government, but they may provide greater protection. (I like the often-referenced image that the federal Constitution is a floor, not a ceiling.) It may well be that *Lopez* and *Leeb* discuss greater protections afforded under the Franklin Constitution, Franklin statutes, and Franklin courts than in *Hazelwood*. Still, *Hazelwood* is factually very similar to our subject and helpful for our client, as the Supreme Court in *Hazelwood* reversed the circuit court and affirmed the district court's ruling that favored the school district.

Hazelwood gives a great deal of deference to the principal and to the school board. For example, note the language in *Hazelwood* that "A school need not tolerate student speech that is inconsistent with its basic educational mission, even though the government could not censor similar speech outside the school." The court recognized the school's right to remain neutral in areas of public controversy and says that only when censorship "has no valid educational purpose" will the First Amendment be implicated and "require judicial intervention to protect students'" constitutional rights.

Lopez again favors our client, allowing the school the right to restrict expression that includes profanity on the grounds that it violates "the professional standards of English and journalism" under the Franklin Education Act. *Lopez* does note that the restriction is to be of the objectionable language (in that case, certain "four-letter words") and not the content of the student speech; in other words, not the ideas or opinions expressed. *Lopez* confirms that its holding that § 48 of the FEA allows "prior restraint of profane student language" is consistent with both the United States and Franklin Constitutions. The *Lopez* court also provides very useful analysis of the public, nonpublic, and limited public forum standards. The court says that school publications (and here the court defines these broadly to include school newspapers, yearbooks, and theatrical productions) are a limited public forum, and as such the school, in order to regulate student expression, must show that the "regulations are narrowly drawn" to achieve "compelling state interests" and must be "sufficiently precise" so they are not vague. This should have given you a great deal of food for thought in reviewing provisions of the proposed Code, as many of them were far too vague to let stand.

Lastly, a few highlights from the *Leeb* case underscore that the State of Franklin provides greater protection to students than the Supreme Court did in *Hazelwood*. Even with greater deference to students, though, the *Leeb* court nonetheless ruled in the school's favor, finding that the principal had justifiable concerns supporting his prohibition on distribution of a student newspaper edition that included photos the principal considered "damaging" to certain students' reputations. *Leeb* did remind us that under the leading Supreme Court case, *New York Times v. Sullivan*, even a school "may not censor defamatory material that is not actionable because it is privileged or deals with a public figure without malice." Reading this should have led you directly to advise editing or deleting Provision 5c, that part of the proposed Code prohibiting criticism of public officials. *Leeb* concluded with some useful dicta about revising school communications codes to comport with legal requirements—our exact task in this PT.

Again, those are just some highlights. You should have seen a great deal more in each of those cases. With that backdrop, though, take a few minutes to study the grader's point sheet in the Online Question and Answer Bank, and compare this to your own answer to see how you did on this exam. Investigate how these comments analyzing the legality of each provision compare to what you wrote in your answer.

SPIN-OFF EXERCISES

Spin-off exercises provide exposure to different document types without taking time to learn new facts and law. Spend a few minutes, now that you have completed *Gardenton*, thinking of other tasks you might have been given and how you would have handled them. Here are a few suggestions.

1. Draft a persuasive document instead of a neutral one. Imagine that the Board had adopted the proposed Code as is, without ever consulting you, and is now being sued by a free-speech organization on behalf of students who were censored. Draft a persuasive memo to help Frank Eisner argue in court that the Code is constitutional.

2. Draft a persuasive statement opposing the Code that might be made orally by a student group or a civil rights group at the Board meeting that is open to public comment. Then, draft an equally persuasive statement that would be read aloud by a parent committee supporting the Code.

3. Represent a student instead of the Board of Education. Pretend that a Gardenton High School student ("Student") wrote and wants to star in a one-person play dealing with high school angst. The script includes themes relating to the lack of funding for the arts in public schools, teenage stress and anxiety, drug usage, sex, and gender identity issues. The drama teacher showed the principal the script, and the principal said that Student would not be allowed to perform the show. Student and his parents want to sue High School and Principal and come to you for legal consultation:

   a. Draft a two-part memo that (i) advises Student of his rights, and suggests alternative courses of action Student might pursue, and the pros and cons of each, and (ii) asks Student any follow-up questions you need answered to know how best to advise Student going forward. For example, would you want to know if the language used in the play is profane (i.e., is it filled with "four-letter words"), or is it simply about a mature subject matter that is worded in socially appropriate terminology?

   b. Draft a persuasive letter on Student's behalf to the school principal urging that the student be allowed to perform the play. For the purposes of this exercise only, assume that (i) you are a junior associate in the Franklin law firm of Allen, Eisner & Thomas, (ii) that neither you nor your law firm has any conflict of interest with your firm's having advised the Board and that you may freely represent Student, (iii) that the proposed Communications Code has not yet been adopted, but that (iv) all the constitutional and case law in the Gardenton Library controls.

PRACTICE, LAW SCHOOL, AND PTs: COMPARE AND CONTRAST

Gardenton provides a scenario that differs greatly from many typical law exams. In many ways, it reflects much of what certain lawyers actually do in practice. Clients often bring documents to their lawyers to edit to make sure they comply with legal requirements. The exercise you were asked to complete in *Gardenton* is not much different in principle from reviewing a contract, provision by provision, to determine if each is lawful and in the best interests of your client. (You saw just that sort of an exercise in Chapter 6 of this book on contracts.) Here, of course, you were analyzing the document in terms of constitutional restrictions, but the same type of thinking was required. Also, it is easy to picture clients coming to you to ask about how to draft and/or edit contracts. If your client is a school board, you can see that they might come to you for advice on all sorts of policies and documents, from employment and building contracts to communications codes.

Unless you took a drafting course (an elective in most law schools), or unless you work for a law office that does transactional work, you are probably much more familiar with essay and analytical legal memo formats than you are with deleting, adding, or modifying language to achieve a client's goals. Nevertheless, drafting and editing work is the lifeblood of many law practices.

CLIENT COUNSELING

If you enjoy these sorts of tasks and are interested in client counseling, look into the ABA Law Student Division's Client Counseling Competition at http://www.americanbar.org/groups/law_students/events_competitions/practical_skills_competitions/ccc.html. This competition was inspired by the career of one of my mentors, the late Louis M. Brown, an attorney and professor fondly referred to as "the father of preventive law."

This PT provides a great tool to help you transition to thinking as a transactional lawyer would at this early stage of representation: ensuring that documents are drafted so as to prevent later litigation rather than looking at what has already occurred and determining the legal rights and remedies of the parties at that stage.

PT Pep Talk

PTs are open book and, at least to a certain extent, "real world." Take a moment to appreciate this exam. Hopefully, you had fun with it! I would love to see you get to a place of confidence in how to approach and tackle these PTs where you are certain you can handle anything they throw at you. Wrestle with and master the time and data management challenges now, ahead of time, so that you can actually have fun with the PT on your bar exam.

PTs are not contrived hypotheticals designed to see how many rules you memorized, as some essays seem to be. Nor do PTs require the extreme speed with which you must analyze and pick the best answers on multiple-choice questions.

You must complete essays and MBEs on your exam. They too can be fun. For many, the issue spotting and the strategy of taking MBEs, eliminating wrong answers by ferreting out inconsistencies and errors, make the MBEs like a game, challenging in a way that is similar to other tricky word games. Many also view the legal analysis portion of essays as an intriguing puzzle—issue spotting and seeing how facts prove or disprove particular elements of rules of law.

Try to enjoy all the practice tests you complete, and learning process generally. As with most work and study, to the extent you can have fun with the process, the more engaged you will be and the more likely you will be to succeed.

A Word on Memory and Enjoying the Process

Essays and MBEs test critical reading and analytical skills, and can help immensely in training you to be a successful lawyer. These testing forms also depend heavily on memory, though much of today's lawyering does not. Lawyers use tablets, computers, and smartphones to help them remember a lot of what they need on a day-to-day basis. PTs by contrast, like much of law practice, are open book. You can look up rules, and you can take some time to actually think about them. (Ninety minutes on a PT does not allow time for deep reflection but it feels more leisurely a pace than 1.8 minutes per MBE question.) Again, though, I am not knocking MBEs at all. For many, taking the MBE is an exhilarating experience, albeit exhausting; it is empowering to know that you can read rapidly through 200 legal scenarios in a single day and be able to critically reason through each one.

Again, if you let yourself, you can really enjoy all of bar preparation, especially PTs. Your memory gets to relax a little because they are open book, and you get to dive right into real-world struggles and help your clients. *Gardenton* is a perfect example. This happens all over the country: students want to express themselves, and parents and other community members are often offended by what students say. Schools and school boards are frequently stuck in the middle, as in *Gardenton*: they must follow education laws and guidelines, but they do not want to alienate the community or become ensnared in scandals that can disrupt their basic task of educating students. You get the opportunity to jump into the thick of the situation, learn what both the state and federal governments require and permit, and provide useful advice in a very realistic scenario.

Tell me honestly: If you could complete this exam as part of a pass/fail class, not worrying about your "grade," wouldn't you have fun? Even though the bar exam is a high-pressure, high-stakes exam, I urge you to get into that mindset. *Have fun.* Get into the role-play. You will do just as well, if not better, than if you are totally stressed out. Also, if you are enjoying yourself you will stay awake, focused, and not get as easily distracted as people often do with this long an exam.

Remember, too, that even on the bar exam, you are still in the "safe" world of simulation as compared with law practice. What do I mean? You have stimulating cases to work on, with fascinating and sometimes complicated facts and/or law, but you will be awarded points for identifying the issues and theorizing logically about the likely outcomes, without actually being responsible for the results. So long as you explain your reasoning, you likely will do well on the exam, if you do just that: answer thoroughly and logically, often no matter what your exact conclusion is. Students often return and tell me after graduation that the best part of law school was getting "credit" for seeing both sides of issues and not having to worry about who would actually "win," as they do in practice.

I hope you enjoyed the *Gardenton* practice test and saw it as part real-world and part simulation role-play, but entirely useful, as you continue your training to succeed on both the performance tests and in law practice.

KEY TAKEAWAYS

- This PT was set in a different context than many of the typical litigation-oriented PTs. In this exam, you were proactively counseling your client (the School Board) about what would likely be permissible in their proposed communications code and what would not be. Your tone and presentation had to take this into account.

- When writing to a judge or opposing counsel, your job may be to persuade. Here, you were writing to your senior partner to help advise the client, so your job was to analyze as more of a neutral observer and counselor. For that reason, it was just as important to note which provisions were likely permissible as it was to note which had to be revised and why.

- This PT task was also a problem-solving and a drafting/editing exercise, in that you were asked to make suggestions about deleting or adding particular language that would help your client achieve its goals.

10

PROFESSIONAL RESPONSIBILITY

OVERVIEW OF PROFESSIONAL RESPONSIBILITY

Professional responsibility (PR) or legal ethics are not only required courses in law school, but also required for licensure in nearly every state. Specifically, almost every state requires you to pass the Multistate Professional Responsibility Examination (MPRE) in addition to passing your state's bar exam. Because you have so much exposure to ethics rules during law school, it is possible that most of what you will learn in bar review will actually be a review in this subject. That said, there may be areas that are new to you, or that you did not fully understand or see the implications of in law school.

The MPRE tests rules regulating attorneys and judges, whereas most bar exam PR essays test ethics issues relating mostly to lawyers. (In fact, the easiest way to spot a PR issue on a bar exam essay is the presence of a lawyer in the fact pattern!) The most heavily tested PR areas on bar exams include:

- How you gain and how you can lose the right to practice law
- Working with and/or supervising other lawyers and nonlawyers
- Advertising for and soliciting clients
- Managing client money (fees and funds)
- Becoming and staying competent to represent clients
- Zealously representing clients
- Conflicts of interest
- Confidentiality

For a comprehensive list of the subjects covered on the MPRE, consult the most recent MPRE Subject Matter Outline published by the National Conference of Bar Examiners on their website, ncbex.org/exams/mpre/preparing/. Many of these are fair game for bar exam essays and could also be tested in a PT.

SIMULATED PROFESSIONAL RESPONSIBILITY–BASED PERFORMANCE TEST

Take three hours and complete the *In re: Deale* performance test found in the Online Question and Answer Bank at **http://ambar.org/barexamprep**.

TIME-CRUNCH TIPS

This PT requires you to complete one single task chock full of ethical issues. Professional responsibility is tested on almost all bar exams in some form or other, so I urge you if at all possible to find three hours and complete this test in full. If you cannot find that time now, please read the entire File and Library (using the SS-BROW system you learned in Chapter 2) and outline the memo. In your outline, be sure to identify all the ethical problems that have occurred and the potential ethical problems, and note what points you would have discussed if you had had the full three hours to analyze them. You can do this in about 90 to 100 minutes. Plan to come back and write out your answer in full when you have more time.

INSIDE THIS TEST: TIPS AND STRATEGIES

Now that you have tackled *Deale*, let's look together at its File and Library, and see how you did. As noted in previous chapters, you find instructions in the first pages in General Instructions, a Task Memo, and/or Format Pages.

Deale included a standard (nearly boilerplate) set of General Instructions. These Instructions noted that there were statutory authorities as well as cases, but there was nothing unusual (no third set of material beyond the File and Library, for example) and no percentage split, as there was only one assignment to produce.

The Task Memo

The Task Memo gives background about Ms. Amanda Deale, our client, and the City Council she serves on; it further states that she also serves on a property development subcommittee that has been under investigation. The language used by Jim Klein, the partner giving you the assignment, is interesting: "After reading over the transcript of the interview [between Deale and Mark Craven, another lawyer in our firm], I think there may be some ethical problems." The first time you read this, you may have just thought, "Oh, OK, perhaps I'll see some ethical issues." Going back to this, after reading the File and the Library, you were likely screaming to yourself, "*Really*, Mr. Klein? You think there were problems?! Duh! Mark Craven will be lucky if he's not disbarred!" Note I said "screaming to yourself." Whatever you think when you read, make certain that your answer is written in a professional and respectful manner.

Mark Craven's words and actions were deeply troubling, and in a number of instances appear to clearly have violated ethical rules and principles. If you did not see the problems on your initial skim of the File, you would have seen them on your re-read of the File after you investigated the Library contents.

Jim Klein next indicates that while still zealously protecting Deale's rights and adequately preparing her for the grand jury, "it is imperative that our representation of her be totally consistent with the demands of professional responsibility." That comment sets the stage for your careful review of the last paragraph, which explicitly gives you your task:

> Based upon your review of the file, write a memo to me that identifies and analyzes ethical problems that have already occurred and potential ethical issues affecting either our client or our firm. To the extent that these issues present problems to our client or to us, describe how I should solve them.

Right in this assignment language, you have a structure for your answer and a rough draft outline. Here is the skeletal framework:

To: Jim Klein

From: Bar Applicant

Re: *In re: Deale*: Past and Potential Ethical Problems Affecting Client and Law Firm.

Date: [date of the exam]

Memo

I. Ethical problems that have occurred

II. Potential ethical issues affecting client/firm

Conclusion

To make your memo easy to follow, you will include descriptive subheadings that identify past problems and potential issues and list them under each appropriate main heading. Based on your knowledge of the PT generally, you should expect to see ethical rules in the Library, and facts in the File, that trigger ethical issues. (If you keep this outline as an open document on your computer, you can note issues right in the outline as you see them.)

Once you understood the directions, following the steps outlined in Chapter 2, you should have skimmed the File, studied the Library, then returned to the File to flesh out your outline and pick up enough factual information to write a thorough answer.

Skim the File

Why again do we skim the File? You should see right away, here in *Deale*, why that step is so important. There is so much in the File! If you don't know more precisely what you're looking for, you will get bogged down in irrelevancies. That is precious time you cannot spare. Also, although your instincts and general knowledge of PR law may help you see some of the ethical issues, you will not see them all or be able to fully analyze them until after you read the Library. That is why you skim the File first, then study the Library, and then re-read the File.

Before checking out each of the File documents, I suggest a quick look at the File table of contents, to see what your world is. There are six documents, including the Task Memo. The first File document (after the Task Memo) is the interview that Craven conducted with Deale, our client. You know from the Task Memo that there are problems in Craven's interview; Jim Klein said so specifically. For now, though, just flip through it and get a flavor. If anything pops out at you, fine, but don't spend time trying to make all the facts make sense yet. (When you return to the File after reading the Library, you will study Craven's interview word for word, because Klein told you that is where the problems are. At that time, what is significant will be obvious.)

You see there is a lot of discussion about property called the "Wharf Building." You might have noticed Craven asking to keep a document and might have made a mental note to review attorney duties with respect to retaining physical evidence.

You see Craven speculating on what is and is not covered under the subpoena. (You might recall from your look at the File table of contents that the subpoena itself is in the File.)

Other things will become obvious in the transcript, if you didn't see them on the first skim, including: (1) Craven's revealing to Deale confidential information, a "hush-hush deal," about another client; and (2) Craven seemingly counseling Deale that she can hide documents and/or evade responding to questions at the grand jury. These are both very significant problems that you need to look at carefully when you re-read the File. (The examiners were undoubtedly giving you a hint that confidentiality duties were violated by having Craven refer to the other client matter as a "hush-hush" deal.)

The next document is the partnership agreement, which, among other things, lists who owns what percentage interest in the Wharf Building.

Next is the subpoena. You might have noted the language in Paragraphs 1 and 2, which appears to request a fairly broad sweep of documents.

The next document is an internal memo from Mark Craven to Jim Klein (the person to whom we are writing), in which Craven lets us know that Deale wants us to represent her secretary, Stuart Levy. Craven says Deale wants Stuart "to have a lawyer who is sensitive to [Deale's] interests." This should scream out at you as problematic. Even without looking in the Library, you know that an attorney must zealously represent the client. If we represent Levy, then Levy is the client—and if his interests are potentially adverse to Deale's, then there may be a conflict of interest issue with our current client, Ms. Deale. You might have written something just like this paragraph as draft notes the minute you saw this, and then edited the point into a more thorough paragraph in your answer after reviewing the Library authorities.

The last File document is a newspaper article that gives you a bit more background on the city council's alleged favoritism with respect to the city development.

The Library

The table of contents shows that the Library contains five authorities: two statutes and three cases. The statutes are from the U.S. Code and the Columbia Rules of Professional Conduct, which Rules the table of contents states are identical to California Rules of Professional Responsibility. Because this was a California bar exam, this signaled to applicants that they were already familiar with these rules (as this was law they would have had to apply on a PR essay). An MPT could easily note that Library statutes are substantially similar to statutes you are familiar with, such as the Model Rules of Professional Responsibility.

Caveat: Do not study PTs to master specific rules of law. It is true that many of the PR rules in this Library are similar to those in other jurisdictions, and it is hoped that completing this PT helped bolster your general knowledge of PR at the same time it helped train key lawyering skills. Nevertheless, as we have said throughout this book, you must not expect to use practice PTs to master particular rules for your bar exam. Examiners may use fictitious law for PT exam purposes. Even if a PT is from your own jurisdiction, case holdings may have been changed for exam purposes, or the Library law may be outdated. So remember, practice PTs provide excellent skills training in the context of subjects you need to master, and they help you gain fluency in general areas of law that will help in turn when you go to master the rules in your jurisdiction.

In this Library, as always, read the cases in full as if they were new to you, and brief them using the surgical briefing method described in Chapter 2. Still, because of your presumed general familiarity with professional responsibility statutes, it makes sense here to first read the titles or headings of the statutes before spending time studying each provision.

Scanning these headings, you see from the criminal code sections that the following are crimes: Tampering with a witness, victim, or an informant; Perjury;

Subornation of perjury; and Destruction of evidence. If Mark Craven (the lawyer in our firm whose actions we are writing about in our PT answer) counseled any of those things, then he acted in a way that advised a violation of the law. Again, you know from your general knowledge of PR rules that advising someone to violate the law is itself a violation of an ethical rule, and you see that specifically set forth in the Library in Rule 3-210.

Looking next at the Columbia Rules of Professional Conduct, among other things you see:

- A duty to maintain client confidences (3-100)
- Prohibitions against acting incompetently (3-110) and against bringing actions that are not in good faith (3-200)
- Obligations not to advise someone to violate the law (3-210), to avoid representing parties with adverse interests without informed consent, and certain other requirements (3-310)
- Duties to the tribunal (5-200) and a prohibition, with some exceptions, not to act as a witness in a case in which you are representing a party (5-210)
- A prohibition against suppressing evidence (5-220)
- Rules about prohibited contact with witnesses (5-310)

Again, all of the titles of these code sections raise possible ethical violations, most of which occurred or will potentially occur given the facts in this File. You might note as subheadings in your outline, right when you see them, any violations you think Craven committed.

> **Note:** All of these provisions deal with ethical obligations of lawyers. The task you must wrestle with is what the lawyer in our own firm, Craven, did or said that raises or potentially raises issues for our firm or our client. Nothing in this Library is about the city council's obligations or about what Deale's obligations as a government official may be. (Students frequently make the mistake of focusing not on what Craven did wrong but on what Deale did wrong. If you were confused about this, let the Library be your guide. It's nearly all about the duties of lawyers.)

The cases are interesting, and each raises different areas of ethical concern. I will walk through them here, in this debriefing, case by case, but in your answer, you want to reference the cases as they relate to possibly unethical behavior in the past and potential future ethical violations committed by Craven and/or our law firm. As I have warned in nearly every chapter of this book, you do not want to write a summary of each case, case by case, in your answer. (Here your answer should have been organized violation-by-violation.)

Bronston, a Supreme Court case, holds that it is the responsibility of the questioner, the lawyer, to ask precise questions and ferret out the truth when a witness answers a question in a literally honest manner but in a manner that nonetheless misleads by what it leaves out. The burden is on the lawyer to ask follow-up questions and get the full picture. So long as the witness is honest, she or he is not committing perjury.

When you go back to the File, what will pop out is that Craven starts to advise Deale accurately about her obligation to answer truthfully but without obligation to volunteer information. Then, however, Craven goes on and tells Deale she "can always say she doesn't remember." What? (Did you stop yourself wondering if you read this wrong? I remember reading it five times the first time I saw this PT, thinking, "Did Craven really just say what it looks like he said?") I hope this jumped out at you as very wrong. If you remember something and under oath say you do not remember, you are committing perjury. By advising Deale that she "can always say she doesn't remember," Craven seems essentially to be telling her to perjure herself. Big problem!

The next case, *Edwards*, reminds us that physical evidence does not become privileged simply because it is given to or taken into custody by an attorney. The attorney may keep evidence in a criminal case only long enough to prepare a defense, but then must turn over the evidence to the prosecution. You may remember, and the rules tell you, that this may be done anonymously. There is no need to say how the evidence came into the lawyer's possession. However, an attorney cannot keep the evidence for too long. Reading *Edwards* should have made you think, when you went back into the File, about the partnership agreement that Craven took from Deale.

The last case, *Elliott Saul*, reiterates (in the context of a grand jury situation) that so long as the client knowingly and intelligently consents, an attorney may represent more than one person subpoenaed before the grand jury. Here, this basically points us in the direction of making certain we have informed consent from Stuart Levy, whom Deale wants us to represent. Although there may be ethical issues with that representation (the one we looked at earlier of Deale wanting us to be "sensitive" to Deale's issues in representing Levy, rather than Levy's, and the possible conflict of interest), it still may be possible to represent both Deale and Levy if the proper consents are obtained. This is another issue you would study carefully, perhaps moving back and forth between re-reading the relevant pages in the File and reviewing the relevant law as you write.

Study the sample answers in the Online Question and Answer Bank and compare and contrast them to your answer.

SPIN-OFF EXERCISES

Using the same facts and law as in *Deale*, try drafting the following assignments:

1. A letter to Amanda Deale advising her specifically about her obligations with respect to the grand jury subpoena and her obligation to answer questions truthfully. Also inform her explicitly in your letter that if Stuart Levy wants us

to represent him, we will owe a duty to him and not to her during that representation. Discuss, as well, the potential conflict of interest in representing both her and Levy. Note that even though Deale is a politician, to our knowledge she is not a lawyer, so write in a tone appropriate for Deale.

2. A letter to Mark Craven notifying him of ethical violations you believe he committed and what must now be done about those violations.

Note that in this case, the senior partner, Jim Klein, would likely deal directly with his partner, Mark Craven. But what if this were a small firm, or if Mark Craven were a solo practitioner you worked for? How do you think you would handle this situation? What would you do if Mark Craven were your boss and had directed you to file frivolous motions for the purposes of delay?

Related Substance Abuse Concerns

What if you have reason to believe that part of why Craven engaged in such egregiously unethical conduct (including revealing client confidences and counseling our client to hide documents and evade responding to questions) is that Craven has an alcohol or drug problem? What do you do with that information? Do you talk with Craven? Do you talk with another, more senior, attorney for advice? Do you report Craven to an ethics hotline?

Let's say further that you are a new junior associate, just out of law school. Craven and your boss Jim Klein are much older than you, and they are close friends. You think that Klein does not see or does not want to see or admit that Craven has a substance abuse problem. But Craven has taken you to lunch and ordered far too many drinks on a number of occasions, you have seen Craven stumbling in the elevator when he leaves at the end of the day, and you are certain that Craven needs help. Draft a paragraph of the dialogue you might have with Jim Klein about Craven.

Another scenario: What if Craven is much older than Klein? Craven, now in his eighties, was Klein's mentor, and Klein does not at all want to see that Craven is slowing down. How do you handle expressing your concerns about Craven's behavior? (Note that the American Academy of Neurology estimated that up to 50% of people over the age of 85 experience some dementia.[1])

Lastly, what if working for Klein and Craven is so stressful that you find yourself drinking to calm yourself down each afternoon, or that you drink before meeting with them, or before going to court on matters they send you on that you are not comfortable with? What if they both drink often during the work day and pressure you to join them?

---

[1] From Richard Carlton, *A Closer Look at Depression and Cognitive Decline in Senior Attorneys*, CAL. B.J., Apr. 2016, https://apps.calbar.ca.gov/mcleselfstudy/mcle_home.aspx?testID=108.

Would you be able to recognize if you have a substance abuse problem? What steps might you take to help yourself?

Note: If you think I am making up unrealistic scenarios here, think again. Substance abuse is an enormous problem in our profession and one you must be aware of. You must actively work to stay healthy yourself and to understand and comply with ethical obligations when you encounter others who are using and possibly abusing drugs or alcohol. (I don't say "if" but "when.")

In addition to spinning off assignments based on the *Deale* File and Library, while you are thinking practically about professional responsibility, try to answer these few short PR-related hypotheticals.

1. You are Plaintiff's counsel. You just received a request from Defense counsel to continue the hearing you had set for tomorrow morning. You went to some length rearranging your own calendar to make the hearing date and time work, and you believe that opposing counsel attorney is asking for the continuance to stall. How do you handle the situation?

2. You are in court on your first case ever. You are speaking to the court clerk, who is rude. The clerk says that you and your client are wasting the court's time, and suggests that you do not know how to handle yourself as a lawyer. What do you say or do?

3. You are in court litigating a particularly thorny issue, and, on a quick break from the proceedings, your client tells you that he intends to just "skip certain details" if the court asks him about them. How do you handle the situation? Is this a *Bronston*-type situation where it would be up to the court to ask the right questions? Should you advise your client to answer truthfully but not volunteer additional information? Write a short paragraph on how you would respond to your client.

4. You have met with your client once. At the close of the initial meeting, after telling you a bit about her case, and after your explaining how you could potentially help her, she gave you a large retainer. Before your next meeting, she tells you that she and her adversary have tried going to a mediator and hope to resolve things without a lawyer and no longer need your services. How do you handle the situation?

5. You are acting as the mediator for two parties. With your help, they have reached a preliminary agreement, and you have encouraged them each to have outside counsel read it before they sign it, if they wish. One of the attorneys phones to yell at you, insinuating that you are biased or being "paid off" because the agreement is so one-sided. How do you handle the situation?

6. The court is set to hear your argument, and the judge says, "Counselors, I have a docket full of important matters this morning, and you both are wasting my

time. Go out in the hallway and figure this out. Come back in 30 minutes with a solution." You are taken aback by the judge's tone. Opposing counsel (who is a much more experienced lawyer than you are) tries to push you into a compromise, but you really believe, based on the facts and law, that your client should prevail. How do you handle the situation?

PTs and PT spin-off exercises are among the best places and times to think about ethical issues and prepare yourself to face trying situations.

PRACTICE, LAW SCHOOL, AND PTs:
COMPARE AND CONTRAST

Ethical issues in real life do not typically come wrapped in neat packages the way they do on law exams. (Even in this fairly realistic PT, the bulk of the many professional violations nearly all appeared in one short transcript.) In actual practice, PR issues may sneak up on you. You may not know for certain if something is permissible or not; it may be a gray area and you may need advice. If so, seek advice from another trusted lawyer. Lawyers are typically very generous with their time in terms of mentoring less experienced colleagues. There are also ethics hotlines at many state bar offices, where you can call and get advice anonymously. If you sense that something isn't right, make some inquiries, do some research, and find out for certain what you must do, what you may do, and what you may not do. Trust yourself.

Ethics issues in practice may be laden with peer pressure, or heavy-handed top-down intimidation—some with veiled (or not-so-veiled) threats that you may lose your job unless you engage in the prohibited conduct. The hypothetical I suggested earlier (where you pretended Mark Craven was your boss and was pushing you to file frivolous lawsuits) is all too realistic. I have heard many lawyers discuss how they were asked to engage in unethical behavior when they were new to practice, including being directed by more senior lawyers to mishandle client trust funds, disregard contrary legal authorities, and/or delay proceedings to gain a competitive advantage. Things you might think would only come up on an exam unfortunately do arise in practice. Protect your license and your reputation, at the same time as you fight for your clients.

Bottom line: The price of failing to understand ethical rules (and follow them) in practice is far higher than on exams. The worst you can typically do on an exam when you don't see or understand what is at issue is fail and have to retake the exam or course. This is not something I want for any of you, but it is not tragic. In practice, however, you may lose your license, your reputation, and all that you have worked for your whole life—not to mention what your client may lose as a result of your behavior. As you well know, some attorneys end up in prison. So, do everything in your power to protect this law license that you are working so hard now to earn. Guard it as one of the most precious things you will ever have the privilege of calling yours.

Further protect your ability to become licensed by following all Honor Code and other rules in law school, and keeping your moral character record such that you will be deemed fit to practice law by the jurisdiction of your choosing.

KEEP YOUR OWN PRIVATE LISTS

A very senior and extremely experienced attorney I knew advised young lawyers to keep two private lists, and to update those lists every time they worked with another attorney (in or outside of their own practice):

1. A list of attorneys you want to work with in the future, people to whom you would give the benefit of the doubt if they ever need it. (Jot notes to remind yourself of particularly reputable actions the attorney took while you were interacting with him or her.)

2. A list of attorneys you do not want to work with, or, if forced to work with, whom you will not trust or give the benefit of the doubt. (On this list, note anything the attorney did that was underhanded, unprofessional, or unethical, so that you remember why you do not trust this person in the future.)

Whether we keep them as written lists or mental lists, we all keep such lists. People will remember what you do that is right and honorable, and what you do that is not, starting in law school (and even earlier). It takes a lifetime to cultivate a good reputation, but only a moment to destroy one.

Bottom line: PR issues on PTs and essays are often derived from real life. Many of the scenarios you will have to identify and analyze, and sometimes make recommendations about, are problems and violations you see regularly reported against practicing lawyers. The difference between both types of exams and real life is that the consequences in the latter can be devastating, even irreparable. Learn your rules of ethics, and learn them well!

KEY TAKEAWAYS

- This practice exam helped raise your awareness of the types of ethical issues that may well arise on a PT. In this PT, the underlying legal backdrop was professional responsibility, but any one of the concerns in this PT may be planted in a PT based on any other legal subject as just a single issue for you to identify and discuss. For example, you could have a wills and trusts problem where you were drafting an estate plan and a lawyer in your firm revealed the confidences of another client.

- Having completed this PT, you should have your antennae up for potential ethical issues and a good sense of how to address ethical issues in future PTs.
- This PT showed a very realistic (unfortunate but realistic) scenario of a client pushing the attorney to "bend" or outright break the rules for that client. In real life, it can be tremendously difficult to call out (or report) the unethical behavior of a colleague. Nonetheless, you must know what your own duties are, and follow the rules of professional conduct. You work too hard for your law license to lose it.

11

REAL PROPERTY

OVERVIEW OF REAL PROPERTY

The term *real property* connotes land, as opposed to "personal property" or moveable items also known as *chattel*. Law school property classes and the bar exam both focus on the former: land. (On bar exams, issues relating to personal property most often arise in torts contexts, where someone may be interfering with or destroying personal property or in criminal law contexts, where someone may be trying to steal it.)

Chattel that is attached to real property will likely be deemed a fixture and part of the real property, not separate personal property. Likewise, growing crops are considered part of the land until they are cut (such as for harvest), after which time they become personal property.

In law school, often in 1L, you learn about how real property is acquired (often by sale), and you need to know a fair amount about land sale contracts.

> **Note:** In contracts class, you learn that contracts for the sale of land must typically be in writing. You will likely also pick this up in your property course with further study of the Statute of Frauds and its exceptions, as it applies to interests in land.

Land can also be acquired by adverse possession, and the government can acquire land by eminent domain; the former you will probably study in law school, but, depending on your professor, the latter you might not get to until bar review.

You will learn about deeds or land ownership documents; what constitutes a valid deed; and rules with respect to delivering deeds, transferring deeds, and recording deeds. You will also learn about different types of recording statutes.

In law school property classes, you study restrictions on the use of land such as easements, profits, covenants, and equitable servitudes. You learn about present possessory estates and future interests in land. (These terms should seem familiar: fee simple, fee tail, life estate, possibility of reverter, and remainders.) Most law school classes and bar exams also test concurrent estates, including joint ownership such as joint tenancy, tenancy by the entirety, and tenancy in common. You may have studied and should know rules about present landowners protecting the interests of future owners (waste), and rules that would prevent unreasonable restraints on transferability (alienation) of property, such as the rule against perpetuities.

You may or may not cover landlord-tenant rules in law school, but they are often tested on bar exam essays and on the MBE. Mortgages also end up frequently tested on the MBE. For a list of the topics covered on the MBE in real property, consult the most recent MBE Subject Matter Outlines published by the National Conference of Bar Examiners on their website at ncbex.org/exams/mbe/preparing.

SIMULATED REAL PROPERTY–BASED PERFORMANCE TEST

I chose the *Westside Community Corporation* (*Westside*) PT for confidence-building reasons. In it, you will tackle the dreaded "rule against perpetuities" (RAP). It is not that difficult to understand, but it has gotten a bad "rap" (pun intended!). It seems odd to say that I picked what some view as an impossibly tricky topic to build confidence, but what I want is for you to get to a place where you believe that you can handle anything the examiners throw at you, even the RAP.

Go ahead and take three hours and complete the *Westside* PT found in the Online Question and Answer Bank at **http://ambar.org/barexamprep**. We'll debrief it together after you finish and you will see that it isn't that bad at all!

TIME-CRUNCH TIPS

If you do not have time now for a full three-hour PT, but still want to do some work with this practice exam, read all the materials and complete just the first memo, comparing the prior Columbia law and new Columbia statutes. Skip the second memo advising the board about the proposed alternatives. This should trim off at least 30 minutes of the time needed to complete this exam.

INSIDE THIS TEST: TIPS AND STRATEGIES

Walking through the *Westside* File, as always the first and most important document is the Task Memo. In the Task Memo, we learn that the partner (Meherrin, the person to whom we are to deliver our assignment) has met with the executive director of our client, the Westside Community Development Corporation (Westside). Immediately, knowing our client is a corporation, we can expect to hear about the board of directors. Sure enough, in the next sentence we learn that the board is negotiating with the Lewiston Historic Preservation Society (LHPS) about "the transfer" of the old Lewiston High School property (High School).

I suggest starting a "cast of characters" on your scratch paper. You may end up having lots of people and parties to keep track of in a PT. It can be helpful to start notes on who is whom, like a program for a play. Here, you can begin that already, reading the Task Memo.

- Meherrin = our boss (partner in our firm)
- Westside = our client
- Paulette Wade = Westside's executive director
- LHPS = party negotiating potential lease/sale of high school with our client

Did you wonder why Meherrin used the word "transfer" rather than "sale"? The next sentence provides a hint. Our boss refers immediately to the lease that is in the File, but says that the board is considering two alternatives. The lease must be one. We will find out more as we read.

Some students freak out when next they see mention of the rule against perpetuities (RAP). It is imperative to stay calm and not panic. Just keep reading, and think as you read; talk yourself through the instructions:

> *What is my exact task? Draft a memo that analyzes the prior and new Columbia law on the RAP. (I do not have to know this by heart. The Library will have everything I need.) Then, I need to draft a second memo analyzing the two alternatives, and determining which is better and why, to help my boss to best advise the Westside board.*

At this point, at what would be only about two minutes or less into reading this PT, you can start a draft outline. You can either write this outline on scratch paper or type it into a blank document file on your computer that will eventually become your final answer.

Header and Introduction to Meherrin

Memo I

Analysis of prior law and new law of RAP and how it affects Westside's alternatives. Does new law eliminate old problems?

Memo II

Analysis of alternatives. Which is better for Westside and why?

Conclude Memo II with advice to give to board.

Most often, Instructions tell you how much each task is worth. When they do not, make an educated guess based on how much material relates to each task and how complex each is: *Here, the first memo is the law–heavy document; it incorporates analysis of both prior and new law, so likely there is more to say here than in the second memo, which is more of a problem-solving and factual analysis document. In that second memo, I must evaluate the pros and cons of each of the two alternatives. Sounds like something that can be written more quickly than the first memo.* This is how your reasoning might lead you to allocate a bit more time to the first task, if the percentages are not specified. Here, it is likely that the first memo would have been worth about 60% (with about 40% of that 60% focused on prior law and 20% on the new law) and the second memo worth about 40% of the total.

The next File document is a short letter to our boss from Westside's executive director, Paulette Wade. It tells us that her main goal is to obtain access to the Fine Arts Building to get started constructing a new cultural and arts center. Wade says that the board is interested in getting control of the entire school property. She also spells out very precisely the two alternatives that our boss noted in the Task Memo:

1. Lease the High School's Fine Arts Building, with an option to purchase the entire property (lease-option), or
2. Purchase the entire school, with LHPS retaining an option to buy it back (sale-buy back).

You can update your draft outline with this new information.

Header and Intro

Memo I

Analysis of prior law and new law of RAP and how it affects Westside's lease-option and sale-buy back. Does new law eliminate old problems?

Memo II

Analysis of alternatives: which is better for Westside and why?

1) Pros and cons of leasing the High School's Fine Arts Building, with an option to purchase the entire property (lease-option), or

2) Pros and cons of purchasing the entire school with LHPS retaining an option to buy it back (sale-buy back).

Conclude Memo II with advice to give to board.

Note that the letter tells our boss not to "worry about the specific dollars and cents." We might learn more about the money in later File documents, but this also may be a hint that the money is not the biggest factor in this decision.

The next document is a draft lease. Before knowing all the law in the Library and having more familiarity with the rest of the facts, you may want to just make a mental note that the lease is here in the File for you to return and read it when you have more context for fully understanding it.

The next document is a letter from the LHPS to the board. Among other key facts, you learn in this correspondence that the Historical Society has already rejected two offers from prospective buyers offering $3 million because those buyers were not willing to commit to preserving the historical character of the school. That is LHPS's primary concern. We also learn that LHPS acquired the property from the school district precisely because of concern that a new buyer would destroy the character of the property, but that when LHPS does sell the property it will have to pay 75% of the proceeds to the school district.

LHPS explains that it cannot sell only a part of the school, as our client seemingly wants, but would consider leasing us just the Fine Arts Building. (Notice how I am jumping into the role-play and thinking of the client as "us." The more "into" these PTs you get, the easier they will be to understand.)

LHPS further suggests that a sale of the entire property may be possible even at a "modest" below-market price, if there were a buy-back option (on an equally modest basis). That way LHPS could later find a buyer that was willing to both keep the history preserved and pay market value.

You should already be beginning to see some of the pros and cons of each alternative. If not, do not be concerned. Keep reading and re-reading. The minutes of the Westside Board clearly set out the positions of different board members. Remember, too, that the whole File will make more sense after you read the Library.

The next document is another letter, this one from Westside to a foundation seeking money for a grant. This provides a lot of background on both Westside and on the high school site. It will come in handy when exploring the pros and cons of the various alternatives, in your second task. For example, you learn from this letter that the Fine Arts Building needs extensive renovations, and you learn that although Westside immediately wants just that one building, it may eventually need the whole property.

The next document is minutes from a July 1 Westside Board meeting. Skim it now and come back to it after you have read the Library. Some points will make sense on this first skim. Others will not be clear until after you know the law. As you read, add to the cast of characters you started when you began the Task Memo, to keep everyone straight. Next to each name, you can jot down the person's position vis-à-vis the two alternatives:

- Meherrin = our boss (partner in our firm)
- Westside = our client

- LHPS = party negotiating potential lease/sale of high school with our client
- Paulette Wade = Westside's executive director
- Ashleigh McKenzie = Chair of Westside Board
- Wade Herndon = Secretary of Westside Board
- Jane Kovnat = President of LHPS
- Reverend S.C. James Dawes = Board member
- Jenny Alley = former dancer and presumably board member
- Ellis Hart = lawyer
- Nicole Figures = CPA

In the minutes, in addition to learning different board members' positions, we also learn that although the million-dollar grant request was not approved, Westside was awarded $250,000 for renovations to the Fine Arts Building if Westside leases or buys it.

The minutes go on to detail several people's positions on a lease versus a sale. You could have started writing some of these positions right into your outline under the pros and cons of each alternative.

The minutes end by authorizing Wade to negotiate either the lease or a sale, so long as the board approves.

The last File document is language from LHPS about each option. You can look at this now, but you will need to come back to the specific language after studying the RAP law in the Library in order to determine how these provisions do or do not comply with the rules.

Note: If your lawyering instincts saw a red flag by the language "at any time" in both the lease and sale language, you are on the right track! Perhaps you were thinking: *Does that really mean any time? Any time at all in the far distant future? In other words, they could have this right in perpetuity? That would mean they could essentially keep their interest in the property locked up forever...* Ah, now that you see it, this rule against perpetuities won't be that hard to understand! (If you did not see this yet, do not be concerned; the first case, *Symphony*, and later cases, especially *Citgo*, should have started to make the RAP clear.)

Off to the Library to tackle the RAP in more detail.

Library

This Library contains sections of the Probate Code and four cases. I will highlight some points in each, specifically places you might have gotten detoured and points you should have seen.

Probate Code

The first section listed, § 21201, tells you that this chapter supersedes prior common law. Thinking back to your directions, you already might sense that the statutes will primarily give you the information you need on the second part of Memo 1 (the analysis of the new law). Logically, you might deduce that the cases will then provide what you need for the first part of Memo 1 (the analysis of prior law). What this means is that you really must read the cases and then come back to the statutes to see how the statutes fix problems that occurred under the old law. (Note how, as you read, you want to continually think about what your exact assignment is, and ask yourself how pieces of the Library and File fit into that assignment.)

I will review the rest of the statutes now, but you might well just have skimmed the statutes at first and then come back to them after reading the rest of the Library. They make much more sense when you have the context.

The second section listed, § 21205, gives the modern rule against perpetuities.

The next section, § 21220, provides for a remedy; in the case of a violation, the court "shall reform a disposition in the manner that most closely approximates the transferor's manifested plan distribution." Under this section, the court will also limit the nonalienation period to 90 years. You may not see the significance of this at first read, but after reading all the cases, and going back to the Task Memo, File, and thinking about how they all connect, you will see that this allows for the possibility of the court coming in and fixing a RAP problem should the transfer to Westside pose such a problem.

Perhaps the most interesting section, § 21225 lists exceptions or interests that are specifically excluded from the rule. This is gold. Your assignment (in the second part of Memo 1) is to describe how the new law eliminates problems with prior law. Reading carefully, you will see a few exceptions that potentially apply here, namely:

- § 21225(a) on non-vested ... arising out of nondonative [or "commercial"] transfer, and
- § 21225(e) on charity-to-charity giving.

Also note that § 21225(g) excludes interests that would have been exempt under prior law; as you learn from reading the case law, in the lease alternative, if the option is considered part of the lease and not independent (or "in gross"), it will be excluded under prior law and under current law via § 21225(g). You will note in the sample answers in the Online Question and Answer Bank how some of these points were mentioned only briefly.

Again, if the statutes were not clear on first read, it would help to read the cases and then come back to the statutes. Note too that only some, but not all, of the subsections in § 21225 were applicable to our case. So, if you did not see how a section applied, it was important not to spend too much time trying to make it fit. (Always remember that on PTs, you will be sorting relevant from irrelevant material.)

All of the cases were applicable and I hope you saw how at least some of the statutes applied. Let's look at the cases now.

> **Note:** Remember, the directions tell you that you can abbreviate cases. You get no "extra credit" for providing full cites. Do not waste time writing complete case citations.

Symphony

This case provided the old RAP rule: that prior to the adoption of the Uniform Statutory Rule Against Perpetuities (USRP), a future property interest was invalid "unless it must vest, if at all, not later than 21 years after one or more of the lives in being at the creation of the estate and any period of gestation involved."

In addition to literally stating the rule, *Symphony* also helped explain the purpose of the RAP in plain English. Did you begin to see it? The basic idea of the RAP is to invalidate interests in property that vest too remotely (generations into the future); the rule thereby stops landowners from excessively restraining the free transfer of property in the far-off future. Very descriptively, *Symphony* explains how 17th-century judges used the RAP to try to limit the "dead hand of landowners [from] reaching into future generations."

Think about it in the terms of the facts of our case. Do we as a society want this (albeit historic) high school property site locked up forever in the hands of LHPS? Do we want them controlling the property for generations to come? Or do we want new owners, such as our client Westside, to be able to come in and reinvigorate the property and help it grow to meet the present community's needs? I realize I am oversimplifying, but no matter what law you find in the Library on PTs, you need to step back, see the big picture, and try to make the rules make sense to you in the context of this role-play.

You cannot allow yourself to be intimidated by any rules you see in a PT Library or any facts you see in a PT File. This is why I included *Westside* in this book!

Again, though, you may have had to read this and the language of each alternative (on the last File page) several times to see their significance. Eventually, you would see that the lease option is potentially problematic as worded because it allows for indefinite renewals and so could continue beyond lives in being plus 21 years. The sale-buy back may also pose problems because, under the current wording, LHPS could exercise its option "at any time after sale."

Symphony also cites *MTA*, a case that distinguishes options from preemptive rights, and explains why the latter (also called *rights of first refusal*) do not violate the RAP. A right of first refusal would likely provide another way to possibly get around the RAP problems under prior law, something we will write about in Memo 1.

Temple Hoyne Buell (Temple)

The *Temple* case provides "fixes" for the RAP problems, namely adding a savings clause (or time limitation language) or deleting language that makes an option binding on heirs, successors, and assigns. This is also a very important problem-solving tool that we may want to write about in Memo 1.

Citgo

In the *Citgo* case, you learn that purchase options (such as the one contemplated by Westside) may be exempt from the (old) RAP if they are adjunct to a valid long-term commercial and nondonative lease. (Is this a commercial lease? It might be considered one, or it might be analogous to one, though it could also be considered a charitable venture.) You will see how the sample answers in the Online Question and Answer Bank analyzed this.

However, *Citgo* may not apply because, in *Citgo*, the option could be exercised any time *during* the lease; whereas, in our case, the language allows LHPS to exercise the option *at any time* starting two years *after* the lease.

Even if *Citgo* is distinguishable, we might still argue that some of the policy applies and should help save the lease because it furthers the goals behind the RAP, namely stimulating improvement and development of the property. This property has been unused for nearly 20 years, and our client is offering to come in and bring the location to life with arts and culture.

Shaver

This is the only case that discusses the new law. *Shaver* discusses USRP § 21225, giving insight into its nonapplicability to commercial nondonative transactions. Hence, you might reference *Shaver* in your discussion in Part 2 of Memo 1 regarding how the new law eliminates RAP problems.

THE BIGGEST CHALLENGES IN THIS PT

What many found challenging here included:

1. Finishing, as there was a lot to discuss. A success strategy here (and with other PTs that seem overwhelming) is to write briefly on each part, finish, and then return to add more detail if time permits.

2. Getting "thrown" by the RAP. Just read it and analyze it like any other rule of law. Do not assume that you cannot understand it. It is no more complicated than much of the rest of what you study in real property. (Of course, depending on your professor and the casebook you use, you may study some RAP cases that are extremely complex, but if tested on the bar exam, RAP issues will likely be fairly straightforward. Also, as the USRP is adopted in more states, casebooks seem to be dropping many of the particularly complex RAP cases.

PUTTING IT ALL TOGETHER

After initially briefing the cases, go back and look at the Task Memo and remember your assignment. In the first memo, you are to analyze the old law and recommend how to avoid the RAP even under the old law, and then analyze how the new law eliminates RAP problems. After reading these cases, re-reading the File, and maybe re-reading the law (especially if it was confusing on first read), you should have seen several ways to fix the problems under the old law. Then, after putting together Part 1 of Memo 1 (on the old law), go back and review the USRP provisions and *Shaver*. You will immediately see how the new law helps eliminate RAP problems: namely (as noted earlier), with provisions excepting the commercial nondonative transfer and the transfer from charity to charity. After that, move on to the second memo on the pros and cons of each alternative.

How would this all fit into the outline we started earlier?

To: A. Hilliard Meherrin

From: Applicant

Re: Westside Community Development Corp. and Effects of Rule Against Perpetuities on Plans to Lease or Buy Property on the High School Site.

Memo I: Analysis of prior law and new law of RAP and how it affects Westside's lease-option and sale-buy back. Does new law eliminate old problems?

The traditional rule against perpetuities poses potential problems with both the lease option and the sale-buy back. As to the former, because the lease may be renewed indefinitely, it may extend too far into the future. Also, under the second option, because LHPS could exercise its buy-back option at any time in the future, that too would violate the rule as strictly construed.

Analysis of prior law

[Ways to possibly solve lease-option problems under old law]:
• Make option adjunct to the lease and not independent of the lease.

Discuss and cite cases, including *Citgo.*
• Include a termination date for the lease option.

Discuss and cite cases, including *Temple.*
• Make sure the option right does not transfer to successors in perpetuity.

Discuss and cite cases, including *Temple.*
[Ways to possibly solve sale-buy back problems under old law]:
• Show why it is part of a commercial nondonative transaction.

Discuss and cite cases, including *Symphony.*
• Include a termination date for the buy back.

Discuss and cite cases, including *Temple.*
• Insert a preemptive right (or right of first refusal) clause.

Discuss and cite cases, including *Symphony.*

Analysis of new law
Several changes in the new law will help, particularly the following exclusions:
Show why it is part of commercial nondonative transaction.
Discuss, cite *Shaver* and § 21225(a).
Show why it is a charity-to-charity transfer.
Discuss, cite *Shaver* and § 21225(e).

Memo II
Analysis of alternatives: which is better for Westside and why?

Many of the Westside staff and board members expressed strong opinions about Westside's acquiring space on the old high school site. The following is a summary of the pros and cons of each alternative, and a recommendation based on a review of all views as a whole as to which path would best serve our client.

1) Pros and Cons of Leasing the High School's Fine Arts Building, with an option to purchase the entire property ("lease option"), or

Alternative 1 gets Westside the Fine Arts Building right away, and Westside has the money to complete the necessary renovations on that one building from the Rappaport Foundation grant. This alternative also gives Westside a purchase option, which, depending on how the language is read and interpreted, may give Westside the right to buy the property for quite a long time. The purchase option protects Westside in this way, and also allows Westside time to raise more money to fix the rest of the buildings (and perhaps eventually build additional buildings) on the site.

2) Pros and Cons of Purchasing the entire school with LHPS retaining an option to buy it back ("sale–buy back").

Alternative 2 gives Westside the entire property and accordingly the potential to grow and expand further in the future, so at first it may look like the better option (and several board members seem to favor it), but (a) can Westside afford to buy the whole property? And (b) will LHPS come snatch it back (with the buy-back provision as written) and take it all away from Westside? (And will knowledge of the mere existence of LHPS's preemptive right to repurchase cause hesitancy on the part of prospective tenants to rent space on the property? Will this cause similar problems for Westside too in terms of future grant applications?)

Conclude Memo II with advice to give to board.

On balance, after evaluating both the positions of the Westside Board and staff and the soundness of each option, quite likely the lease option is the better of the two alternatives for Westside.

Note: More important than your actual conclusion was that you explained your reasoning and clearly set out the pros and cons, and the importance of avoiding a focus on merely technical compliance with the RAP. Also, although *Holland* discussed legal malpractice, it brings up an important strategy available to a lawyer who has the luxury of drafting documents instead of defending documents after the fact (in litigation). The board members will want to avoid the expensive and distracting litigation that may arise if the RAP issue is questionable. We're looking to stay out of court here, not for a winnable case. Thus, the solution should be clear and obvious compliance with the letter and spirit of the perpetuities rules.

Memo 2 should have been much easier after writing Memo 1, because Memo 1 really already forced you to think about both alternatives. Memo 2 just makes more explicit the task of evaluating the pros and cons of each alternative, and, if you have time, summarizing the specific positions of various Westside staff and board members. Review the sample answers in the Online Question and Answer Bank for more details.

SPIN-OFF EXERCISES

Spin-off exercises are a great way to gain exposure to different types of documents without as much of a time commitment as it would take to complete a whole new performance test. Now that you have completed the *Westside* memos, think about other documents you might have been asked to draft based on the same law and facts. Pay particular attention to how your tone and approach might differ depending on the goal of your assignment and your audience. Consider how you would draft an answer if your task were to:

- Make a presentation to the board advocating the lease option as the better of the two alternatives (and why). Write out your words exactly as you would speak to board members. Anticipate questions that particular board members may ask and indicate how you would respond. How does this assignment differ from writing a memo to your boss about how to advise the board?
- Draft an investigation plan. What, if any, additional information would you like to help choose the best alternative for Westside?
- Edit the draft lease in the File and/or draft a proposed sale agreement.

PRACTICE, LAW SCHOOL, AND PTs: COMPARE AND CONTRAST

This again is a fabulous and realistic transactional problem. You are not set in a litigation context at all; thus, this is a very different type of assignment from a typical law school property essay question where it is likely that facts have already taken place which give rise to a potential lawsuit. Here in *Westside*, you are thinking forward to help your client make a legally sound decision that accomplishes the organization's goals. The perspective you had to adopt in this problem was that of a "preventive lawyer" (planning well to avoid ever having legal issues in the first place), rather than that of a litigator. Though some clients do not seek the advice of a lawyer until litigation is inevitable, the client here was smart to get counsel involved early on to help determine which alternative was better. We see similar assignments that ask you to role-play as attorneys with a similar perspective in the constitutional law and contracts chapters of this book (Chapters 9 and 6). If you enjoy these sorts of tasks, you might take additional transactional courses in law school and intern for or get a job in a firm that does transactional work.

Congratulations, too, on grappling with a tough area of the law on this practice exam. There is a tendency, both on exams and in real life, especially for beginning lawyers, to get nervous when they don't have all the answers—but this is normal. Do not pretend. Competency of counsel does not mean you know everything off the top of your head. You may have to study to become competent, or associate with more knowledgeable and experienced counsel.

In law school and in studying for the bar exam, it is very important not to get frustrated. Do not even think that there are areas of law that you cannot understand. If you were smart enough to be accepted by a reputable law school, there is an overwhelming likelihood that you are smart enough to understand every rule or concept you encounter in law school and studying for the bar exam. That does not mean it will be easy! You may have to read things many times over. You may have to seek help and ask for explanations, possibly from multiple sources (professors, classmates, and academic support faculty). You may also need to read trustworthy explanatory resources such as hornbooks or treatises. Still, with enough dedicated, focused hard work, you *will* get it.

KEY TAKEAWAYS

- This practice exam helped steel you for the worst, and hopefully empowered you to see that you must not "freeze" on the PT portion of the bar exam if a PT is set in the context of a subject of law that you either do not know or do not like. (There may even be subjects you dread or fear, though I urge you not to fear anything on the bar exam; just prepare well and face the beasts!) Note this applies on essays and MBEs as well. There may be subjects you like more or feel more comfortable with, but you cannot panic or turn off when faced with questions in your least favorite subjects. In fact, I would recommend that as part of your practice, you complete extra questions in any subjects you secretly hope will not be on the bar exam, so that you are well prepared (and not psyched out) if they are.
- This PT gave you some further exposure to statutory as well as case analysis in that part of the exam that required you to analyze the new and old laws.
- Although the first memo task was heavy on legal analysis skills, the second memo task also worked your problem-solving skills. You needed to consider how each alternative would help your clients or not, and why, and conclude by giving them advice.

12

FAMILY LAW

OVERVIEW OF FAMILY LAW

Family law comprises both divorce and marital property division laws, as well as laws about child support, child custody and visitation, and related family issues. Family law matters are handled in state court, and family laws differ from state to state. There are some threads that are common with child custody and visitation concerns generally, namely that family courts typically look at what is in the best interests of the child. However, the law discussed in the performance test in this chapter may or may not be similar to your state's laws, and should be used *only* to provide a legal context for this hypothetical case and *not* for purposes of learning what law might govern in any other case.

SIMULATED FAMILY LAW–BASED PERFORMANCE TEST

Take three hours, and complete the memo requested in the *Stolier v. Wallach* performance test located in the Online Question and Answer Bank at **http://ambar .org/barexamprep**. Though set in a family law context (the main question you are concerned with is visitation rights), your assignment is essentially an investigation/ discovery plan (implicating civil procedure rules). Thus, it is good practice in both family law and civil procedure.

This is yet another reason why PTs are realistic: They often cross over different subjects. Law school divides study into distinct subjects, but all kinds of matters may arise in the context of family law practice, including bankruptcy, criminal concerns, education law, tax law, and more.

Enjoy the *Stolier* exam (located, again, in the Online Question and Answer Bank), and after you have drafted your answer, read the rest of this chapter.

TIME-CRUNCH TIPS

This PT requires you to complete one memo (essentially a discovery plan). If you cannot take a full three hours to do this, please read the entire File and Library and outline your answer. Try to at least quickly identify the legal elements at issue, evidence that proves or disproves facts related to each element, and sources of obtaining such evidence. You can do this in about 90 to 100 minutes.

INSIDE THIS TEST: TIPS AND STRATEGIES

Now that you have tackled the *Stolier* PT, let's look together at the File, starting with the Task Memo and the Library, and see how you did.

The Task Memo

The Task Memo is written to you, Applicant (who you are on the PT) from Marsha Pushkin. A quick glance at the letterhead shows Pushkin as the third named partner. Assuming Marsha is that partner, we understand we are in a private law firm and working for one of the named partners.

The very first sentence is the most critical of the entire PT. "We represent Celia Stolier and are trying to help her establish the right to regular visitation with her granddaughter, Joanna Wallach." It would have helped to have returned to that sentence, and everything in this Task Memo, several times as you read, outlined, and wrote, to keep your eyes on the bottom line.

In PTs, as in practice, what your client wants is the baseline. The bar examiners use the PT in part to see if you can help the client achieve the client's desired objectives.

Your boss, Pushkin, then goes on to provide some background about the parties and how the parties got to the point they are now. Joanna's mother died, and her father and stepmother refuse to let Celia (our client and the grandmother) see Joanna (the granddaughter who is now living with her father). Pushkin outlines a history of "bad blood" between the father and grandmother, but suggests that Celia and Joanna had an "excellent" relationship.

When you first read this, were you wondering how Pushkin knows this? If so, your lawyering instincts are excellent. So often, our concerns in PTs and in law practice are with how facts are proven.

Note: Pushkin goes on to indicate that litigation is now the only choice. Remember, the Task Memo is helping define your task by situating you in context, telling you what your assignment is and also what it is not. This language lets you know not to write about settlement or alternative dispute resolution (both viable possibilities in real life, even given the fact that reconciliation has thus far failed). The PT is an exam, though, and the examiners write the questions to be answerable within the time limits, so you want to be sure to pick up on clues regarding what to write about and what not to write about.

Your boss (Pushkin) then says she has gathered some cases and statutes (what you will find in the Library) and that she has communicated with some of the players (opposing counsel and our client's brother-in law), giving a preview of what we will find in the File, with a very important hint.

Pushkin tells you, "There is no doubt that the facts here are seriously in dispute." What a wonderful sentence! First, this underscores another great difference between PTs on the one hand, and essays and multiple-choice questions on the other. PTs often set up that very real-life situation where different people see things differently, where there are two or more sides to every story, and where a huge part of the job of a lawyer is determining what happened and how that can be proven. You do not want to "fight the facts" on MBEs and essays; they are fixed, set in stone. Your job on essays is to determine how you will use the facts as given to prove or disprove the applicable legal rules raised by the relevant legal issues. Second, and more specifically relating to this PT, this sentence hints that you should expect to see contradictions in the File, and perhaps provides a hint that your task may involve some determination about what facts can credibly be established. You of course hold that last thought until you read exactly what your boss wants you to draft. Still, this sort of thinking gets you primed to understand your assignment, something underscored in the next paragraph.

"Before we draft the Petition … I need your thoughts on how we should go about gathering the facts." This is followed by a paragraph that starts: "What I need from you is … ." Underline or highlight that part of the Task Memo; it is your guide, your bible. Here is where those who read slowly and carefully will do so much better than those who are hurrying to get to the File and Library. Slow down now, and read every word. Why? You will be graded in large part on whether you give the examiners what they want (whether you follow directions!). Here, Pushkin is (or, really, the bar examiners are) telling you precisely what your assignment is: "a well-organized, thorough but not unduly repetitive statement as to how we can obtain the evidence needed to show the court that our client should be granted the right to visit her grandchild." That is your precise assignment.

Equally important is the next sentence telling you what the assignment is *not*: "Please do not burden this memorandum with a general discussion of the legal right to visitation, as I am aware of those requirements." This is critical for PT purposes because you will typically be able to finish the PT only if you give the graders what they want and only what they want. If you give them extras, you will not be rewarded, unless you have first thoroughly covered everything that was requested. This really is important. You may well appear before a judge who asks you to speak on one thing and not another; you will likely annoy the judge, and perhaps lose, if you do not comply.

The next part of the Task Memo is really a Format Memo in disguise. It sets forth exactly how to set up your answer, with examples. (Examples on PTs are gifts!)

Note: If you were confused about how to organize your response on this exam, I would ask how carefully you read the last two paragraphs of the Task Memo.

This is how I would have translated that information immediately into my rough draft outline, before I even began skimming the File or reading the Library:

I. Elements that must be established to grant visitation rights

II. Element #1

—Items of evidence to prove or disprove facts relating to element #1, and
—Source(s) of such evidence

Element #2

—Items of evidence to prove or disprove facts relating to element #2, and
—Source(s) of such evidence

Element #3

—Items of evidence to prove or disprove facts relating to element #3, and

—Source(s) of such evidence

And so on for however many elements we have.

This, of course, is a most basic skeletal outline, but it starts helping me visualize what I will need to draft to be responsive to the directions. I urge you to get into the habit of outlining as soon as you see an organizational structure or a directive to respond to.

Next, I would actually have mapped out the examples given in the Task Memo so I have a format to follow that makes sense in context, not just a skeletal outline. Pushkin gives one required element, facts that might establish that element, and how we might prove those facts. I translated those examples into outline form as follows:

I. Elements that must be established to grant visitation rights

II. Element #1

—Items of evidence to prove or disprove facts relating to element #1, and

—Source(s) of such evidence

Element #___: Joanna has a desire to visit her grandmother.

—Fact that proves this element: Joanna wrote a letter expressing this desire to her grandma.

—Discovery/investigation needed to establish this fact: Have Joanna's letter authenticated, possibly by Celia or by admission of father.

—Fact that proves this element: If Joanna had told one of her teachers that she wanted to see her grandma.

—Discovery/investigation needed to establish this fact: Interviewing and perhaps taking depositions of Joanna's teachers.

Element #___

—Items of evidence to prove or disprove facts relating to this element, and

—Source(s) of such evidence

Element #___

—Items of evidence to prove or disprove facts relating to this element, and

—Source(s) of such evidence

III. Conclusion

I would have kept this outline, with examples, as sort of a "cheat sheet" in front of me as an open document, so that I could type in ideas as I thought of what facts to investigate, and place them into the logically related part of my memo.

> **Note:** I added space for a conclusion at the end of my memo. It will not be long because it was not specifically requested, but it will wrap up and serve to notify the grader that I completed the assignment.

Because it was not requested, you would not want to waste precious time writing a statement of facts in this Memo. That was easy to see (we hope!) and something we have stressed throughout this book: *follow the directions*. They will tell you what they want. Write the assignments as the bar examiners direct you, and not as you learned in school or at work. (That said, I do realize that just previously I said to add a very short conclusion even if that wasn't requested; but doing so will not take time away from your work and it adds substantial value in showing the grader that you finished.)

What may have been a bit trickier was determining how much to put into the first part of the memo that your boss requested: the setting forth of the required legal elements. We will look at that in more detail after exploring the File and Library.

For now, with a big-picture sense of what our client wants and what she is fighting, and a fairly detailed sense of the type of document we are to produce, you want to get the lay of the land: first factually, by quickly skimming the File; second, by briefing the authorities in the Library and understanding what those critical elements are that will frame your whole task; and third, by going back and carefully reading the File to pick up what you need to write your answer.

Skim the File

If you flip back to the table of contents of the File, you see that the File consists of all notes and letters. You see from your careful read of the Task Memo that the facts are in dispute and that your job will be to organize facts as they establish elements. Here, a very quick look at the File is all you want to do until you get to the Library and identify those elements.

You might want to get into the habit of thinking of the File as just general background, much of which may be irrelevant, until you know what the legal framework is. Only then can you pull out what is truly significant from your File. So, at this first skim, just familiarize yourself with what is in the File, eyeballing for a sense of each document.

Notes of Interview with Our Client

Again, you do not yet know what is critical in this document; until you understand the law, you won't. Still, this document does give you background on a number of different people. As you read, you may want to write a "cast of characters" on scratch paper (or in part of your answer file that you will delete before uploading), so you remember everyone. Just as a program names the actors who play certain roles in a play, you can add quick notes about each person as you see him or her described in the File documents. For example:

- Marsha Pushkin: senior partner and my boss, person I am writing task to
- Celia Stolier: client
- Joanna Wallach: client's granddaughter, person client wants to be able to visit
- David Wallach: Joanna's father, opposes Celia's visitation requests
- Fred Andrews: Wallach's attorney
- Elizabeth Lawton: deceased mother of Joanna (divorced from David Wallach before she died)
- Harry Breckenridge: Celia's brother-in-law, very ill
- Wanda Breckenridge: Celia's sister, now deceased. Joanna lived with her great-aunt Wanda and great-uncle Harry when Joanna's mother divorced and then after she died, before Joanna moved to live with David Wallach and his new wife. Wanda and Harry wanted and were awarded visitation.

TIP: VISUAL LEARNERS

You can take the related members of your cast-of-characters list and make it into a "family tree" to visualize how the people in this PT are related.[1]

Notes to File

This document is a chronology of sorts. There are some red flags, but nothing you can yet make sense of. There are references to "surprising allegations" about our client in a letter from the Wallachs' lawyer. We don't know what they are, but we know we have a letter from the attorney, so we can look for those when we get to that document. There is also a reference to a new person to add to our cast of characters, Karen Hegel, but we don't know who she is yet. This too will likely become clear as we keep reading, but we can add her name to the list with a question mark for now.

Letter to Fred Andrews, the Wallachs' Attorney

When you first skim the File, you may not see why this letter was important, but after you read the Library, you note that it is critical for thoughts on why Joanna will benefit from visitation with Celia: She benefits from (1) continued contact with maternal blood relatives, and (2) financial and material support that Celia can provide.

LETTER TO ANDREWS AS SAMPLE SETTLEMENT LETTER

There's another important thing about the letter from Pushkin to Andrews: it provides a great sample of a settlement letter. It says what our client wants from Andrews' client, and how his client can benefit from granting our client's request. It concludes by making clear that our client intends to pursue relief in court if an informal agreement cannot be reached. If you end up having a settlement letter assignment on a performance test, this is a very useful example of what you might write in this sort of task.

---

[1] All credit for this suggestion to my colleague Christine Francis, Esq.

Reply Letter from Fred Andrews, the Wallachs' Attorney

This reply letter is easy to read, and again, as with the letter from Pushkin to Andrews, should be read both with an eye toward the facts that we need to look into in this case, and with a sense of how we might draft a reply refusing a settlement request on behalf of our client if that were the task in a future PT. The "surprising allegations" about our client that were alluded to earlier in the File are now clear: the claim is that Celia "abandoned" her own daughter when she was young. We do not know exactly how this fits in to the assignment, because we still have not read the Library and do not yet know the legal framework. We also do not know if this is true or, if it is, whether Celia has a reasonable explanation. Remember, David Wallach is allegedly biased against our client and may have reasons to fabricate statements that hurt her. However, as we are in an investigatory stage, preparing to go to court to make requests for relief on behalf of our client, we must learn about all potentially damaging as well as all helpful evidence.

Notes of Interview with Harry Breckenridge

From these notes we learn a bit more about Harry's physical condition, particularly that it is "precarious," and about the significant contact the Breckenridges had with Joanna (her living with them for a time, etc.), and how Celia often came to visit during that time. Harry spoke very positively about the grandmother-granddaughter relationship. Pushkin asked him about family photos and he said he and Wanda had taken many and thought they were in a box. He also provided some details about Celia's and Elizabeth's backgrounds: how Celia's multiple marriages contributed to why Elizabeth stayed so often with the Breckenridges and how Celia came to be wealthy.

Notes from Second Client Interview

In the second interview, Celia gave our boss more details on her own background, including depression, recent counseling with a psychiatrist named Jane Peters (another person to add to the cast of characters), and time spent 32 years ago in a psychiatric center. Celia also mentioned that Harry had given boxes of Wanda's things to a friend, Karen Hegel (the person we added to our cast of characters earlier but could not identify). Celia notes that she and Hegel are not on speaking terms, but does not say why.

Letter from Joanna to Celia

Lastly, we have a handwritten letter, purportedly from Joanna to Celia, saying she misses Celia. If you remembered, or if you had taken notes on the Task Memo examples, Marsha Pushkin mentioned the letter in connection with proving the element of the child's desire to see her grandmother.

We have now skimmed the File and come full circle. We know a bit about the situation and we know one element of the legal framework (what the senior partner gave us from the Task Memo). We need to see what the Library reveals in terms of what all the other elements are.

The Library

First notice the this Library is a nice mix of statutes and cases. As we have said with statutes, before you study each word of them, figure out whether they are statutes you are familiar with (for example, excerpts from a code you are already charged with knowing for the bar exam, such as the Federal Rules of Evidence; if so, you can treat them more like a reference Library) or whether they are statutes governing a particular area relevant to your PT case (if so, you must read them carefully as if they were brand new to you).

The first rules you have are from the Columbia Rules of Civil Procedure (CRCP). You do not have language specifically telling you that they are substantially similar to the Federal Rules of Civil Procedure, but a quick look reveals that they cover basic discovery tools. You know this! (Or you would by the time of the bar exam.) Each numbered section covers a different discovery device. In case you forget, or blank on the exam about these, you can glance through these to remind yourself what each device is and how and when you can use it. For example, you can see that as a party, you can take depositions of any person (party or nonparty), whereas you as a party can only send interrogatories to other parties.

At this point, I would simply scan the headings of each of the CRPC sections, listing the five formal discovery tools they have provided sections for on scratch paper, or highlighting each heading: depositions, interrogatories, requests for admission, requests for identification/production of documents, and physical/mental examinations.

You may already be matching up these devices in your mind with our cast of characters to determine what sort of further information you might want from whom. Or, you might just hold this list so that when you get to figuring out what facts you want to prove, you can look back to this list to see if any of these rules and devices will help you prove what you want to establish.

Along this line, note that buried in the first paragraph under the code section on depositions is the following: "Upon leave of court, the deposition of a potential witness may be taken, notwithstanding the absence of a pending action, where good cause exists to believe the witness may be unavailable at the time suit is filed." Anything pop out at you? Harry Breckenridge is very ill. He has positive things to say about the relationship between Celia and Joanna, something he witnessed at first hand over many years. We may want to immediately request permission from the court to depose him now, in case he gets sicker and is unable to talk with us on the record, and determine what exactly we will want to ask him.

Next, we have four sections from the Columbia Civil Code. This is not something we are familiar with; it clearly relates directly to the particulars of the *Stolier* visitation issues. We will have to read these sections as if they were brand new. They are not terribly long or complex, though, so we may want to glance at them now and then go back and re-read them carefully after we read the three cases.

Two of the cases, *Whitaker* and *Hawkins*, are Columbia Supreme Court cases, and thus binding in our case, which will be filed in state court in Columbia. The third case, *Douglas*, is from the Court of Appeals of Indiana, so it is merely persuasive authority in Columbia. However, *Douglas* is cited by the *Hawkins* court, so its reasoning appears to be compelling to our Columbia Supreme Court.

Remember, per the Task Memo, we are not supposed to be writing a treatise on grandparental visitation, simply a quick summary of the elements we must establish. (Other PTs have asked for lengthier legal memos; this is more of a discovery plan organized by the components of the applicable legal standard.)

Looking strictly at § 3108, we see it applies in certain proceedings (not how Celia's matter arises) and only to parents. However, the court may order, "in its discretion," certain "reasonable companionship or visitation rights" to "any other person having an interest in the welfare of the child." Also, *Hawkins* allows the court-ordered grandparental visitation in special circumstances in situations such as *Stolier's* where there is no pending divorce proceeding.

Whitaker holds that "grandparents may be granted visitation rights under Section 3108 if the trial court finds that such visitation is in the child's best interest." *Whitaker* further holds that the § 3108 factors for determining the "best interest of the child" for custody apply for visitation purposes as well.

So, Marsha Pushkin in the Task Memo asks for "elements." Those essentially appear to be two: whether Celia is a person "having an interest in the welfare of Joanna," and whether ordering visitation with Joanna is in Joanna's "best interests" as determined by a set of five factors that the court will look to as guidelines.

Note: Factors are not the same as elements. Elements must each be proven in order to establish a cause of action, defense, or other legal theory. Factors are not applied rigidly, but typically assessed on a sliding scale: if most of the factors are clearly established, the standard may be found to be satisfied even if proof of a certain factor or factors is weak. Taking the cases and statutes as a whole, it appears clear that the standard the court will be looking to in making its determination will be whether or not the visitation would be in the best interest of Joanna.

Armed with the legal framework, I would revise my outline before I go back into the File and look for facts that prove each factor.

Updated Outline

<u>Legal standard that must be established to grant visitation rights</u>

First that Celia qualifies, as Joanna's maternal grandmother, as "any other person having an interest in the welfare of the child" under § 3108. And, next, considering the following five factors in § 3108, that ordering visitation with her grandmother is in Joanna's best interest:

(a) <u>Joanna's wishes</u> [and note that she is only eight years old, so this is not mandatory but within the court's discretion to consider]

—Brainstorm here, listing items of evidence to prove or disprove facts relating to Joanna's wishes, and sources of proof for each such item of evidence.

(b) <u>The wishes of Joanna's parents</u>. [Get creative here and consider not only her one living blood parent, but perhaps her stepparent and perhaps Breckenridge who stood for some time in a parental role.]

—Items of evidence to prove or disprove facts relating to Joanna's wishes, and sources of proof for each such item of evidence.

(c) <u>The child's interaction and interrelationship with her parents</u> and any other person (such as grandparent) who may significantly affect the child's best interests.

—Items of evidence to prove or disprove facts relating to Joanna's wishes, and sources of proof for each such item of evidence.

(d) <u>The child's adjustment to home, school, and community</u>.

—Items of evidence to prove or disprove facts relating to this factor, and source(s) of such evidence.

(e) <u>The mental and physical health of all persons involved in the situation</u>.

—Items of evidence to prove or disprove facts relating to this factor, and source(s) of such evidence.

Conclusion

TIP: PAY ATTENTION TO INFORMATION THAT IS REPEATED

The § 3108 factors are set forth both under the Civil Code Sections and again in *Whitaker*. This is a hint that the factors are important and should be used in your answer. (As I've said throughout this book, lists, especially lists of elements or factors, are often organizational gifts in PTs! Also, anything the bar examiners repeat within a question is worth paying special attention to.)

PUTTING IT ALL TOGETHER

With that sort of an outline, I go back into the File and essentially begin plucking out facts (and ideas on how to prove them) to plug into the appropriate section of my outline.

Because we are in the first stages of planning what to investigate rather than at the stage where we are arguing before the court, we can brainstorm here and be fairly creative. As long as the graders see that you are suggesting facts that are relevant to proving each factor and are proposing ethical and lawful ways of gathering and establishing those facts, you should get points for all your ideas.

For example, for the fourth factor, Child's Adjustment to Home/School/Community, my first thought was to show that Joanna is not as well-adjusted where she is now and that she would be better off if she were allowed to visit with her grandmother.

- Review court records if they can be unsealed, reports and accounts of teachers, counselors, and clergy people to find out how well-adjusted Joanna is. (Are there "Grandparent and Me" classes at the local community center that Joanna could be a part of if Celia were in her life?) Much of this information could be collected informally through simply talking with people, though some we might need to depose; for sealed records we would seek leave of court under Columbia Civil Code § 3121.
- Request a physical inspection of the father's home to determine if Joanna is comfortable there and also if there is anything lacking that perhaps Celia's material resources might help provide.
- Mental evaluation of Joanna, perhaps. Have a counselor talk with her and see if she is well adjusted, if she misses her grandmother, and so on.

You can see from this list that it is brainstorming, but in a way that shows what information we are seeking, why, and from what sources: responding exactly to the directions and what was asked of us in the Task Memo.

Go ahead now and study the sample answers in the Online Question and Answer Bank. Compare and contrast them to your own answer, looking for ideas on how to improve what you wrote. Pay special attention to the organization of your answer.

SPIN-OFF EXERCISES

Taking the same facts and law as you had in the *Stolier* PT, try drafting the following:

- A dialogue of a mediation between Celia Stolier and David Wallach. Be sure to note what the mediator would say, and what each party would say, both when they are together and when each meets privately with the neutral mediator.
- A second settlement letter from Marsha Pushkin to Fred Andrews, in addition to the letter on June 15, 1989, to Fred Andrews, again requesting and pushing harder on visitation rights for Celia Stolier.
- Next, assume for the sake of this assignment only that David Wallach fired Fred Andrews; write a letter from Marsha Pushkin directly to David Wallach.

How would the content and tone of your letter to Mr. Wallach differ if you were writing to his attorney or if he was unrepresented? Both of these suggested exercises are designed to help you think about the differences between writing in plain English, so that a lay person can easily understand your points, and writing to fellow lawyers. (Remember, you are a lawyer on this exam!)

The PT often requires an awareness and appreciation of the differences in communication with lay people versus lawyers. Are there any bits of jargon or terms you have come across that you might need to define? Lastly, how does the goal of mediation differ from what the goal in your settlement letter would be?

Next, assume that a hearing on visitation has been set and the court requests both briefing before the hearing and oral argument at the hearing. Draft the following:

- A brief to the family court urging that Celia Stolier be granted visitation rights
- An oral argument to the family court judge arguing that Celia Stolier should be granted visitation rights

How would the last two assignments differ? What might you include in a written brief in advance of a hearing that you would not say orally, or vice versa? In both instances your audience is the judge, but in the former the judge will presumably sit and read what you wrote, whereas in the latter the judge is listening to what will likely be a fairly quick statement in open court.

PRACTICE, LAW SCHOOL, AND PTs:
COMPARE AND CONTRAST

This exam posed a problem that is not uncommon, especially in today's world of frequent divorces, blended families, grandparents living longer, and so on. However, unless a grandmother like Celia Stolier were very wealthy (and here note that built into the File was the fact that Celia had inherited substantial wealth), it is not likely that she would have the money to engage in discovery and have an extended court battle to visit her granddaughter. More likely, in the real world, this would be a matter handled either informally, with or without the brief intervention of a lawyer, or through some sort of mediation. Nevertheless, the *Stolier* problem is a great exercise for a law student, because it combines a basic governing principle of family law (best interests of the child) with fact-gathering work using informal and formal discovery tools.

Family lawyers often work with both issues relating to divorce and property division and issues relating to children. All kinds of other matters may arise in the context of family law consultations, including bankruptcy, criminal concerns, education law, and more. Family lawyers may specialize, but they often are called on to refer parts of their cases to others who know more about particular slices of their clients' problems. Law school courses may be more siloed: some might focus more extensively on marital property division, which may be tested more heavily on bar exams; others might focus on issues relating to children and families. Some law schools include children's rights courses and clinics, where the issues that students grapple with may extend to children facing violence, educational or health care challenges, neglect, and other problems (civil and/or criminal), both within their families and outside the family setting such as in foster care or schools settings.

As you work your way through law school, if this is an area that interests you, look both at what family law–related courses and/or clinics your school offers. Look also at externships or clerkships that may be available in local legal organizations, clinics, or law offices. Consider both paid and volunteer positions, so you can gain as much experience as possible. You might also consider getting trained as a mediator and helping with some family law mediations; this is something you can do without a law license.

Family law is an important area on many state bar exams and in real life. Whether you end up practicing in the area or not, some exposure to the area can be helpful, as you will inevitably encounter questions at some point from family, friends, or colleagues who need advice in family law matters.

KEY TAKEAWAYS

- This practice exam helped train your factual analysis skills. It was less "law-heavy" and much more focused on seeing which facts (and finding new facts) that help prove the elements your client has to establish to secure her visitation rights. This is an excellent skills-training PT even if you have no interest at all in family law. Just having to pull the key rules out of the Library, and then think of facts to prove each element, was superb PT success training.

- Breaking down the facts that prove or disprove each element and the sources of such evidence (how and where you find and establish such facts) provided an excellent exercise and training for any PT that involves discovery or fact investigation. Studying the answers, you see that this question asked you to consider both formal and informal discovery—a very realistic exercise.

- This PT also provided very explicit directions, with a specific format, and thus tested your ability and willingness to follow instructions as well as your other lawyering skills.

13

CONCLUSION AND STRATEGIC REVIEW

If you completed all the performance tests in this book, you are well on your way to mastering this portion of your bar exam. You have also made serious strides on the path toward establishing a foundation of competency in certain basic lawyering skills.

THE PT AS A "TRIAL RUN" OF YOU AS A LAWYER

After role-playing the lawyer in all the PTs in this book, you now have an extensive and diverse "portfolio" of cases. Here is a small sampling of the work you completed in this book:

- You "represented" almost a dozen clients, from an injured teenager to a local school board.
- You served as a prosecutor twice: once opposing a motion to suppress evidence based on alleged *Miranda* violations in a murder case, and again in investigating the facts in a heated political case involving alleged assault and trespass in a newsworthy local labor union dispute.
- You worked on various aspects of several negligence cases: *Carelton* (where you wrestled with varying duties owed by landowners to trespassers), *Dodson* (which required you to analyze evidentiary and procedural rules in a case stemming from a serious car accident that left your client a paraplegic and put your client in an adversarial position not only against the car manufacturer but also against her own sister), and *Piccolo* (where you helped fight a discovery battle in another car-accident case where a passenger in your client's car was killed).
- You dealt with litigation matters, and you also reviewed a contract, analyzed a lease, and scrutinized a proposed communications code as you addressed free speech and other concerns of a school-board client.
- You helped a grandmother trying to win visitation rights to see and have a relationship with her granddaughter.
- You counseled a colleague about ethical concerns in representing a client who is a local politician.

Your work history in these role-plays was varied. You worked as an associate in several private firms for private clients and at least one charitable organization; you also served as a prosecutor in criminal matters. You wrote several legal memos, and you drafted both opening and responsive briefs. You analyzed documents. You drafted discovery plans and fact-gathering memos for use in pretrial investigation and you drafted a cross-examination plan to question a witness during trial.

Sounds like a lot more than just reading a book, right? You bet! I hope that, after completing these PT assignments, you are starting to see yourself as a beginning attorney, rather than as "just" a law student. You will be making that transition shortly. The bar exam will not be a "bar" to your entry into practice but a door of opportunity that leads to a bright future, filled with potential for you to both better your own life and to help make the world a better place.

Additionally, the bar review study period you are headed toward before you sit for the exam is not the torture some describe it as. Bar review can be an empowering experience, an opportunity to review everything you learned in law school, to pull disparate legal threads together, and to get ready to prove to the bar examiners that you are capable of effectively serving clients. Rules and areas of law that may have been murky in school will become crystal clear. And, when you pass, you will feel a sense of achievement and accomplishment that is incomparable. If I haven't yet convinced you and you are still dreading the bar exam, please read *Pass The Bar Exam*.[1]

USING PRACTICE PERFORMANCE TESTS AS WRITING SAMPLES

In addition to helping train your writing, analytical, and practical knowledge and getting you ready for the bar exam, PT answers can sometimes be adapted to serve as writing samples for job interviews. This is a nice way to get extra mileage out of work you did while taking practice tests. Showing an employer several answers may demonstrate the range of your writing ability, especially if you choose both a persuasive and an analytical sample. Work with professionals in your law school's career development office and your academic support faculty to help you determine if one of your PT answers might be effectively edited into an appropriate writing sample.

IMPROVING YOUR PERFORMANCE TEST WRITING TO GET READY FOR SUCCESS ON THE BAR EXAM

Self-assessment is a critical part of training for success on the bar exam. For every practice question you take (essays, MBEs, and PTs), set aside time to study answers and find ways to improve.

---

[1] Sara J. Berman, *Pass the Bar Exam: A Practical Guide to Achieving Academic & Professional Goals* (American Bar Association, 2014).

As you complete practice PTs, ask yourself the following key questions to self-assess your work. Also, be sure to compare and contrast your answer to reliable sample answers to find any ways to improve your own answers.

PT SELF-ASSESSMENT CHECKLIST

1. Did I finish the assignment within the allotted time?
2. Did I follow the directions, completing the specific task(s) requested in the Task Memo and only those tasks (being cognizant of the respective weights of different tasks if applicable)?
3. Did I produce a well-written, thoughtful, and organized answer? (Is my answer easy for the grader to read? Did I write in short paragraphs and include headings so that my grader can easily see my organization and main points?)
4. Did I use the authorities (citing to all the main cases and key statutes in the Library)?
5. Did I incorporate sufficient facts to support my analysis or argument?
6. Did I employ the proper tone given the audience I am writing to? (If I am writing a letter to a lay client, did I define legal jargon? If writing a brief to the court, did I write in a persuasive, lawyerly manner?)

This a good time to return to and re-read Chapter 2 of this book. The information about performance test skills and test-taking strategies will make so much more sense now that you have completed a number of practice tests. You will pick up tools to arm yourself for success.

Keep writing practice PTs until you have it down, until you are consistently producing passing-quality answers under timed conditions. Keep self-assessing and studying sample answers after every practice question you complete. Reverse-engineer: look at those answers and then back at the File and Library to determine how to reference enough of the facts and law to write a complete answer without getting so bogged down that you don't finish.

"CHEAT SHEETS"

A favorite law professor of mine advised that by two weeks before the bar exam, applicants should have drafted one page on each subject.[2] (The intellectual tool he used to explain what to write on the page was this: "**Pretend** you were going to cheat on the bar and could fit only one page per subject in your pocket." He

---

[2]Thank you UCLA Professor Emeritus Ken Graham.

emphasized the word **pretend**, and asked, "What would you want on your contracts cheat sheet if you were hit with a contracts essay? Write that on your contracts cheat sheet and do the same for each bar-tested subject.") About two weeks before your bar, draft your own "cheat sheets" for every subject tested on your exam. You might find these pages invaluable when you want something quick and useful to review on the mornings before and breaks between each testing session. I loved this advice so much that I not only drafted subject-specific cheat sheets but also a "PT Strategy Sheet." Here below is a sample of what you might want to remind yourself of before taking a PT.

Sample PT Strategy Sheet

INSTRUCTIONS—Skim any general instructions quickly to see if this is a "normal" PT with a File and Library, to note which jurisdiction I am in, and to glean any other information about my task(s).

TASK MEMO—Paper clip (if permitted) or bend the corner of this page so I can easily refer back to it. **Do NOT tear the page.** Read this slowly and carefully. This is the most important page of this test. Look for: 1) Who am I? 2) Who am I writing for? 3) What type of writing is this and what is the goal of the writing task(s)? 4) What exactly am I expected to produce by the end of these 90 minutes? 5) Are they giving me any formats or tips on how to organize my answers—in the Task Memo or any format pages? If so, study them carefully.

CASE—Big picture. Who is my client and what does my client want? What if anything is preventing my client from getting what my client wants? If the case involves litigation, who is suing whom over what? If transactional, what is my client's main objective(s)?

LAW—1) Try to find the main legal issues and figure out the legal analytical framework—how do the Library rules fit together? 2) Figure out what the legal issues are really about: Is the analysis mainly procedural or substantive or both? Is it expanding or narrowing a legal policy? Is it building a prima facie case or defense theories? Is it distilling a rule from a long line of cases, or finding an exception to a general rule? Is it arguing why our case doesn't fit some particular statutory scheme? What is the legal analysis I am to perform? And, again, how does the Library seem to fit together? (The law often provides the key to a logical organizing principle to write my answer.)

FACTS—On my first skim through the File, find out my client's basic story. Second read through, after studying the Library, let me think: 1) After knowing what is in the Library and isolating (and if possible breaking down) the main legal rule(s) into element or component parts, let me find some relevant facts that tie up to (relate to by proving or disproving) each legal element or component. Remember, there may be irrelevant and duplicative facts. No worries. Just look for some relevant facts on every key component of every main rule. 2) If appropriate, think about how we might gather additional facts that might help my client. Note any inconsistent facts. Note which facts (and which sources of facts) are or are not particularly reliable and why. 3) Again, expect many irrelevant or duplicative facts. Don't get bogged down in anything I don't understand the relevance of; I can always come back to it. It's all here right in front of me. Everything I need to answer this question is in my File and Library.

PROFESSIONAL RESPONSIBLITY —Look for conflicts and rule violations, actual and potential; think about client consent and communications and other possible ways of resolving client problems and/or any ethical concerns facing lawyers.

SOLVE CLIENT'S PROBLEMS —1) Keep my client's objectives in mind. 2) Present alternative strategies; give client at least two choices. 3) Recommend tactics and strategies as well as substantive courses of action.

CONCLUDE!!! —1) Finish with some obvious concluding line. 2) Be sure to regularly ask myself, as I am writing, "Did I perform the task(s) I was asked to in the Instructions and Task Memo? Did I help whomever I'm supposed to help on this project?"

I often say that PTs would not be difficult for most law students if you had several days to complete them. But finishing a thorough answer in only 90 minutes often proves to be a great challenge. Do not get frustrated. Working thoroughly yet quickly is what clients most often expect in this fast-paced world. Just as answering clients in a timely and accurate manner will become easier as you become more experienced, so too will PTs become easier as you practice them.

This book has given you the tools to produce passing-quality answers. If after completing these practice exams you are already writing thorough answers in 90 minutes, you are in great shape. You may need a brief PT refresher during bar review, but you likely have all the skills you need to pass this portion of your bar exam. If timing is still a challenge, work on shaving off time with each additional practice exam you complete. *Pass the Bar Exam*[3] also includes many time-saving strategies that are applicable to PTs, bar essays, and multiple-choice questions.

---

[3] Sara J. Berman, *Pass the Bar Exam: A Practical Guide to Achieving Academic & Professional Goals* (American Bar Association, 2014).

Bottom line: Work hard and work smart. Invest the time with practice tests now to master the PT and make this open-book portion of the bar exam your ally on the actual test. With PT portion under control, you will be free to focus on conquering the rest of what you need to learn and memorize to pass your bar exam.

KEY TAKEAWAYS

- Performance Tests are:
  - Open-book and thus fair in that they truly test your skills and not your memory. Once you master the skills, you don't forget them.
  - Realistic. They prepare you for law practice as well as for the bar exam.
  - Fun for many students because they allow for some creative expression, not often as big a part of law essays or multiple-choice questions.

- The best general strategy for completing a PT is to use the SS-BROW approach: **S**tudy, **S**kim, **B**rief, **R**e-Read, **O**utline, and **W**rite.
- To become competent in writing effective PT answers within the allotted time constraints, *practice, practice, practice.*
- Get a head start on performance tests during law school:
  - To help make law school come alive,
  - To see yourself as a lawyer (not "just" a law student), and
  - To give yourself a down payment for success on the bar exam.

You've got this! The bar exam is yours to pass. Best of luck, on the exam and in law practice!

INDEX

Also from the ABA...

Pass the Bar
A Practical Guide to Achieving Academic & Professional Goals
Sara Berman

From Law School to Lawyer
Jonathan D. McDowell

More from the ABA...

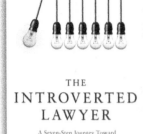

The Introverted Lawyer
A Seven-Step Journey Toward
Authentically Empowered Advocacy
Heidi K Brown

Solo Lawyer
By Design
A Plan for Success
in Any Practice
Gary Paul Bauer

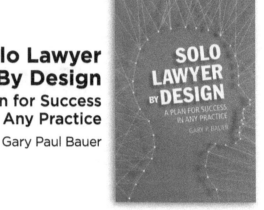

To order 🌐 visit **www.ShopABA.org**
or call 📞 **(800) 285-2221.**